# Management in Scandinavia

# Management in Scandinavia

Culture, Context and Change

Jette Schramm-Nielsen

*PhD, Associate Professor, Copenhagen Business School, Denmark*

Peter Lawrence

*Emeritus Professor of International Management, Loughborough University, UK*

Karl Henrik Sivesind

*PhD, Senior Researcher, Institute for Social Research, Norway*

**Edward Elgar**

Cheltenham, UK • Northampton, MA, USA

Published by
Edward Elgar Publishing Limited
Glensanda House
Montpellier Parade
Cheltenham
Glos GL50 1UA
UK

Edward Elgar Publishing, Inc.
136 West Street
Suite 202
Northampton
Massachusetts 01060
USA

A catalogue record for this book
is available from the British Library

ISBN 1 84376 431 8

Printed and bound in Great Britain by MPG Books Ltd, Bodmin, Cornwall

# Contents

# List of figures and tables

**Figures**

**Tables**

# Acknowledgements

First of all we wish to acknowledge our gratitude to the heads of our case study companies for letting us have access to their enterprises, and more specifically to all our respondents, managers, employees and union representatives who gave up hours of their valuable time to talk to us, answer our questions and show us production sites. Special thanks go to ekon.lic. Pavla Kruzela, Lund University, for being extremely helpful in establishing contact with a number of our Swedish case companies and for participating in interviews in a very competent manner. Next we wish to thank colleagues and peers who have given us valuable feed back and comments in their specific areas of expertise: Staffan Åkerblom, Programme Director of IFL AB – Swedish Institute of Management, Stockholm, Professor Even Lange, Department of History, Oslo University, and Assistant Professor Anette Risberg, Department of Intercultural Communication and Management, Copenhagen Business School. During the actual writing of the book Peter Lawrence visited some additional companies in Norway and Denmark, and he would like to thank these companies for their friendly cooperation. He also wishes to acknowledge financial support from the Loughborough University Business School, which facilitated participation in the fieldwork. Extensive reference has been made in Chapter 7 to research by R. Inglehart, commencing on p. 171. Permission to print excerpts from his work, which originally appeared as Chapter 3, 'Culture and democracy', in L.E. Harrison and S.P. Huntington (eds) (2000), *Culture Matters: How Values Shape Human Progress*, has been given by Basic Books of New York, © 2000 by Lawrence Harrison and Samuel Huntington.

J. Schramm-Nielsen, P.A. Lawrence, K.H. Sivesind
February 2004

# 1.   Making the case

This book is a contribution to the expanding field of cross-cultural/comparative management. It addresses the issue of whether the main Scandinavian countries – Norway, Sweden and Denmark – exhibit such similarities in management style and practice that it is meaningful to speak of a Scandinavian management. This means that on the one hand we explore the homogeneity thesis, and on the other hand, as a consequence, we engage in the cluster theory discussion in the sense of asking if these three Scandinavian states constitute a country cluster.

Scandinavia is a fascinating region to study. First, because it is one of the richest and most advanced areas in the world in terms of development and use of technology; second, because these countries have done away with the flagrant inequalities that we find in most other countries around the world; and third, and not least, because these countries have developed a management style which is extraordinarily participative and process oriented without losing the battle for efficiency.

A country cluster theory based on attitudinal variables was first formulated in the early days of research on cross cultural management by Haire et al. (1966). Their theory of clusters of similar countries went against the accepted wisdom of the period, which was that of trust in universal management methods and standards. The 1970s saw a number of country cluster studies, but they did not attract much attention at the time. It was only when Hofstede started publishing his results from the comprehensive IBM study in 1976, and especially in his 1980 book on work related values, that the business research community and managers alike were shaken in their conviction about management universals, a thesis that Hofstede elaborated and enlarged in a later book (2001). It was as path breaking as the Haire et al. study. We will come back to these studies in Chapter 7.

Besides the country cluster studies, a number of studies have been conducted, which include one or more of the Scandinavian countries compared with countries outside Scandinavia, but none of these studies make a comprehensive synthesis of what is distinctly Scandinavian, nor do they try to distinguish clearly between commonalities within Scandinavia and what might be specific for each of the three countries here considered. This is exactly what we aim to do in this book. Whereas the studies hitherto published on Scandinavian values leading to the country cluster theory are all quantitative, our study is qualitative and based on multiple field interviews, to our knowledge the first study to do that. Our results we hope show what it means in terms of management practice and business culture to be a cluster.

The common sense justification for asking these questions is that over the years there has been a certain discourse on Scandinavian management, implying the existence of a distinct Scandinavian style of management. Outside Scandinavia this has often been explicitly or implicitly synonymous with Swedish management, represented by high flyers such as Chief Executive Officer (CEO) of SAS 1981–93 Jan Carlzon (b. 1941), a charismatic figure who described his management philosophy in his widely read book *Riv pyramiderne ned!*, 'Pull down the pyramids' (Carlzon, 1985); Pehr Gyllenhammar (b. 1935), CEO of Volvo 1971–90, who took an active part in the public debate about corporate ethics and responsibility, or the former ABB star Percy Barnevik (b. 1941). They were all heroes of the 1980s, when Sweden was still enjoying the reputation of a strong, industrialized, and rich welfare state, a role model for many other countries. When these companies started to fall behind, their management style was questioned, and since then they have all fallen from grace for various reasons. Actually, in our view, the individuals cited were rather un-Swedish or un-Scandinavian in their style, outstanding exceptions and not really representative of what we have come to consider mainstream Swedish or Scandinavian management. This we hope to illustrate in the following chapters.

Inside Scandinavia, the people of the three countries have a more or less diffuse picture of what the distinct Scandinavian style might be, each one probably thinking in terms of his or her own national culture.

The homogeneity thesis takes as its starting point the fact that these three countries represent a number of core values on different levels of analysis: at the societal level, where we expect to find institutions with similar basic philosophical and ethical attitudes; at the level of the labour market, already documented by other researchers; and not least at the organizational level and the level of people management.

Now, if we want to establish at least a probable link between these levels of analysis, it follows that we have to search more widely than is usually the case in comparative studies, which typically probe into specific themes such as that of welfare states (Esping-Andersen, 1990), labour market issues (Galenson, 1998) or human resource management (Jackson, 2002). In this book we cast the net wider by including (in Chapter 2) the context, in the sense of the main features of history, state building, religion, natural resources, the economy including historical development of the economy, the political forces of recent decades, and even key national personalities, where we find them indicative of each country. The purpose is to provide readers, especially the non-Scandinavian readers, with the necessary overview of the three countries in order for them to be able to understand how and why the countries exhibit the characteristics that we find today. These descriptions are not intended to be comprehensive, but rather indicative.

Chapter 2 also shows that our three countries share a certain number of basic cultural variables such as history, the protestant-evangelical religion, which shapes the ethical values, and similar but not identical languages, all of which give the inhabitants a vague feeling of togetherness and commonality. This of course has contributed to our choice of these countries.

In view of the movement towards European integration in politics as well as in economic coordination, where we already see a much stronger input from these North European countries than we have seen before, and in order for the Scandinavians themselves to understand what distinctness they bring with them into the European cooperation, we hope to fill in some of the gaps in the knowledge and understanding of these northernmost countries of Europe.

This book is based on what is arguably unique, certainly new empirical data in the form of 70 interviews with managers in the three countries – top managers, middle managers, foremen and trade union representatives – on a broad spectrum of issues including strategy, production, management–workforce relations, human resources, company culture, conflicts and management *esprit de corps*. The interviews lasted from one to three hours each; they were tape-recorded and transcribed in full for analysis. The mean age of our interviewees was 44.7, and they had from three to 41 years of work experience. The respondents were almost equally divided between the three countries. All interviews were conducted in English apart from a few with union representatives who were less comfortable speaking English. One of the interviewers, however, understands all three Scandinavian languages and translated on the spot with the respondent controlling for meaning.

As well as the interviews, we had published materials on each company, such as the company history, personnel magazines, up-to-date financial performance data and information on the organizational structure, pay systems and so on. We never visited a head office alone, but always included a production unit to see how things worked and gained an impression of how the production was organized. On average we spent two days in each company.

The research design is based on a number of matched companies in a limited number of industries across the three countries. This design was pioneered by the researchers at Laboratoire d'Economie et de Sociologie du Travail (LEST) at Aix-en-Provence in southern France. In a famous study LEST compared matched companies in France and Germany. The design has the obvious advantage of allowing us to see whether there are differences between the countries when we hold industry constant, at the same time allowing us to ask whether there are differences between the industries if not between the countries. Our definition of an industry is a set of firms manufacturing products which are of a like function and nature. Critics of the idea of distinct characteristics of national or regional business cultures have often argued that industries or professions cross country have more in common than have different nation-based industries or professions. As a result of our research we will be able to say whether this is the case in the industries that we have chosen. The industries that we will report on here are brewing, furniture, confectionery and shipbuilding, which will each be documented in separate chapters: brewing in Chapter 3, furniture in Chapter 4, confectionery in Chapter 5 and shipbuilding in Chapter 6. Each of these chapters will start by setting the scene in the shape of an overview of recent international development of the industry in question, against which backdrop our case study companies will be described. Each industry will have three case examples, one from each country.

The criteria for choosing the industries were several. First, we wanted industries that would be as old as possible, that is, traditionally country based in the hope that they would show cultural characteristics, if these existed. Second, they would have to be present in each of the three countries; as readers will see from Chapter 2, discussing the Scandinavian context, this greatly limited the choice available since the natural resources are very different from one country to the other and so consequently are the variety of industries represented. Third, the case companies had to be of a certain size, big enough to have a reasonable organization structure and important enough to contribute to the national economy. Fourth, the companies should be nationally owned. All of these criteria aimed at isolating, as far as possible, *national* characteristics. The last criterion, however, turned out to be a stumbling block in our research design, since in this era of internationalization and economic expansion, we saw a number of mergers and acquisitions taking place, many of them inter-Scandinavian, but in the case of Sweden nearly the whole sample of Swedish companies are in foreign ownership. This is partly due to the economic crisis that Sweden went through in the 1990s and partly due to the structure of Swedish industry, as will be explained later. This is not just a mishap in our research design, but a general feature of recent Swedish economic development. Consider these examples of corporate Sweden being merged with or acquired by foreign investors: Kockums was merged with German HDW. The steel company Avesta was merged with Corus, formerly British Steel. Saab automobiles was bought by General Motors. Volvo was acquired by Ford Motor Company. Astra Laboratories were merged with British Zeneca and another pharmaceutical company, Pharmacia, was merged with US Upjohn. Many of the head offices have been transferred to somewhere outside Sweden.

As it turned out, however, this fact did not influence our interview data much, since all of our respondents were natives of the particular country, except for one, and he was from one of the other Scandinavian countries.

However, some of the criteria did work to our advantage. Take the shipbuilding industry; from Chapter 2 it will appear that this industry has lasted more than a millennium, that it has played a major role in the history of all three countries and still does, although Swedish shipbuilding has recently been limited to military vessels, which incidentally blocked our access to data. Or consider the brewing industry, which goes back to the early Middle Ages, first as production on each farm and later as production at the local township level. In Denmark alone, breweries could be counted by the hundreds for many centuries. Or the furniture industry. Until the cost of transportation was reduced dramatically, it was essentially a local industry, and even today we see distinct differences in style between the three countries.

In Chapter 7, which discusses differences and similarities, we will turn round the perspective and focus on countries instead of industries. The chapter will summarize the findings from the previous industry chapters by reconsidering the main themes treated in Chapters 3, 4, 5 and 6, and especially draw on Chapter 2 for possible explanations of our findings, or to put it differently look for deep structures in history, state building and political development that might help explain similarities as well as differences between the countries. This will also be the opportunity to re-examine the homogeneity thesis and the country cluster theory.

Finally, in Chapter 8, 'Present and prospect', we will answer our main question of whether there is such a thing as a distinctive Scandinavian style of management, and if so, how it can be compared with other national styles of management. We will attempt some judgements on the strengths and weaknesses of the Scandinavian style(s), point out changes that are in process, and we will venture some predictions on the future of Scandinavian-style management in view of the up-coming deeper integration into the enlarged European Community and the involvement of Scandinavians in international affairs, such as peace initiatives, international trade negotiations and the engagement in the economic development of poorer countries.

The three authors are all experienced writers and researchers in this field. We represent three different nationalities, British, Danish and Norwegian, which we like to think is an asset in any cross cultural endeavour, serving to reduce the risk of ethnocentrism. All of us have international experience, having lived and worked outside our country of origin, and each of us have expertise in a number of countries and cultures, enabling us to situate Scandinavia in the wider international context.

What audiences do we have in mind?

Our target groups are academics and practitioners. Within academia this book is of interest to researchers and teachers in comparative/cross-cultural management and to students and teachers of international business or general management, as well as to executive training programmes with an international focus. Other likely groups are teachers and students in corporate governance, international human resource management, operations management, inter-cultural communication, inter-cultural management and organizational issues.

It will also be useful for practising managers, all those operating in a Scandinavian context inside or outside Scandinavia, to people working with Scandinavians in international organizations or in foreign affairs. In this connection we also have in mind politicians and civil servants in the European Union (EU) administration, and other international organizations where Scandinavians are involved. It might also be helpful for civil servants in Scandinavia who would like to understand the background of their institutions in a short historical perspective.

## REFERENCES

Carlzon, J. (1985), *Riv pyramiderne ned!*, Copenhagen: Gyldendal.

Esping-Andersen, G. (1990), *The Three Worlds of Welfare Capitalism*, Cambridge: Polity Press.

Galenson, W. (1998), *The World's Strongest Trade Unions – The Scandinavian Labour Movement*, Westport, CT: Quorum.

Haire, M., Ghiselli, E. and Porter, L. (1966), *Managerial Thinking: An International Study*, New York, NY: Wiley.

Hofstede, G. (1980), *Culture's Consequences – International Differences in Work-related Values*, Beverly Hills, CA: Sage.

Hofstede, G. (2001), *Culture's Consequences – Comparing Values, Behaviours, Institutions and Organizations Across Nations*, 2nd edn, London: Sage.

Jackson, T. (2002), *International HRM - A Cross-cultural Approach*, London: Sage.

# 2. Context

## COMMON FACTS AMONG THE THREE COUNTRIES

Our three countries have a number of features in common, albeit they are all constitutional hereditary monarchies, the first born automatically being the heir in Norway and Sweden, whether a son or a daughter. In Denmark, a son has priority so far, but this will no doubt be changed should the present crown prince have a daughter as first-born. The three royal families have intertwined family relations, although these days spouses are mostly chosen outside family circles. Power lies with Parliament, and the roles of the members of the royal families are mostly representative and are an undeniable asset in campaigns for foreign trade.

The three main Scandinavian countries have been nation-like entities for at least a thousand years, and they can look back on at least a millennium of historical bonds and changing coalitions and unions, although this shared history has not been devoid of conflicts and even wars.

The first historical period for which there are records is the Viking period, from around AD 800 till about AD 1050 during which adventurous expeditions set out from the Scandinavian coasts to raid and trade on neighbouring shores, especially those of England, Scotland, Ireland and France, and also eastbound to the Baltic countries and Russia, reaching as far as the Court of Constantinople and the Italian shores, all thanks to their famous longships and navigation techniques. The Norwegians even went as far as the northeast coast of North America, without settling. Apart from worldly things the Vikings eventually brought back Christianity, late by European standards, and the introduction of the Christian faith really meant the end of the Viking period. But it certainly did not end the skills and traditions of the sea, including shipbuilding, which is one of the industries that is subject to our scrutiny.

Today the Scandinavian people share Protestantism of the Lutheran-Evangelical branch as an ethical and moral foundation. Scandinavians do not demonstrate their religious adherence by frequent church attendance, and faith is considered a private matter that one would not ask about in ordinary conversation. Rather, religious adherence points to a deeper level of shared philosophical worldviews.

In terms of civilization these countries were long on the outskirts of Europe, but the elites were always in contact with the cultural movements of Central and Southern Europe and did not escape the political turmoil and shifting power relations shaped by what natural resources were in demand and what political constellations were formed.

## Similar Languages

The Scandinavian languages (Danish, Norwegian and Swedish) are part of the larger group of Nordic languages, including also Icelandic and Faeroese, all part of the Germanic family of languages. Originally, up till around AD 1200, the present Nordic languages were considered one common language, but during the Viking age (AD 800–1100) divergence started that eventually led to the present single languages. The Scandinavian languages are similar to a certain extent, especially Danish and Norwegian, but not always immediately comprehensible without some training and exposure.

## Welfare States and Wage Equality

All three countries are welfare states of the Scandinavian type. The main difference between this type and a continental European type or Anglo-Saxon type is that it follows a universal principle, meaning that everybody is entitled to social security benefits independent of income, prior or present. In other words, a person is entitled to social benefits whether he or she has ever had a job or an income.

The Scandinavian countries have often been considered too generous. High average wages combined with a high level of public social insurance and welfare services must, so to say, be too expensive in an age of globalization. If labour-costs are too high, increased capital mobility would mean that production would move elsewhere. At least it should mean no establishment of new activities in Scandinavia, goes the argument. This sounds reasonable, but it is contradicted by the fact that Norway, Sweden and Denmark have recovered from the economic slump at the end of the 1980s or the beginning of the 1990s. Unemployment now is lower than in the rest of the EU. The small but open economies of the Scandinavian countries have had to adapt to changes in international markets since the process of industrialization started. An integrated European economic area and deregulation of finance and credit markets did not in fact mean the end of the Scandinavian model. At least not yet.

To understand why, we need to take a closer look. It is the case that wages for low-wage groups are higher in Scandinavia than elsewhere. However, wages for high-wage groups are also lower. Norway, Sweden and Denmark have the most compressed wage distribution among 17 Organisation for Economic Co-operation and Development (OECD) countries, if we look at the difference between the top 10 per cent and the bottom 10 per cent (Barth et al., 2003). In the United States and Canada, the top wages are more than four times higher than the bottom wages, whereas in Scandinavia they are little more than two times higher.

A different study shows that the basic pay for US top managers in the Standard and Poor's 500 index was 90 times higher than that of the average production-worker in 1996 (Murphy, 1999). Norwegian top managers' basic pay was just eight times higher (Dale-Olsen, 2003). If pensions, stocks and options were to be included, the difference between the United States and Norway would be even more extreme (Hall and Murphy, 2003).

A survey of 12 OECD countries shows that the average of the top 5 per cent wages in Sweden is just US$150 000 (Abowd and Kaplan, 1999). Norwegian top wages in similar companies are even lower, just US$120 159 (Dale-Olsen, 2002). Scandinavian wage differentials may have increased slightly in recent years, but it does not really change the situation. Managers and highly educated personnel have relatively low wages. Wages are compressed in the middle in Scandinavia.

According to Barth et al., countries with highly coordinated wage determination tend to have smaller wage differentials. The highest rates of union membership in the world, the fact that on average three-fourths of the working population are covered by collective agreements, combined with frequent centralized wage negotiations means that the Scandinavian wage determination is extremely coordinated (Barth et al., 2003). In national wage negotiations, trade unions take employment and prices into account. Coordination leads to moderation – and in Scandinavia this includes aversion to inequality. Normally employers would want to outbid each other for the best labour. This gives them a free-rider problem. However, in centralized negotiation they prefer to keep the average wages as low as possible. This is why highly coordinated wage formation results in smaller wage differentials and moderation when there is an understanding of crises in the economy (Sivesind, 1996). Contrary to common wisdom, coordination is good for adaptation to rapidly changing world markets. It makes transfer of labour between industries easier, it rewards highly productive industries with low wage-costs and thus facilitates entrepreneurial activities, and it reduces unemployment.

It seems paradoxical that the Scandinavian countries with small differences in wages also have fairly generous welfare states. Why level out the differences between people when the differences are so small? It seems as though the welfare states in general are more generous in countries with small differences in income (Barth et al., 2003). One reason is that small and open economies are vulnerable to external shocks, which makes it sensible to distribute the risks between different industries and types of employees through welfare arrangements (Katzenstein, 1985). Social insurance is not primarily motivated by an urge to increase equality, but by a need for insurance against temporary hardship. When there are small wage differences, a larger share of the population feel a need for such insurance, in particular in countries exposed to the rapid changes in an internationalized economy.

Barth et al. argue that generous welfare arrangements contribute to a compressed wage structure because they strengthen the position of marginal groups in the labour market. People are less vulnerable to threats about losing their job, which gives more power and increased pay. Higher minimum wages increases the motivation to get a job, and hence reduces unemployment. An egalitarian wage structure creates support for a generous welfare state. Consequently, there is an institutional balance between coordinated wage formation and social insurance that results from an adaptation to an open economy. Globalization and increased exchange of goods does not threaten this institutional balance, on the contrary.

The Scandinavian model is primarily threatened by its own success. By creating a well-educated middle class, competition between the trade unions and federations has increased. Employers' incentives for outbidding each other for the best employees increase knowledge-based production. In addition, knowledge-workers with confidence in their own market value and ability to guard themselves against misfortunes may no longer want compressed wages or expensive, universal social insurances. They may be better off with individualized wages and insurance. Consequently, increased inequality may reduce support for the welfare state, and a less generous welfare state may weaken marginal groups in the labour market and further increase wage-differences.

**Trade Unionism**

The power of the labour movement is legendary in Scandinavia. It reflects the relative balance of power between capital and labour both in political and industrial relations implemented by strong social-democratic parties (Ibsen, 1997).

The industrial relations system in Scandinavia was based on 'basic agreements', first in Denmark in 1899, then later in Norway in 1936 and Sweden 1938 (Saltsjöbadavtalet). The basic agreements stipulated the ways of regulating the labour market: basic union rights, the managerial prerogative, the collective agreement as the way to regulate wages and work conditions, and ways to solve industrial conflicts. Another key element in the Scandinavian model is the union structure and the high density (Ibsen, 1997). Union membership is especially high in Sweden and Denmark (around 80 per cent for blue- as well as white-collar workers, and somewhat lower in Norway

(57 per cent). Indeed, Scandinavian union membership rates are among the highest in the world, equalled only in Israel. The two main parties, the employers and the workers, soon became so well organized that often both realized that neither of them would be able to win an open fight, and consequently the compromise became the solution *par excellence*. Should a compromise not be reached in the first place, social-democratic governments tended to intervene, directly or indirectly, often at the expense of the employers. Their common desire to keep government intervention at a minimum has facilitated orderly and responsible collective bargaining. On the other hand the close relationship between social-democratic governments and the labour unions has also led to a comradeship and complicity between them, which may have blocked the way for solutions not invented by either of them (Schramm-Nielsen and Lawrence, 1998).

The interaction also comprises the political sector, and in this respect the Scandinavian countries and, until recently, especially Sweden represented a corporatist model, where the interest organizations on the labour market initiated and created a system of representation in political bodies and where we still find an intensive cooperation between these organizations and the state. Thus the two central labour market organizations cooperate with government bodies to formulate the main guidelines for the implementation of economic and social policies. This tripartite cooperation has been institutionalized, a routine has developed over the years, and the result is an integrated consensual decision-making system, in which the interests of the large majority of citizens are recognized. This pattern of relationships is especially marked in Sweden (SOU, 1990:94).

All this contributes to a deliberate restraint and regulation of open conflicts, where the bargaining power of each party is decisive and calls for moderation but where, on the other hand, trade unions and other interest groups may influence government policies (Schramm-Nielsen and Lawrence, 1998).

The bargaining structure in the Scandinavian countries has historically been a combination of centralization and decentralization, centralized agreements on the national level between the two national federations on the employer and employee side, and decentralized at the local branch or enterprise (Ibsen, 1997). The tendency is now towards decentralization and individualization of the wage formation process.

**Economies in High Gear**

Today the region is one of the most active economic concentrations in Europe, as will be seen from Tables 2.1 and 2.2 which show real growth rates in the period 1993–2001 and per capita gross domestic product (GDP) above the EU average in 2001.

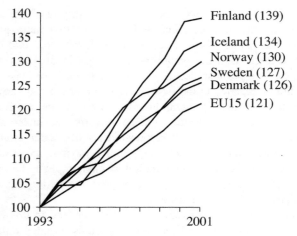

*Source*:   Eurostat/Hanell et al., 2002.

*Figure 2.1    Real GDP growths 1993–2001 (index 1993 = 100)*

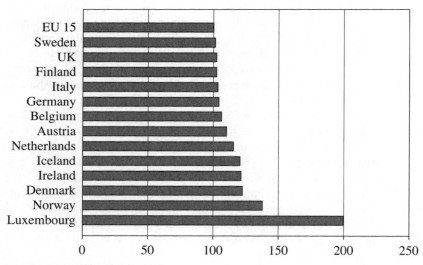

*Source*:   Eurostat/Hanell et al., 2002.

*Figure 2.2    Nordic and European GDP per capita in PPS 2001
(index EU 15 = 100)*

The World Economic Forum evaluates the economic competitiveness of a
large number of countries. In its annual report for 2003–2004 it comprised
102 countries, which account for 97.8 per cent of the world's GDP in total, and

*Table 2.1   Competitiveness rankings*

| Growth competitiveness index | | Business competitiveness index | |
|---|---|---|---|
| 1. | Finland | 1. | Finland |
| 2. | United States | 2. | United States |
| 3. | Sweden | 3. | Sweden |
| 4. | Denmark | 4. | Denmark |
| 5. | Taiwan | 5. | Germany |
| 6. | Singapore | 6. | United Kingdom |
| 7. | Switzerland | 7. | Switzerland |
| 8. | Iceland | | ........ |
| 9. | Norway | 22. | Norway |
| 10. | Australia | | |

*Source*:   World Economic Forum, 2003–04.

it comprises two overall rankings as shown in Table 2.3. One is the growth competitiveness index, in which our three Scandinavian countries are among the top ten, Sweden and Denmark being surpassed only by another Nordic country, Finland, and the United States. The second is an index that measures the business competitiveness. While the first one analyses the macro-economic environment, the quality of public institutions and technology, the second identifies key obstacles to economic growth, or said positively the ability of firms to create valuable goods and services using efficient methods; here again we find Sweden and Denmark among the top four, whereas Norway only scores 22nd.

The possession of a well-educated labour force is one of the major explanations for the high level of competitiveness, and this goes for blue-collar as well as white-collar people. Many blue-collar workers have an apprenticeship education or technical schooling of three years on top of nine or ten years of compulsory school. These days this will necessarily imply a certain level of information technology (IT) knowledge. As for white-collar employees, the share of persons of working age who have a tertiary level education (age 18+) is almost 30 per cent, which is higher than the OECD country mean, and compared with EU countries this gap is even larger, according to Eurostat estimates. As in a number of other countries, there has been an explosion in higher education since the 1970s, and the number of students in higher education is still growing. An interesting feature here is that, in the younger age groups, females are better educated than males, whereas the opposite holds true for the older age group. Among the three countries Sweden here stands out as an exception, since also in the older age group (55–64 years)

*Management in Scandinavia*

*Table 2.2    Percentages of women in national parliaments of the EU member states (2001)*

| Country | Women |
| --- | --- |
| Sweden | 44.3 |
| Norway | 41.2 |
| Denmark | 38.3 |
| Finland | 37.0 |
| Netherlands | 34.7 |
| Germany | 31.5 |
| Austria | 27.9 |
| Spain | 27.7 |
| Belgium | 23.2 |
| Portugal | 20.0 |
| UK | 18.2 |
| Luxembourg | 16.7 |
| Ireland | 12.7 |
| Italy | 11.3 |
| France | 9.6 |
| Greece | 8.7 |

*Source*:   European Database, 2001.

the share of females having a tertiary level education is higher. This is also reflected in the representation of females in the national parliaments (Table 2.4), which is 44.3 for Sweden, 38.3 for Denmark and 41.2 for Norway (European Database, 2001).

Another characteristic of our three Scandinavian countries is that women take an active part in the creation of national wealth.

As will be seen from Table 2.5, female participation in the workforce is very high in all of the three Scandinavian countries and at the similarly high level of 76 per cent of all women of working age; it is the highest in the industrialized world (Ellingsæter, 2000), and this is probably one of the criteria of wealthy industrialized countries. This high proportion of females on the labour market does of course put pressure on the need for childcare institutions provided by the state, which again is one of the reasons for high taxation. A large proportion of the women are employed in social care, which means that taking care of, for instance, children and elderly people has moved from the private to the public sphere. However, women are increasingly better educated; in many university studies such as medicine, law, dentistry and even some areas of business studies, the proportion of female

*Table 2.3    Labour force participation rates age 15–64 in percentages
(2001) (selected countries)*

|             | Men  | Women |            |
|-------------|------|-------|------------|
| Denmark     | 84.4 | 76.0  |            |
| Norway      | 84.5 | 76.0  |            |
| Sweden      | 79.7 | 75.5  |            |
| USA         | 84.7 | 71.8  | (year 2000)|
| Canada      | 82.3 | 70.6  |            |
| UK          | 82.5 | 67.7  | (year 2000)|
| Netherlands | 83.9 | 66.3  |            |
| Australia   | 84.3 | 66.2  |            |
| Germany     | 80.3 | 64.4  |            |
| Japan       | 92.4 | 64.4  |            |
| France      | 75.7 | 63.5  |            |
| Spain       | 78.7 | 50.9  |            |
| Italy       | 75.6 | 47.8  |            |

*Source*:   OECD Labour Market Statistics, June 2003.

students is higher than male. In short they are pushing upwards in the employment hierarchy.

In international perception the Scandinavian societies are by and large viewed as efficient and untainted by corruption (Hanell et al., 2002), although of course personal and professional networks that may facilitate business do exist. Since the countries are relatively small, the same influential people meet in all kinds of circles. Business people form networks with politicians and public administration personnel on practical matters and problem solving. To give an example: one of our case companies in Norway joined with the local county administration to build a bridge across a fjord, a bridge that would facilitate traffic between residential areas and the company's production facility to the benefit of all parties involved. The company contributed with the same amount of money as the county. The president of the company also convinced the politicians not to close down the only technical school in the area that specialized in furniture production. Such networks are not used for nepotism or favouritism, but to solve practical problems.

**Cross-border Cooperation, Post-Second World War**

Today the Scandinavian countries have cooperation in a number of areas such as a common labour market, a passport union and in regional development, especially in border regions. They coordinate some of their political and administrative activities through the Nordic Council of Ministers, a common parliamentary body established in 1952, cooperating on projects and the exchange of experience in virtually all fields of public administration. The members are: Denmark, Finland, Iceland, Norway, Sweden and the self-governing areas Greenland (part of Denmark), the Faeroe Islands (part of Denmark) and Åland (part of Finland) (Nordic Statistics, 2001).

SAS (the Scandinavian Airlines System) was established in 1946 and is jointly owned by the three countries, now operating with both public and private capital. Since 1997 it is part of the Star Alliance, which also includes Lufthansa, United Airlines and Singapore Airlines, among others. SAS dominates the inter-country as well as domestic civil aviation.

More recently, a joint Nordic market for the production and distribution of electricity has been established, including Finland as well. Demand and supply is efficiently coordinated as a free market, where electricity is sold at market prices. For instance in dry periods resulting in low water levels in the Norwegian and Swedish rivers fuelling the hydro-electric power stations, their demands will be covered by Denmark and vice versa.

In 2004 a joint Internet based job bank will be created in the border regions as well as a joint Nordic electronic tax calculation model, so that individuals may see what the consequences would be in terms of taxation if they were to choose to work in or move to one of the other countries.

In the years since the collapse of the USSR, special attention has been paid to environmental protection and restoration in the Baltic Sea region.

## NORWAY

### Geography, Demography and Company Sites

Norway occupies the western half of the Scandinavian peninsula. Two-thirds of Norway is mountainous, and off its much-indented coastline, carved by deep glacial fjords, lie some 50 000 islands. The country has been inhabited for about 6000 years, since the first Indo-Europeans settled along the coast, establishing a permanent settlement near the present capital of Oslo. The interior was more sparsely settled, owing to extremes of climate and difficult terrain, and even today the country's population of 4.3 million is concentrated in coastal areas and in the south, especially around the Oslo fjord, where we find about one-fifth (22 per cent) of the population.[1] In fact as much as 81 per cent of Norway is completely uninhabited. The other three major cities are Bergen, Trondheim and Stavanger, all on the coast.

The sites of our companies are no exception, since they are all situated along the coast: the shipyard, on one of the numerous islands along the west coast; furniture and confectionery, in deep fjords on the west coast, one of them with direct access to the sea; and the brewery, near Norway's second biggest town Bergen, again on the west coast.

The great majority of the inhabitants are ethnic Norwegians (96 per cent), plus a number of Danes, Swedes and British. Over the last decades there has been an influx of people from other nations such as Pakistan, Vietnam and Arab countries.

Communication by road is very complicated, narrow roads winding along fjords and sinuously over mountains. Fjords are crossed by boat or through numerous tunnels that are also carved through mountains, but in spite of the long distances and rough terrain, the roads are extremely well built and well maintained. In 2000 the world's longest road tunnel, 24.5 km, opened to ensure year-round connection between the two biggest cities Oslo and Bergen. The train service is also complicated, with low standard speed and double tracks on only a few stretches, whereas the bus service is dense, and an extensive net of ferries and a well functioning air service between top modern airports help overcome the difficulties. This is a country where an ambulance may well come in the shape of a helicopter.

## History, State Building and Religion

Norway is exceptional among the Scandinavian countries in having been an independent state only for short periods of time from around 1000 till 1320 and again after 1905. After a period of decline the country formed a union with Sweden from 1320 for the next 60 years, when it entered into a union with Denmark lasting for more than 400 years until 1814. At this point Denmark and Norway were separated, and Norway was given to Sweden as a result of Denmark having joined the losing side in the Napoleonic War. During the more than 400 years of personal union with Denmark, the so-called twin-monarchy, Norway kept its own laws but was administered by Denmark and most of the civil servants in Norway were Danes. This inevitably had the effect that the written administrative language was Danish, influencing also the spoken language. When finally Norway became independent in 1905, a nationalistic movement wanted to do away with the still Danish inspired influence in administrative language and to introduce a genuinely Norwegian tongue. The result was that from 1929 Norway has two official tongues: *bokmål* (book language) which is commonly spoken and *nynorsk* (new Norwegian) used by about ten per cent of the population.

In reaction to 'being given away' by the winning side at the end of the Napoleonic wars, the demand for independence grew rapidly, and that same year an assembly was called that formulated a constitution which at that time was very liberal and democratic. Parliamentarism was introduced in 1814; since then the date of 17 May is celebrated as Independence Day in Norway. The Danish prince Christian Frederik, who was also heir to the Danish throne, was chosen as king of Norway. This step would obviously in time have led to yet another personal union with Denmark. This development, however, was opposed by Sweden who threatened to use military force, and instead Norway was forced into a personal union with Sweden. However, only minor modifications were made in Norway's new constitution, that was more democratic than the Swedish one at the time.

Towards the end of the century, not least inspired by poets such as Henrik Wergeland (1808–45) and Bjørnstjerne Bjørnson (1832–1910), the grass root movement demanding independence and reforms had grown into a strong political movement, and in the summer of 1905 the Norwegian Parliament unanimously declared the union with Sweden dissolved. After a full military Swedish mobilization, and on the brink of war, the Swedish king gave in and Norway's independent status took effect from September that same year after having been approved by the Norwegian people in a referendum.

Again a Danish prince, Carl, brother to the later Christian X of Denmark, was chosen for King of Norway under the name Haakon VII.

The struggle for independence and for the emergence of an unmistakably national cultural identity, boosted by pride in the successes of polar explorers Fridtjof Nansen (1861–1930) and Roald Amundsen (1872–1928), undoubtedly plays an important role in the Norwegians' rejection of becoming a member of the EU, the word 'union' having a decidedly negative connotation to Norwegians.

During the First World War, Norway was neutral, whereas the Norwegians fought bravely against the Nazi Occupation during the Second World War. After a short military resistance, the king and the government went into exile in London. Like Denmark, the country was occupied from April 1940 to May 1945.

In religion, the Norwegians followed the development of Northern Europe, being Catholics from the Christianization of Scandinavia at the end of the Viking period around 1050 and then Lutherans from the time of the Reformation in 1536, during the twin-monarchy period. As in Denmark, there was a religious revival in the late eighteenth through to the nineteenth century, a revival which was especially strong along the western and southern coasts where the population had to face a rough climate and the dangers from the sea, living mostly from fishing, whaling and sea transportation. This area is still strongly marked by the Protestant work ethic, the rugged islands and the fjords bustling with activity. We found four of our companies in that area. The stern religious movement of Inner Mission, a contemporary evangelical expression of Pietism, and other religious communities was somewhat mitigated by the Danish religious leader, historian and author Grundtvig, who advocated a worldly, joyous and happy life on Earth in opposition to the Pietist movement of the late eighteenth and early nineteenth centuries. Along with the Pietist and puritan religious movements, a non-alcoholic movement developed, which is still rather strong, influencing the restrictive policy of Parliament on alcohol consumption (see Chapter 3 on breweries).

## Natural Resources

In 1970, Norway started on an era of unprecedented wealth, when the exploitation of oil deposits in the North Sea began. The country experienced a decline in the petroleum industry in the late 1980s, only to rebound in the 1990s benefiting from increased production and higher prices. Also in the 1980s, Norway went through an economic crisis caused by overheating of the economy, resulting in a negative balance of payments. In response the government introduced harsh measures, which came too late and were too radical, so that subsequently it had to stimulate the economy. From 1996, Norway is the third biggest exporter of oil and gas, surpassed only by Saudi Arabia and Russia. Thanks to this resource Norway has the highest GDP of the three Scandinavian countries, with NKr304 000 in 2002 (about US$38 000), and is among the highest in the world. The oil and gas industry accounts for up to 25 per cent of GDP. In order to reduce the risk of economic overheating along the lines of the 1980s crisis, the government in 1990 established the Government Petroleum Fund, into which budget surpluses are deposited (OECD, 2003c).

Thus, in spite of great wealth, successive governments have kept tight budgets controlling the increase in welfare expenditures and, paradoxically, due to green taxes, Norwegians pay Europe's highest price for gasoline, to the dismay of most Norwegians.

Other natural resources are hydro-electricity, forestry, forming the basis for the wood-processing industry, fishing, including fish-farming, the basis of a large fish-processing industry, and some minerals (iron, silver, copper, manganese). The fishing industry also offers seasonal employment for many farmers, since half of all Norwegian farms are so small (about 10 hectares) that a second source of income is necessary. Inland this could also be in forestry. Only about 1 per cent of the farms have more than 50 hectares. Since as little as about 3 per cent of Norway's total area is arable, the country never developed a landed aristocracy. Agriculture, forestry and fishery account for only 2 per cent of GNP; industry, including the oil industry, about 40 per cent; and the service sector constitutes some 60 per cent.

## Economy, Strengths and Weaknesses

From the second half of the 1990s, after a recession in 1989–93, Norway has become the richest economy in Europe. In 1996 all foreign debts were paid, the state budget and the foreign exchange reserves had surpluses, and inflation was as low as 1 per cent. Since then, Norway has full or nearly full employment, which shows in the difficulties our companies experienced in hiring personnel, especially for management positions. On top of this, the oil industry and related industries are absorbing many well-educated people, and so is the large public sector (OECD, 2003c).

The strength of the Norwegian economy, the dominating petroleum industry, is also its vulnerable point, dependent as it is on the ups and downs of the oil prices and the international politics of other regions in the world. Eighty per cent of the Norwegian oil income ends up in the coffers of the state, and on top of this the public sector owns large parts of other sectors such as electrical power stations, banking and telecommunication. The state owns significant shares in the top five companies listed on the Oslo Stock Exchange. These companies represent 65 per cent of the total market value of the stocks. Private individuals on the other hand have only about 8 per cent of the shares, as opposed to 15 on the Copenhagen stock exchange and 12 in Stockholm, all of which is low compared with the Anglo-Saxon world. This leaves a mere 27 per cent of the shares for institutional investors in Norway, one of the lowest rates in Western Europe. In the period 1990–2002 public ownership actually went up from 15 to 44 per cent of the market value (Engelstad et al., 2003). The main reason for this increase is the introduction of the formerly fully state-owned companies of Statoil and Telenor to the stock market. In recent years the wave of privatization has also reached the Norwegian shores, but for two reasons the politicians have been reluctant to privatize. The first reason is that since the state has been the major investor in most business sectors, not least in oil production, there is a lack of private capital in Norway. The second reason is a consequence of the first: since there is little available private capital among Norwegians, ownership would probably go to international institutional investors and thus not stay Norwegian. This is indeed in sharp contrast to the situation in Sweden, where about one-third of the 250 large Swedish companies are now in foreign ownership, and headquarters moved to other countries. The Norwegian state does not need foreign capital.

Due to the geography of the country, Norwegian engineers have specialized in the construction of power stations, dams, tunnels and bridges. Add to this the demand for technicians and experts for the oil industry, it comes as no surprise that today the country has a high level of advanced technology that has benefited all sectors. Cheap electrical power has been used to develop an important electro-metal and electro-chemical industry, notably one of the big exporting companies Norsk Hydro, which is partly state owned, specializing in oil, aluminium and chemicals, including fertilizers. The aluminium industry is worth mentioning as one of the industries that has benefited from cheap energy up till now. In spite of the fact that the raw material is imported, this industry is competitive on the world market.

## Membership of International Organizations

Norway is a member of most of the international and regional organizations, such as the UN, NATO, WEU, OECD, OSCE, WTO, the Nordic Council and the Baltic Council.

Unlike Sweden and Denmark, Norway is a member of the much diminished European Free Trade Association (EFTA) and not the EU. Since the 1960s the question of Norway's relations with the EU has split the country's population across traditional party lines and even within families. In 1972 when Denmark, Britain and Ireland decided to join the then EEC, Norwegian voters defeated the referendum on membership by more than 53 per cent. In 1994 Norwegians again had the chance of joining along with Sweden and Finland, and again the voters turned down the idea, this time with a slightly thinner margin.

How can we explain this? There is probably a variety of reasons not necessarily valid for all no-voters:

- One is psychological: the no-voters did not want to enter into another 'union', the word having a negative connotation reminiscent of the 1814–1905 'union' of Norway with Sweden.
- Second, many – especially in the small communities – were suspicious of a union of the bureaucratic type, strongly influenced by France and Latin countries, and the centralizing tendencies thought to go with it. This is the centre-periphery problem.
- Third, they did not want their Parliament, the Stortinget, to lose its independence of action.
- Fourth, by 1994 the country had gained confidence that thanks to its economic strength it could stand on its own feet and did not need partners.

It is true that although 75 per cent of all Norwegian exports go to EU countries, economically Norway has no problem standing outside the EU. This is due to the fact that it is part of the European Economic Area (EEA), established in 1994 to ensure free movement across borders for goods, persons, services and capital, and common rules on competition and state subsidies. It means that for all practical purposes it is a member of EU internal market, the only exceptions being fish and agricultural products.

The only place in the EU where Norway is absent is in the political decision making. In practice the country implements all EU directives (OECD, 2003c), and this was confirmed by our case companies. The consequence is that if/when at some point Norway does become a member, it will make little difference to business life. In conclusion we can say that the large political parties (Høyre and part of Arbeiderpartiet), the Employers' Federation and the trade unions are pro EU, whereas a slight majority of the population is against.

Since 2001, Norway is also part of the Schengen agreement of 1989, doing away with control at the national borders in exchange for more strict control at the outer borders of the EU, particularly the Norwegian–Russian border, although it is insignificant in comparison to influx by sea and air. Norway is a member of the EU's military and defence policy (the Western European Union) as well as its foreign policy, but again has no vote.

## Industry Structure and Labour Market

Norway is characterized by a business structure of mainly small and medium sized enterprises. Indeed fewer than 5 per cent of the companies have more than 100 employees. Nonetheless, these companies account for half of the industrial labour force and for more than half of production. The smaller companies are usually family owned, whereas most of the larger ones are joint-stock companies. Foreign interests control companies accounting for about 10 per cent of total production.

Traditionally the government has a significant ownership control over sectors such as oil, telecommunications and rail transport, strengthening the state-capitalist features of the Norwegian political economy (Mjøset et al., 2000), but in recent years some of the companies have been partially or fully privatized; one such example is Telenor (telecommunication).

Trade unions, which play an important role in society due to the system of collective bargaining, are traditionally strong and highly centralized, although the central authority of the LO (Landsorganisasjonen, the Norwegian Confederation of Trade Unions, established in 1899) has been broken, since it now represents only about 30 per cent of members of unions. Also central union power is somewhat mitigated by local negotiations conducted by the local union representative and by ballots among members. Other important labour unions are the Confederation of Vocational Unions and the Confederation of Academics and Professional Union of Norway. The unions and the employer associations respect one another, as well as the government guidelines, and this helps to control the rapidly expanding economy.

By Nordic standards, trade union membership in Norway is relatively low, 57 per cent, but it is still high seen in an international perspective.

There is a perennial shortage of labour, especially of skilled workers. Our case companies make up for this by training unskilled workers.

## National Heroes

*Roald Amundsen (1872–1928)*
Polar explorer.

| | |
|---|---|
| 1897–99 | Expedition to the Antarctic. |
| 1903–06 | The first to sail through the Northwest Passage. |
| 1911 | On 14 December he reached the South Pole – one month before Captain Scott of Britain. |
| 1926 | Flew over the North Pole in an airship. |
| 1928 | Died/perished searching for the Italia Expedition. |

*Bjørnstjerne Bjørnson (1832–1910)*
Writer.
Patriotism; wrote national anthem, *Ja, vi elsker dette landet*.
Nobel prize in literature in 1903.

*Gro Harlem Brundtland (b. 1939)*
Educated as a doctor, politician for the Norwegian Labour Party.

| | |
|---|---|
| 1981 | First woman to become Prime Minister in Norway. |
| 1984–87 | President of the UN world commission on environment and development. |
| 1987 | Responsible for the Brundtland Report *Our Common Future*. |
| 1998–2003 | General Manager of World Health Organization (WHO). |

*Henrik Ibsen (1828–1906)*
Dramatist. Internationally known for *The Doll's House* among others.

*Edvard Munch (1863–1944)*
Internationally known expressionist painter.

*Fridtjof Nansen (1861–1930)*
Polar explorer, oceanographer and diplomat. Educated as a zoologist.

| | |
|---|---|
| 1888 | The first to cross the Greenland ice cap on skis. |
| 1893–96 | Polar expedition on the Fram. The plan was to float with the ice from Siberia across the North Pole. Not successful, but … |
| 1895 | He reached 86 degrees and 14 minutes north on dog sledge. |
| 1922 | He was awarded the Nobel Prize for humanitarian aid in sending |

450 000 prisoners of war home from Russia and Central Europe, for relief help for famined people and refugees in the Soviet Union and exchange of large groups of people between Greece and Turkey.

*Henrik Wergeland (1808–45)*
Democrat and liberal. Author, opponent of Danish influence and language and Swedish authority, especially active 1830–40.

# SWEDEN

## Geography, Demography, Natural Resources and Company Sites

Sweden is the largest of our three countries, in area (449 960 square kilometres) as well as in population (8.9 million inhabitants in 2003). Part of the Scandinavian peninsula, it stretches some 1600 km from north to south and about 500 km across. This vast area is sparsely populated (20 per sq km), especially in the northern half, which accounts for only 10 per cent of the population. In fact as much as 71 per cent of Sweden is completely uninhabited. Thus the population is concentrated in the southern part, the relative low lands of Svealand and Götaland, around the major cities of Stockholm (the capital), Göteborg, Malmö and Uppsala. Along the Norwegian border we find high mountains covering about 25 per cent of the country, and more than half of the country is covered with coniferous trees, another 10 per cent with lakes, leaving only about 7 per cent of the area for agricultural purposes. In natural resources Sweden is rich in wood, hydro-electric power and a number of minerals such as iron, copper, lead, zinc and silver, and these resources were exploited in Sweden's early industrialization, forming the basis of the manufacturing industry which was long Sweden's strength par excellence.

As a consequence of the geographical concentration of the activities, we found our companies north-west of Stockholm and Uppsala (the steel company) and in the south-western part of the country, the brewery in a small town along the west coast, and the other companies in the busy south-western part of the country across from Denmark.

## History, State Building and Foreign Affairs

Sweden has been inhabited for at least 10 000 years and has been subject to a unitary government for about 1000 years, but its territorial expanse changed often until 1809. During the period from 1397 to 1523, known as the Kalmar

Union, Norway, Sweden and Denmark were actually unified under an elected Danish regent, the first of whom was Queen Margrethe I (1353–1412). Each country, however, had its own set of laws and it was largely a defensive union directed towards the Hanseatic League and the north German states. From the dissolution of the Kalmar Union, starting with Gustav I Vasa (1496–1560), the Swedes came to know a strong and centralized state that sought expansion in the Baltic Sea area. During the period from 1611 to 1721 Sweden was undeniably the great power in the Baltic area, gradually gaining control over Finland, part of what is now Russia, Estonia, Latvia, Lithuania and even parts of north Germany. All this came to an end in 1721 with the peace treaty after the so-called Great Nordic War against most of the other Northern European powers: Denmark, Poland-Saxony and Russia (1709–21). This war incidentally was also the last belligerent event between the two neighbours, Sweden and Denmark.

During this period of expansion and wars, the central power started exploiting the rich iron deposits in the country, and what could be more logical under the circumstances than to create an arms industry, an industry which is still very much alive, and which poses a paradox when one considers Sweden's present foreign policy based on neutrality, non-alliance, peace seeking and conflict solving efforts on the international scene. For the present authors it had the effect that the only large remaining shipyard in Sweden, Kockums in Malmö, which dates back to 1840, had been turned into one producing only highly sophisticated military naval systems and vessels such as submarines, which again meant that we could not have full access to data.

Swedish society and administration was long marked by its military past with a top-down command structure and rigid rule orientation.

Indicative of this tradition is the fact that after the Napoleonic wars, the Swedes chose a French marshal for king in 1818 under the name of Karl XIV Johan, the beginning of the Bernadotte dynasty. From 1809, however, the power of the king was gradually reduced, and today King Carl XVI Gustav, who is a descendant of Marshal Bernadotte, has only symbolic status. Another feature that has marked Swedish society is that of the system of the Estates of the Realm, which was abolished as late as in 1866, 77 years after the French Revolution that did away with the system in France. From a society governed by Estates, the distance was short to a society governed by corporations, and this was for long a characteristic of modern Swedish society. The state and the big interest organizations representing employers, employees, agriculture and industry still engage in effective cooperation (SOU, 1990:94 p.183), although the corporatist model has changed over the years. From this we can trace the tendency towards compromise and consensus seeking, which is especially pronounced in Sweden and which also entails a relatively high confidence in the state, a characteristic of all the Scandinavian countries in sharp contrast to most other European countries, especially France, Italy and Greece just to mention a few examples.

An institution which is also indicative of the relationship between citizens and the state is the ombudsman, which is a Swedish invention, created as early as 1809–10 as a development of a law dating back to 1776 which offered the general public some insight into the state administration. The ombudsman is a legislative commissioner, but the legislature may not interfere with his handling of particular cases. He is politically independent and his task is to verify the correctness of decisions made by public administrative bodies, civil as well as military. He may do so on his own initiative or at the request of any citizen (Schramm-Nielsen and Lawrence, 1998). Sweden now has a number of ombudsmen in diverse areas such as the administration of justice, childcare, consumer affairs and equal treatment, and this institution has been copied by many other countries, making the word part of the international vocabulary.

Sweden is exceptional in the fact that its territory has not been seriously threatened by outside powers for the past almost 300 years; indeed it has not suffered military occupation since 1523 by the Danes, has not been at war since 1814, and been at peace with its neighbours for almost 100 years, that is, since the conflict with Norway was finally solved in 1905. Sweden declared itself neutral during the two World Wars. Thus Sweden has long ago disavowed military aggressiveness, and instead it has chosen to play a balancing role among the world's conflicting ideological and political systems. Indicative of this attitude is the fact that one of the greatest Swedish industrialists, Alfred Nobel (1833–96), who invented a method for large-scale production of nitroglycerin, dynamite and explosives, dedicated a large fortune to a fund that distributes prizes to people that have 'done most good for mankind in the previous year', now in chemistry, physics, medicine and literature, and not least the Nobel peace prize, which incidentally is distributed by the Norwegian parliament (Stortinget). For economics the Bank of Sweden Prize is given in memory of Alfred Nobel.

Today's reputation of the Swedes as compromise and peace-seeking people has also led to a number of Swedish statesmen having been sought to fill major positions in the United Nations (UN) and in political conflicts round the world, for instance Dag Hammarskjöld (1905–61), secretary general of the UN (1948–53) after having filled several other posts in the UN administration. Or Raoul Wallenberg (1912–47), who went to Hungary in 1944 at the invitation of the US administration to rescue Hungarian Jews. When Budapest was conquered by the Russians, he was arrested on suspicion for being a spy for the Germans, and he died in a Russian prison. The latest example would be Hans Blix (b. 1929), who was sent to Iraq to lead the team looking for weapons of mass destruction, one of the main reasons for the recent war against Iraq in 2003.

Over the years, leading Swedish politicians have taken active part in the discussion of world politics, often criticizing belligerent powers. Examples would include Prime Minister Olof Palme (1927–86) and Anna Lindh (1957–2003), minister of foreign affairs, both highly respected Social Democrats and both murdered, the first in the street and the second in a shopping centre by a psychologically unstable young second-generation immigrant. The murderer of Olof Palme was never found.

**Foreign Policy**

The Swedish neutrality policy means that the country is not a member of the North Atlantic Treaty Organization (NATO) nor the Western European Union (WEU). It does, however, take part in peace-seeking and peace-keeping operations in NATO, this being called 'partnership with NATO', in the European Partnership for Peace (EPP), and is a member of the EU. Membership of the OECD, on the other hand, was never in conflict with Sweden's neutrality policy. Sweden only joined the EU in 1995, in a rapid change of opinion among the leading politicians as a consequence of the discussions leading to the Single European Market (SEM), which became effective from 1994. During this period it became clear that Sweden, with its small domestic market and dependence on exports, could no longer stay outside (Nedström, 2000). In 1994 a national referendum was held, giving a small majority of 52 per cent for membership. This was a decisive step in the movement away from the neutrality policy. However, there is quite an amount of EU scepticism in the Swedish population, as is also the case in Norway and Denmark, and a referendum on adopting the euro was turned down in September 2003 by a majority of 66 per cent.

In 2002, the Social Democratic government and the three main non-socialist parties in opposition formulated a new version of Sweden's security policy, reflecting the new realities, by saying in essence that Sweden pursues a policy of non-participation in military alliances. This would make it possible for the country to remain neutral in the event of conflicts in its vicinity. Thus the intention of neutrality is maintained.

Since 1991, after the fall of Communism in Eastern Europe, Sweden has concentrated its efforts in foreign policy and security policy on the Baltic Sea area, and it has expressed a special concern and responsibility for the small Baltic countries of Estonia, Latvia and Lithuania, where it is active in economic development and military security questions. As part of this security policy Sweden would like to draw these countries and Russia closer to Western Europe.

Several of our Scandinavian companies (in furniture, brewing, shipbuilding and confectionery) invest in Eastern Europe, but this is more from a purely business point of view, although it is applauded by the respective governments and benefits from certain incentives.

## Economy, Strengths and Weaknesses

Sweden long struggled with general poverty. As late as 1840–1930 this led to massive emigration, in fact over some 15 years more than one-third of the Swedish population left the country for more prosperous lands, especially to America (Nedström, 2000). This has been depicted by the great Swedish film-maker Jan Troell (b. 1931) in his 1971 epic film *The Emigrants*, based on a novel by Vilhelm Moberg. However, after a number of reforms in education, agriculture and business a long and continuous progress of the economy took place from around 1850, only interrupted by the economic world crisis of the 1930s. Serious industrialization gained momentum from the 1890s, assisted by a new infrastructure of canals and railways.

The economic history of Sweden is remarkable in several respects. First of all it achieved something many developing countries have struggled and failed to do: it made the transition from a raw materials economy to a manufacturing economy. Such manufacture as Sweden enjoyed in the 1700s and 1800s was based on raw materials, principally timber, pulp, iron ore and some processing of agricultural produce. These were also the mainstay of Swedish exports. Nelson's fleet which bombarded Copenhagen in the Napoleonic Wars used Swedish timber, and without imports of Swedish oats British horse-drawn transportation would have come to a halt.

Second, Sweden's manufacturing economy was founded extensively on a series of inventions and discoveries in the late 1800s and early 1900s. These included most famously Ericsson's invention of the telephone in 1876, von Platen's invention of the gas-driven refrigerator, the development of the revolving lighthouse, the perfecting of the ball-bearing, the development of the cream separator by Gustaf de Laval, the pioneering of powered mining equipment, and the vigorous exploitation of the internal combustion engine. In the 1890–1920 period a raft of big name Swedish companies were founded, including Ericsson, ASEA, Electrolux, SKF, Alfa Laval and AGA.

Third, Swedish industry internationalized at an early stage, in various senses:

● becoming strong exporters;
● establishing manufacturing operations in other countries;
● earning the larger share of their revenue outside Sweden;
● having a non-Swedish workforce (in other countries) that exceeded the number of Swedish employees; and

- developing a management cadre with substantial international experience.
- In this connection it is worth mentioning that the Stockholm School of Economics (Handelshögskolan i Stockholm) was established as early as 1909.

Fourth, Sweden did particularly well in the aftermath of the Second World War (1939–45). As a neutral country Sweden sold to both sides during the War (and increased its exports to Nazi Germany very much in the early stages of the conflict), but its real opportunity came in the years after the War. A deeply industrialized country that had not been occupied or fought over, whose plant and equipment had suffered no damage, Sweden was wonderfully well-placed to respond to the post-War demand for goods of all kinds. In the Nordiska Museet in Stockholm there is a room devoted to capturing the spirit and lifestyle of the early post-War period, and not for nothing is this room entitled The Golden Age.

But it is the breadth and range of Swedish industry that is most striking. Consider that Sweden:

- makes cars, trucks, buses and aeroplanes;
- is a leader in power generation/power engineering;
- has a leading telecommunications company in Ericsson;
- has one of the world's leading electrical consumer goods companies (Electrolux);
- has an enormous range of metal and mechanical engineering and industrial products including mining equipment, rock drills, welding equipment, rolling stock, ball-bearings, instruments, lighthouses, industrial gases, turbines, diesel engines, cutting tools and process industry equipment;
- has an arms industry;
- has a chemical industry;
- and a pharmaceutical industry;
- as well as a massive presence in wood, wood products, pulp and paper.

In addition it once made its own cigarettes, still brews its own beer and processes a lot of its own food. It even has two retailers, Hennes and Mauritz and the mighty IKEA, that have been very successful abroad.

This is a remarkable achievement for a country of barely 9 million people. To put it in perspective one might compare the breadth and variety of Sweden's industry with that of, say, Switzerland with a nearly equal population or with that of the Netherlands which is demographically nearly twice Sweden's size. Not only would Sweden compare well in these two cases, but it would be fair to say that Sweden more strongly resembles Germany, albeit on a smaller scale.

This period of intense industrial development is also the period when trade unions were formed and the Social Democratic Party was founded (1889). This party came to power in 1932 and kept the reins of government for 44 years until 1974, when the non-Socialist parties won the election, only to make a come-back in 1982 to 1991, and again in 1994, but the hegemony of the party was broken. Thus the Social Democratic Party more than any has dominated Swedish politics and is responsible for the building of the comprehensive Swedish welfare state, known under the name of Folkhemmet (the people's home). Indeed, no other country has been so deeply influenced by social democracy.

Sweden is also known for what has been termed 'the Swedish model'. The word 'model' may be somewhat misleading, since it connotes something static or at least stable, when in fact it has changed over the years since the idea took form roughly from the basic labour market agreement between the principal employers' organization, SAF, and the trade union confederation, LO, in 1938, known as the Saltsjöbaden agreement (SOU, 1990:94). This agreement codified the principle of mutual cooperation and self-regulation of labour market conditions, that is to say, without interference from the state, a kind of peace treaty between the main parties. This concept is not without some ambiguity since it cannot be clearly defined (SOU, 1990:94); however, it has come to mean a way of organizing society and relations between various interest groups in the Swedish society. It came to include such circumstances as (Jönsson, 1995; SOU, 1990:94):

- peaceful conflict resolution of labour market problems through negotiation and compromise;
- centralization of labour market negotiations by LO and SAF leading to wage equalization through the policy of wage solidarity;
- a mutual interest in rational production and a competitive export industry, also seen as a compromise between work and capital;
- an overarching social welfare policy of the universal type, meaning independent of income;
- low level of inequality, partly through income equalization;
- a large public sector providing many jobs, especially for women;
- full employment and simultaneous low inflation;
- the main interest organizations became involved in all steps of the political decision making, that is, cooperation between such organizations and the state, known as the corporatist system.

The different parts of the 'model' were the results of a long process lasting from the late 1930s till the late 1970s (Jönsson, 1995), which is also the heyday of the Social Democrats and the period of the fastest economic growth.

The Swedish model has, however, come increasingly under attack. After a severe economic recession in the early 1990s with large budget deficits, it became clear that the welfare state had gone too far in wanting to look after the Swedes from cradle to grave, and for the first time in living memory the Swedes experienced painful cutbacks in budgets in practically all areas as well as severe unemployment.

It is well known that the international economy has changed dramatically over the last decades, and so has the Swedish model in several ways: wage determination has been decentralized, pay differentials have increased, inequality has increased, unions are not as influential as they used to be, and Sweden increasingly has to change as a consequence of EU membership. With a growing number of immigrants Swedish society is not as homogeneous as it used to be. Even the role of the state has changed in as much as it is no longer expanding and is losing out to other actors. Finally, who these actors, these 'interest groups', are is not as clear-cut as it used to be, when the main players were LO (trade unions), SAF (employers) and the political establishment. With decentralization of wage negotiations more unions are in play, and grass root movements, environmentalists and the media all try to influence the political decision making. In other words, the former balance between work, capital and state has been broken (SOU, 1990:94). If the 'Swedish model' is not dead, at least it has become a shadow of what it used to be.

However, in some areas Sweden still stands out as an exceptional country. Consider that maternity leave is 13 months, including two months paternity leave, the longest in Scandinavia (Norway 12 months including one month paternity leave, Denmark 12 months including two weeks paternity leave). The paternity leave is a testimony of the official policy of equalization of the sexes in the Scandinavian countries. In Sweden, a further step has been taken in a symbolic change in vocabulary to 'parental leave'. It can also be taken as a testimony of the fact that if women are to contribute to the GDP of a country, politicians are well advised to give young families adequate compensation.

One of the reasons for the economic recession mentioned earlier can be found in what is at the same time one of the strengths of the Swedish economy, namely the structure of large industrial corporations; nine of them are among the 400 largest in the world and among those with the best results. For too long the Swedish economy was production driven like those of Japan and Germany, both of whom also have severe economic problems. Almost 50 per cent of employment in Sweden is in large firms, in many cases up-stream products such as forest related industries and ferrous metals (Karnøe et al., 1999). There were signs of structure problems as early as the 1970s, but restructuring was not an issue seriously addressed. In corporate Sweden trade unions played their part in pressing for a solidaristic wage policy, in practice meaning the highest level obtainable. A solidaristic wage policy meant that employees would have the same wages for the same kind of work, independent of whether they worked in more profitable or less profitable companies. In this way, less productive companies would be pushed out (Engstrand, 2001). The ideological foundation was that of full employment and full-time employment as a right for all adults, regardless of age and gender.

When unemployment soared, the state had to step in with job creation, leading to massive deficits in the state budget. At the same time the legislation for the protection of workers and employees was rigid and strictly followed. The last in first out (LIFO) principle was maintained, in other words seniority took precedence over competence. The high wage and salary level, however, had a negative effect on competitiveness and killed small and medium sized companies, companies that in other countries such as Denmark are more flexible in their response to market change.

It is a well-known fact that it takes a long time to turn a large oil tanker around. The Swedes, however, did manage to turn the tanker around, by means of:

- devaluations;
- cuts in budgets, not least on social welfare;
- wage freeze;
- slimming and reorganization of the organizations;
- mergers and acquisitions; and
- large-scale education or retraining programmes.

By the end of the 1990s Swedish economy had regained strength, industry production increased not least due to devaluations of the Swedish currency by 20 per cent, inflation went down to about 2 per cent, GNP increased with an average of around 3 per cent from 1998 to 2000, and unemployment went down from 12–13 in 1993 to around 4 per cent; this combined with fiscal stimulus (tax cuts) had a positive effect on private consumption. At the time of writing (August 2003) the unemployment rate is 5.6.

The knowledge-based service sector is growing, as is the medico-pharmaceutical sector, but manufacturing still plays a leading role and the export performance is still relatively weak (OECD, 2001–02).

All considered though, Sweden's economic performance is robust.

**National Heroes**

*Ingmar Bergman (b. 1918)*
Film-maker and theatre producer. Has made about 50 film and television

productions since 1946. Examples: *Summer nights* (1955), *The Seventh Seal* (1957), *End of the Road* (1957), *Whisper and cries* (1972), *Scenes from a marriage* (1973), *Fanny and Alexander* (1982), *Laterna Magica* (1987). During 1963–66 he was manager of Dramaten, Stockholm's most important theatre.

*Tage Erlander (1901–85)*
Politician.
1932–73   Member of Parliament for the Social Democratic Party.
1946–69   Prime Minister and leader of the Social Democratic Party. Major agent in the creation of the Swedish welfare state called Folkhemmet (people's home).

*Dag Hammarskjöld (1905–61)*
Civil servant and diplomat. UN general secretary 1953–61. Killed in an aircraft crash. Posthumously awarded the Nobel peace prize.

*Ingvar Kamprad (b. 1926)*
Founder of the IKEA company.

*Selma Lagerlöf (1858–1940)*
Author of novels such as *The Tales of Gösta Berling* (1891), *Jerusalem* (1901–02), *The Journey of Nils Holgersson through Sweden* (1906–07, written for children), *The Emperor of Portugal* (1914), *The Löwensköld Family* (1925–28). Was awarded the Nobel Prize in 1909.
   Several of her novels have been translated into film productions.

*Astrid Lindgren (1907–2002)*
Much-loved author of literature for children. Examples: *Pippi Longstocking* (1945), *The Master Detective Blomkvist* (1946), *The Children of Bulderby* (1947), *Mio my Mio* (1954), *Emil from Lönneberg* (1963), *The Brothers Lionheart* (1973), *Ronja the Robber's Daughter* (1981). The funeral ceremony for her was royal-like, with a long procession through the streets of Stockholm attended by large crowds of people showing their last respects. Many of her books have been translated into film and television productions.

*Anna Lindh (1957–2003)*
Politician for the Social Democratic Party. Educated in law, she entered politics as a student. She was a great admirer of Olof Palme, for whom she gave the commemoration speech after he was murdered in 1986. At the time of her death, likewise at the hand of a murderer, she was Minister of Foreign Affairs.

*Alfred Nobel (1833–96)*
Educated in chemistry. Inventor of dynamite and explosives. Founder of the Nobel Foundation awarding Nobel prizes in physics, chemistry, medicine, literature, peace and economics.

*Olof Palme (1927–86)*
Politician.

1969–76   Took over from Tage Erlander as leader of the Social Democratic Party and Prime Minister.

1982–86   Prime Minister again until his death in 1986, when he was murdered in the street coming out from a cinema in Stockholm. The identity of the murderer has never been established, nor has the motive.

He held a number of international positions in peace mediation (Iran–Iraq), and as president of an international commission for disarmament and security.

*August Strindberg (1849–1912)*
Author of dramas and novels, photographer and painter. Best known are theatre plays describing the fight between the sexes such as *Miss Julie* (1888) and the generations *The Father* (1887).

*Wallenberg family*
Finance and industry dynasty for five generations from around 1850, controlling large enterprises. They have been involved with Ericsson, Skandinaviska Enskilda Banken, Electrolux, Saab and Scania.

# DENMARK

## Geography, Demography and Landscape

Denmark is the smallest of our three countries, just 43 000 sq km, ten times smaller than Sweden, but more evenly inhabited in the sense of not having large uninhabited areas like Sweden and Norway. With 5.3 million people the population density is 124 persons per sq km as opposed to Sweden's 20 per sq km. The kingdom of Denmark also comprises Greenland (56 000 inhabitants) and the Faeroe Islands (46 000 inhabitants), both in the North Atlantic Ocean and both enjoying home rule. The country is composed of the peninsula of Jutland attached to Northern Germany by a frontier of just 67 km and some 400 islands, of which the largest are Zeeland (Sjaelland) and Funen (Fyn). Distances are small; no point is more than 50 km from a coast.

The entire country is lowlands, and since the climate is temperate, with mild winters for its latitude and cool summers, it offers excellent opportunities for agriculture, which was indeed for centuries the only natural resource available. Today about 66 per cent of the land is exploited for farming, 12 per cent is covered with forest, and another 10 per cent is meadows, lakes and dunes.

The many fjords and bays along the coasts offer excellent opportunities for harbours, and such places were the natural sites for early settlements, which go back to around 12 500 BC. Agriculture developed from around 4000 BC. Agriculture still constitutes an important part of the Danish economy in terms of exports (10 per cent) and as part of the self-image/national identity of the Danes, although nowadays it occupies only about 4 per cent of the population.

Since the country is more evenly populated than its northern neighbours, the industries are also more evenly distributed than in Norway and Sweden. There is nothing exceptional about the location of the Danish companies that we found north and south of Copenhagen, on the Island of Funen and in south-eastern Jutland.

## History, State Building and Industrialization

The earliest records of a Danish kingdom go back to around AD 700, when a rampart was built along the southern border from the Baltic to the North Sea to protect the country from military aggression from the south. This great building project indicates some kind of central authority, the formation of a state at that early period. From around AD 800 the Frankish annals describe campaigns against Danish kings. This means that Denmark has been a kingdom for more than a thousand years.

What is called the 'Danish birth certificate', however, dates from about AD 940. It is a huge stone with a runic inscription erected by King Harold Bluetooth in commemoration of his parents and at the same time claiming the unification of all Denmark, the conquest of Norway and the Christianization of the Danes. This was in mid-Viking era, when the Vikings from all of Scandinavia went marauding, trading and colonizing neighbouring shores. In East Anglia, Harold's son Sweyn and grandson Canute the Great set up an Anglo-Danish kingdom, the Danelaw, meaning of course the area where Danish law prevailed; it ended in 1042 at the death of the Danish king.

The Kalmar Union of Norway, Sweden and Denmark already mentioned (1397–1523) started with Margarethe I (1353–1412), who served as a regent of both Denmark and Norway during her son's minority. However, he died at the age of 17 in 1387 and she was then acknowledged regent of the two countries. In 1388 rebellious Swedish nobles hailed her as regent of Sweden as well. The Kalmar Union also included the Shetland, Orkney and Fareoe Islands, Iceland, Greenland and Finland (that came with Sweden). Later the province of Holstein in northern Germany joined. Since Margarethe was now childless, her sister's grandson, Eric of Pomerania, was crowned king of Denmark, Norway and Sweden at Kalmar. After a troubled period, actually marked by wars between Denmark and Sweden, the union was finally dissolved in 1523. This was the first experience of coordinated efforts between the three countries, but the time was not ripe for a continuous development along these lines. On the contrary, the period from 1560 to 1720 saw an increasing rivalry between Sweden and Denmark over the hegemony in the Baltic Sea area, leading to no less than six wars between them. From the outset Denmark was the great power, being the richer of the two and having a powerful fleet, but as the conflicts continued Denmark gradually lost territory after territory, especially when the Danish king (Christian IV, 1588–1648) meddled in the Thirty Years War (1618–48) in Europe with no luck at all. At a certain point Denmark was even on the brink of extinction, when in 1658 one of the powerful Swedish warrior kings, Carl X Gustav, marched his army from Poland through Germany up into Jutland and had the incredible luck of being able to cross the straits and belts of Denmark, thanks to an extraordinarily cold winter that covered the sea with ice thick enough to carry soldiers and their equipment. It was due only to the resistance of the citizens and foreign support that Copenhagen was saved from the invading troops. However, the price of peace was the loss of all the provinces of southern Sweden, which diminished the country by one-third and the population from 800 000 to 600 000.

Another result of this catastrophe was that the power of the Danish nobility was irreversibly broken, because they had not lived up to their obligation as military defenders of the realm. Instead, a coalition between the bourgeoisie, the clergy and the king, in a bloodless *coup d'état*, installed a hereditary absolute monarchy, which was to last from 1660 to 1849, when Denmark had its first liberal constitution. It is worth mentioning that both of these turning points were implemented peacefully.

Paradoxically, the one person who was most to be blamed for the fall of Denmark from its position as a great power, King Christian IV (1588–1648), is now regarded as one of the greatest rulers in the long succession of kings of Denmark. How come? Well, the first part of Christian's 60-year-long reign was in every respect a success. He was a typical renaissance monarch who did not only see war as his metier, but who also promoted fine arts, bringing musicians, painters, goldsmiths and architects to the country. A diligent builder/entrepreneur, he has left many beautiful buildings in Copenhagen, such as the Rosenborg Castle, the Stock Exchange, the Church of the Navy, the Armoury and so on, as well as Kronborg Castle in Elsinore (Helsingør) and Frederiksborg Castle in Hillerød, both in North Zealand. He founded the city of Christiania, now Oslo, Kristiansand, also in Norway, and Kristianstad, which is now in Sweden, and left his imprint on innumerable churches and other buildings, industries and institutions. He established trading companies and acquired overseas possessions. In sum he was a brilliant entrepreneur, a colourful person and a poor politician.

During the next period Denmark tried in vain to regain the lost territories in Scania, southern Sweden, most of the time assisted by the Scanians themselves, until the case was finally closed with the peace treaty of 1720. Since then the two neighbours have maintained entirely peaceful relationships with one another, even developing into close cooperation with the establishment of the Nordic Council in 1952, already mentioned.

The next catastrophe to hit Denmark was in connection with the Napoleonic wars, when Denmark, due to intricate international circumstances, joined the losing side. In fact Denmark tried to stay neutral, but England feared that the strong Danish navy could be used against it by the continental powers, and attacked Copenhagen twice, in 1801 and in 1807, the first time destroying most of the fleet and the second time bombarding Copenhagen with fire bombs and sailing away with what was left of the navy.

Not only did this mean the end of Denmark as a great sea power and an international financial and administrative centre, but the Napoleonic Wars also meant the loss of Norway already described. The state went bankrupt in 1813 and over the next decades Denmark was in deep economic crisis. However, it also galvanized the national spirit and set off a slow but steady economic development from around 1830 that only slowed down in the depression of the 1930s.

What triggered this development was in fact important structural land reforms that had been initiated by a small group of enlightened landed aristocracy towards the close of the eighteenth century. Right up until after the Second World War the Danish population was essentially agrarian, the majority of the population living from farming. Towards the end of the eighteenth century, Denmark still had a communal open-field system. Most individual landholders were tenant farmers whose farm buildings and land belonged to the local manor house, and part of the rent was paid in labour on the landlord's domain. The farms were clustered in groups of five to 20 in villages, and the scattered plots of land were located in each of two or three large fields, which were farmed collectively. Therefore it was essential that villagers agreed on the timing of ploughing, harrowing, planting and harvesting. Meeting at a central place in the village, family heads discussed common problems of field management and agreed on mutual responsibilities and cooperation. Each family enjoyed the harvest from its own plots, but also worked with the others to manage the fields. They shared resources and their livestock was grazed as a single village herd. Shared decisions were also made on the use of communal facilities such as the meadow, commons, village square, pond and church. Thus Danish peasants cooperated in much of what they did, strengthening the communal spirit, but productivity was very low.

With the great land reforms the system was changed. The open-field system was replaced by the consolidation of fields into larger individual holdings, and new farmsteads were built in the midst of the area now belonging to each individual farmer, who had been financially aided to purchase the farms. Indeed, 60 per cent of Danish peasants became landowners. At the same time technological improvements, such as the light-weight plough that could be pulled by a single horse, made the individual farm run by one family possible. The agrarian economy now shifted from subsistence to commercial farming. At the same time the 1814 school act made school attendance compulsory for all children between ages seven and 14. The Danish land reforms and school reforms are probably the only example of a successful feat of enlightened European despotism. The result was that a poor and ignorant peasantry was slowly but steadily developing into a class of wealthy independent farmers.

From the middle of the nineteenth century the agricultural exports, which were based on grain and live oxen, came under heavy pressure from overseas cheap cereals, especially from the United States and Canada. It is well known that this was made possible thanks to the technological improvements in railways and steamships that made transportation over long distances possible and profitable. The Danish farmers responded to this competition by changing the production from grain and live oxen to dairy products and processed meat of high standard. Each individual farmer did not have the capital nor the capacity for large-scale production, and certainly not for organizing exports. Instead the farmers were organized in cooperatives, in which they invested small amounts of money for shares, delivered their production and received proportional parts of the overall profits.

The cooperative movement soon gained momentum in the entire country in diverse areas including retail, and it had a number of beneficial effects:

- the cooperatives could demand standardized products of high quality;
- they could hire well-educated specialists to run the dairy or the slaughterhouse;
- they could invest in improved production facilities and machinery;
- they could arrange fast transportation and exportation; and
- not least, the cooperatives were run by the farmers themselves, the managing board was elected from their own midst, and there were regular assemblies where important decisions were put to the vote among all members.

This created a whole new class of consolidated, independent and self-confident farmers that also grew in political awareness, organizing themselves into the liberal party Venstre. This party took over government responsibilities in 1901, when the power of the Conservative Party was finally broken and proper parliamentary government was established.

Another important movement was created during the same period, from around the 1870s, that of the folk high-schools. The inspiration came from one of the monumental figures in Danish cultural and religious life, the churchman, poet, author and educator N.S.F. Grundtvig (1783–1872). 'Grundtvigianism' designates a revitalization movement that inspired a new sense of Christian awareness in the nineteenth century in Denmark and Norway. The folk high-schools were established to further educate especially the daughters and sons of the independent farmers and not least to prepare them to take part in a democratic society. Based on Christian belief and peasant culture they were taught history and literature alongside a number of practical skills, particularly the newest techniques and improvements in agriculture and house-keeping.

Grundtvigianism has made a profound imprint on values and attitudes in Denmark and to a large extent also in Norway, where he was very popular. In religious matters, Grundtvig stood for a joyous Christian life on earth in opposition to stern Pietism. In innumerable hymns he praised God's creations, the happy, joyous, modest life, and the Danish mild and smiling landscape. In pedagogical matters, he saw the main enemy as the classic Latin culture with its drill, rigorous discipline and abstract learning. Instead of just imparting knowledge, he thought that education should inspire personal, national and Christian endeavour, and to Grundtvig the spoken word, not the book, was the best means of education. He was convinced of the paramount importance of dialogue. In Church matters as well as in education Grundtvig played an enormous role in the struggle against authoritarian ways of life, and in both fields he pleaded for freedom, democracy and dialogue.

The development of agriculture and the technical improvements created the need for agricultural machinery and equipment and for a food processing industry, and since the country had a century-old craft tradition with apprenticeship education, the basis was there for a large number of small industries, suppliers to agriculture or buyers of agricultural products.

Right up to the middle of the 1900s, Denmark was decidedly an agricultural country in terms of production, exports and the derived light industry. Indeed, it was only in 1963 that the value of industrial exports surpassed that of agriculture, which is very late compared to most industrialized countries. Even today the food processing industries, including fish products, play a significant role in areas such as beer brewing (Carlsberg, Tuborg, Faxe), sugar (Danisco), dairy products (MD Foods, now Arla) and meat processing (Danish Crown).

In 1972, a new chapter in Danish economic life opened when the exploitation of the oil deposits in the North Sea started, until 1981 as a sole concession for the A.P. Møller company. The fact that the concession was given to a private company is in sharp contrast to the strategy in Norway, where concessions were given to fully or partly state-owned Norwegian companies and multinationals. In 1997 Denmark reached the point of self-sufficiency in oil and gas, and since then the country has been a net exporter of these raw materials, an undeniable asset, although not of the magnitude of the Norwegian petroleum industry.

Since Denmark is deprived of natural resources apart from the soil and lately oil, the Danes have had to resort to other means of income. Over the past two or three decades, knowledge-based industries have developed, taking advantage of the high level of education in the population, be it as craftsmen, technicians or academics. The pharmaceutical industry especially and biotechnology have expanded heavily; examples here would include Novo Nordisk (diabetes products) and H. Lundbeck (specializing in central nervous system products) just to mention the largest ones. Medical equipment and healthcare products would be another example, with large-scale exporters such as Oticon, Rexton, Danavox and Widex (hearing aids) and Coloplast (colostomy products) as prime examples. The IT industry is important (mobile and satellite communication), although it is now under severe pressure from competition and over-production. Engineering, especially consultancy, windmills, water treatment and refinement of measuring and precision instruments with a high content of sophisticated technology such as sensor technology coupled with a pronounced sense of design and aesthetics create the characteristics of modern Danish niche export industries.

Another area where the Danes have a century-old tradition is the so-called 'blue sector' – shipping, shipbuilding and related industries. Shipbuilding has seen a decline in all the Western European countries that used to excel in this industry, giving in to competition from South-east Asian countries, but one Danish shipyard stands, that of the Lindø Shipyard on the island of Funen, which is among our companies and which is part of the huge conglomerate A.P. Møller–Mærsk A/S. This company attracts special attention: it started off as two companies founded in 1904 and 1912 respectively as shipping and transport companies by A.P. Møller and his father. A.P. Møller died in 1965, when his son Mærsk Mc-Kinney Møller took over at the age of 51. The son, who is turning 90 at the time of writing, is still at the head of the group as chairman of the board of directors, which means that the company has had only two captains in its 100 years of existence. The two original companies were merged in 2003, making the group among the 200 largest enterprises in the world, with a total of more than 60 000 employees worldwide, and covering areas as diverse as oil and gas extraction, shipbuilding, shipping (containers, the world's largest), aviation, foods, IT and supermarkets. In particular the daring investment in oil and gas extraction and container traffic has made the company the biggest success in Danish business life in the twentieth century.

This company is an exception in Denmark, since less than 1 per cent of all Danish companies have more than 1000 employees. Consequently, Denmark's industry structure is dominated by small and medium sized companies.

Among the more surprising and up-coming competence and knowledge-intensive industries we find textiles/clothing – not the production but design, planning, logistics and sales – and the film and television industry for all age groups, including children. The dogma school of film-makers have lately aroused much interest in the industry and audiences in many countries.

The Danish state owns no manufacturing companies, but the state is an important player in the distribution of natural gas from the North Sea.

## Economy, Strengths and Weaknesses

The Danish economy is basically healthy. The macro-economic situation is good. The government has been running a steady state budget surplus since 1997 and a steady reduction of public debt relative to GDP since the early 1990s. At the time of writing the budget surplus is 1 per cent of GDP, inflation is 2.9 per cent and unemployment about 6 per cent. In 2003, the balance of payment as well as the trade balance showed surpluses. The authorities follow a policy of fixed rate of exchange *vis-à-vis* the euro, although the country is not presently (2004) part of 'Euroland'. In 2002, the growth of the economy was 2.1 per cent, according to the latest statistics, which is considerably higher than most of its European partners including Sweden's 1.8 and Norway's 1.3 per cent. In fact Denmark was surpassed only by Greece, Ireland and the United States, that could show a growth of 2.4 per cent. Exports went up by no less than 5.8 per cent, especially supported by the so-called 'blue sector', shipping and related industries, but many other sectors also performed well. This is the more surprising in view of the current international slowdown (OECD, 2003a).

Since 1993, after seven years of stagnation, Denmark has been riding on an upward wave, reducing unemployment from 12 per cent to just 5 per cent in 2002. However, unemployment is now slowly increasing and it might be difficult to increase further the number of jobs given the present stagnation of the world economy.

Since the only raw materials available to the Danes are soil and oil, and since the country is heavily dependent on exports, the composition of its labour force becomes critical. Like most other OECD countries, the Danish population will be ageing rapidly between now and 2040, when more than one in four adults will be over 65 years old. At the same time the retirement age tends to go down, and the demands for a highly qualified workforce means that a significant proportion of young Danes are still studying into their late 20s, though many of them combine study with working. At the same time immigrants from less developed countries with little or no qualifications have a considerably lower participation in the workforce than the average. Combine this with relatively generous welfare allowances and high taxation, the incentives to work more and longer are limited.

Adding to this problem is the fact that since the 1950s labour market legislation has prolonged guaranteed holidays from two to more than five weeks, and working hours per week have been reduced from 48 to 37.

The main future challenges to create new jobs and raise productive capacity might therefore prove difficult.

Apart from a well-qualified workforce, thanks to thorough vocational training and a century-long tradition in business education, the strength of the Danish economy lies in its enterprises. As already mentioned, very few companies are of a size that can match large international enterprises or, for instance, the big Swedish corporations. The industry structure is that of small and medium sized companies (SMEs) living from exports of products or services of high-quality design and/or knowledge content. Indeed, about one third of all Danish exports are in services. Knowledge and competence reside in people and are not as easily transferable to other countries such as mere production. Furthermore, it gives a high value added. Even a low technology activity such as the fur industry may have high value added in terms of knowledge sharing on production, animal feeding, the treatment of the furs and organization of marketing and sales.

What might seem to many to be a weak point, the limited size of the companies, turns out to be a strength in the present situation, since SMEs prove to be more flexible in terms of products and not least in relation to changing market conditions. To give an example: Germany is an important client for Danish agriculture, furniture, design, engineering and industrial products, but since Germany is experiencing growing economic problems, the Danish exporters have turned to other markets such as Sweden, the UK, Norway, France, the Netherlands and to other overseas markets. Or, they have changed the product portfolio to fit a stagnating market better.

In sum the strengths of the Danish economy are a prudent and stable macro-economic policy together with a micro economy based on a well-qualified workforce, flexible and innovative SMEs and a few high flyers such as the 'blue sector' and oil and gas extraction. The weaknesses are high taxation, demographic changes and relatively generous welfare provisions that might limit the incentives to work.

## Labour Market

The Danish labour market was organized at a very early stage compared to most industrialized, capitalist countries. Already by 1899 the two counter-posed organizations LO (workers) and DA (employers) were formed, and soon thereafter a centralized collective bargaining system was established, forming the nucleus of the Danish industrial relations system for the next more than 90 years. Indeed, it was only during the 1990s that steps were taken towards more fundamental changes of the structure of the two opposing sets of organizations (Lubanski et al., 2001). In 1910 a State Conciliation Board was added to the system, imposing an institutionalization of conflicts at the workplace.

The system has ensured orderly and peaceful negotiations on the regulation of pay and working conditions for virtually the entire Danish labour market, creating relative peace and stability for employers and constant gains for workers. It is based on two important principles: one is that any form of labour market legislation must be based on a prior agreement reached by the two main organizations LO and DA (Lubanski et al., 2001), and the other is a commitment for both employers and employees to maintain a good, cooperative relationship (Lind, 2000).

The characteristics of the Danish system are (Lubanski et al., 2001):

- a comprehensively organized labour market with strong organizations, for both workers and employers;
- a centralized collective bargaining process, leading to the conclusion of agreements, conducted in a synchronized sequence at regular intervals;
- a consensus-based relationship between LO and DA, a relatively low level of work stoppages and other forms of industrial action; and
- agreement-based regulation of virtually all conditions on the labour market via this voluntary system of collective bargaining, rather than legislation, which is applied only to a very limited extent.

The collective bargaining system exerts a decisive, overarching influence on Danish society. It is rather more than an agreement model for the labour market. It constitutes a part of a broader, welfare-state oriented, institutionalized political system (Due et al., 1994).

Another characteristic of the Danish system is that industrial democracy at the workplace does not provide the employees/workers with any real power, but requires the employers to negotiate and to listen to employee arguments. It also obliges the employer to establish a cooperation committee in companies with more than 50 employees. However, according to Lind (2000), only a small proportion of private sector companies have established such committees. As such, the Danish system cannot be called co-determination at the workplace. It only provides employees with a formal platform to obtain information on the economic situation of the firm, and to negotiate general principles of employment, redundancies and the implementation of new technology (Lind, 2000).

Just as in Sweden, membership rates are extremely high on both sides. Indeed, more than 80 per cent of all wage earners were unionized in the late 1990s, white- as well as blue-collar workers. However, this high percentage can be attributed partly to the fact that the unemployment insurance system is administered by the trade unions, making it an important tool for recruiting members.

As stated by Lubanski et al. (2001), the system has operated effectively for a century albeit at the risk of excessive rigidity and stagnation. The system is still very centralized, but since the late 1990s the tendency is to refer decisions on wages and working conditions to the workplace level, giving the parties directly involved greater influence; in short, decentralization.

Another factor which might change the Danish system is EU membership. An establishment of a future European industrial relations system would probably mean fundamental changes for the Danish labour market, since EU-regulation will be more influenced by countries such as France and Germany with their legacy of the Roman empire, meaning that it will be based more on legislation than what has been the tradition in Denmark (Lubanski et al., 2001). According to the same source, the survival of the Danish industrial relations system might even be threatened, since the direct incentive to join an organization would be removed. Indeed, why pay union dues if all workers are automatically covered by the provisions, as is the case in France?

**Denmark in the EU**

As the only Nordic country to do so, Denmark joined the European Economic Community (EEC) in 1973 at the same time as the United Kingdom, then its most important client for agricultural products. The referendum prior to membership gave a comfortable majority of 63 per cent. In the 1990s, the population became divided over closer economic ties with the European Community (EC) and further European integration. In 1992, the Danish voters rejected the Maastricht Treaty with a slight majority of 50.7 per cent. A second referendum in 1993 approved Danish membership of the EU, but only after Denmark had negotiated exemptions from certain provisions of the treaty, which many Danes thought might erode Danish social benefits or environmental protection and force Denmark to accept a defence policy of which the political establishment could not approve. Again in 2000, Danish voters rejected the single European currency, the euro, by 53.1 per cent.

In spite of these political controversies, Danish economy has greatly benefited from the membership, and EU countries remain the most important trading partners.

## National Heroes

*Hans Christian Andersen (1805–75)*
Author of novels (*The Improvisor* (1835), *O.T.* (1836), *Just a musician* (1837)), poetry, theatre plays, travel books *An Author's Bazaar* (1842), short stories *The Shadow* (1832) and fairy tales. Today he is best known for his fairy tales, which were meant for children and grown ups alike, such as *The Little Mermaid*, *The Emperor's New Clothes*, *The Princess and the Pea*, *The Nightingale*. His hymns describing the Danish landscape and the feeling of belonging are still very popular. He is at the same time a much-loved figure and benignly laughed at for his eccentricity.

*Niels Bohr (1885–1962)*
Physicist. In 1913 he developed a theoretical model of the atom, which became the basis for the development of the theory of quantum mechanics. Both he and his son *Aage Bohr* (b. 1922) were awarded the Nobel Prize in physics.

*Christian IV (1577–1648)*
Charismatic renaissance king of Denmark and Norway from 1588. Wanted to make Denmark a great power in Northern Europe. Built a strong navy, promoted fine arts and architecture, and followed mercantilist principles in economy. In foreign affairs he had no luck and brought the country to the brink of ruin at his death.

*The Dogma School of Film-makers*
*The Dogma Manifest* of 1995 by Lars von Trier and Thomas Vinterberg set down a number of principles to break with traditional film-making US-style. The films are low budget, camera to be carried by a person, with direct sound, without artificial light setting, set pieces or props, superficial action or special effects. Shooting must be done on location. The actors choose their clothes themselves and co-author the dialogue. Dogma film titles include *The Celebration* by Thomas Vinterberg, *Mifune* by Søren Kragh Jacobsen, *The King is Alive* by Kristian Levring, *Italian for Beginners* by Lone Scherfig, and *Love You for Ever* by Susanne Bier.

*N.F.S. Grundtvig (1783–1872)*
Churchman, poet, historian, author and educator. His thoughts and attitudes on

religious and political matters and on education have had an enormous influence on the Danish population in his own period as well as to this day. He was in opposition to the religious and political authorities of his time. Concepts such as 'the school for life' based on dialogue with the pupils, 'Danishness' based on history and interest in the common people, and the development of democracy for all, are part of his philosophy. A large number of word combinations including the syllable 'folk-' is a testimony to his influence. On top of this he wrote about 1500 psalms and hymns praising the Danish landscape, modesty and the simple joyous life.

### Søren Aabye Kirkegaard (1813–55)

Religious philosopher and critic of rationalism, regarded as the founder of the existentialist philosophy. He is famous for his critique of systematic rational philosophy, particularly Hegelianism, on the grounds that actual life cannot be contained within an abstract conceptual system. His works are still the subject of intense research by Danish as well as non-Danish scholars.

### Margarethe I (1353–1412)

Regent of Denmark, Norway and Sweden from 1387 to her death. Although she did not officially have the title of Queen, the present Queen Margarethe of Denmark chose to be named Margarethe II out of respect for her predecessor.

### Mærsk Mc-Kinney Møller (b. 1913)

Head of the huge conglomerate A.P. Møller–Mærsk A/S exploiting the oil deposits in the North Sea, owner of one of the largest container shipping companies in the world, the Lindø Shipyard and a number of companies in industry and distribution of consumer goods. With his wife Chastine he set up a Fund for Common Good, donating buildings, parks, funding the restoration of historic sites, supporting arts museums and other cultural manifestations.

### Carl Nielsen (1865–1931)

Composer, especially and internationally known for his symphonies such as *Sinfonia Semplice*, *The Four Temperaments*, *The Inextinguishable*, *Sinfonia Espansiva*, concertos for flute and orchestra, clarinet and orchestra, and operas such as *Mascarade*.

### Lars von Trier (b. 1956)

Film-maker, one of the founders of the Dogma School. *Epidemic* (1987), *Europe* (1991), *The Idiots* (1995), *Breaking the Waves* (1996), *Dancer in the Dark* (2000), *Dogville* (2003).

# CONCLUSION

Since the Viking age (from around AD 800) the histories of the three countries have been interwoven. There were periods of peaceful co-existence, but also periods of war and conflicts, especially between Denmark and Sweden over territories and the power balance in the Baltic Sea area. This ended with the peace treaty of 1720, and for the past almost 300 years the two countries have been at peace with one another. Armed conflicts between Norway and Sweden ended in 1905 when Norway finally became an independent state, loosened from close ties with either Denmark or Sweden. Thus the state building of Norway has been very different from that of its two neighbours, and the Norwegian population is extremely conscious of that fact, making it one of the reasons for not joining the EU.

The geography of the three countries is very different, in size, in geology and in natural resources: Norway is rich in oil, hydro-electric power, fish, timber and some minerals. Sweden is rich in minerals, hydro-electric power and timber, whereas Denmark's only raw material – until quite recently – was its soil and fish. In Scandinavia it is customary to consider the three countries siblings, where Sweden is given the role of big brother, Norway the younger brother and Denmark sweet little sister, a metaphor which could allude to the geography of the three countries or to their former economic strengths.

So, how have these partly similar, partly different starting points influenced the industry structures and the economies? In Sweden the result of early exploitation of minerals and water power, combined with technical improvements and innovations, was the creation of a dozen very large, competitive and internationalized industrial enterprises and relatively few small and medium sized enterprises (SMEs). The latter live with the difficulties of having to compete with the large groups for a scarce workforce and high salaries.

Norway, until recently the poor little brother, developed a forest of SMEs geographically spread out, except in the 'blue sector', shipping and fishing, until the boom of the now dominating oil industry. The Norwegian state is deeply involved in the petroleum industry as in a number of other industrial enterprises. This is the result of a long lasting hegemony of the Social Democratic Party in Norwegian politics. The Social Democratic Party also dominated Sweden for decade after decade, but the Swedish policy was to create the framework for the big enterprises. When the large enterprises prospered, Sweden prospered.

In little sister Denmark, SMEs dominate the picture. This is the result of an organic growth of cooperatives, light industry based on craftsmanship, and knowledge-intensive service companies and often a combination of the three.

Big brother Sweden was the first to set off on a path of prosperity thanks to its natural resources and an industrious and well-educated population. It also benefited from a world demand for industrial products of high quality, especially after the Second World War. Denmark's economic development was slower, but steady from the 1950s. Changing political coalitions and constellations from left to right and back again over a multi-party spectrum had the effect that the state never gained a dominating position in Danish business life and that it generally followed a more liberal path to the present favourable economic position.

All three had economic crises in the 1980s–1990s. They all recovered. Norway, thanks to wage moderation, by applying strict budget principles and by absorbing most of the surpluses from the oil industry so as not to overheat the economy. Sweden recovered by means of an array of measures such as devaluations, cuts in budgets, large-scale education programmes to enhance competitiveness, and in business by mergers and acquisitions, the slimming and reorganization of companies. Denmark also recovered by applying an array of austerity measures that generally turned the population into savers instead of spenders. To sum up, the key words for all three countries are prudence, restraint and stability.

## NOTE

1.   Stockholm 21 per cent, Copenhagen 34 per cent.

## REFERENCES

Abowd, J.M. and D.S. Kaplan (1999), 'Executive compensations: six questions that need answering', *Journal of Economic Perspectives*, 13, 145–68.
Barth, E., K. Moene and M. Wallerstein (2003), *Likhet under Press: Utfordringer for den Skandinaviske Fordelingsmodellen*, Oslo: Gyldendal Akademisk.
Dale-Olsen, H. (2002), 'Topplønninger i det norske arbeidsliv – store kun i norsk målestokk?', *Søkelys på Arbeidsmarkedet*, 19, 201–210.
Dale-Olsen, H. (2003), 'Avlønning på toppen i arbeidslivet', *Økonomisk Forum*, 59, 1–11.
Due, J., J.S. Madsen, C. Strøby Jensen and L.K. Petersen (1994), *The Survival of the Danish Model. A Historical Sociological Analysis of the Danish System of Collective Bargaining*, Copenhagen: DJØF Publishing.
Ellingsæter, A.L. (2000), 'Scandinavian transformations: labour markets, politics and gender division', in *Economic and Industrial Democracy*, vol. 21, London: Sage, pp. 335–59.
Engelstad, F., E. Ekberg, T. Gulbrandsen and J. Vatnaland (2003), *Næringslivet mellom market og politikk*, Oslo: Gyldendal Akademisk.
Engstrand, Å-K. (2001), 'Sweden's fifty-year debate on the labour market and flexibility', in S. Jefferys, F. Mispelblom Beyer and C. Thörnqvist (eds), *European Working Lives*, Cheltenham: Edward Elgar.

European Database (2001), 'Fact sheet: women in the national parliaments', accessed at www.db-decision.de.

Hall, B.J. and K.J. Murphy (2003), 'The trouble with stock options', *Journal of Economic Perspectives*, 17, 49–70.

Hanell, T., H. Aalbu and J. Neubauer (2002), 'Regional development in the Nordic countries', Nordregio report 2002:2.

Ibsen, F. (1997), 'The role of the state in industrial relations in the Nordic countries', in J. Browne (ed.), *The Role of the State in Industrial Relations*, vol. 3 of the official proceedings of the Fifth IIRA European Regional Industrial Relations Congress, Dublin: Oak Tree Press.

Jönsson, S. (1995), *Goda Utsikter: Svenskt Management i Perspektiv*, Stockholm: Nerenius and Santérus.

Karnøe, P., P. Hull Kristensen and P. Houman Andersen (1999), *Mobilizing Resources and Generating Competencies – The Remarkable Success of Small and Medium-sized Enterprises in the Danish Business System*, Copenhagen: Copenhagen Business School Press.

Katzenstein, P.J. (1985), *Small states in world markets – industrial policy in Europe*, Ithaca, NY: Cornell University Press.

Lind, J. (2000), 'Denmark. Still the century of trade unionism', in J. Waddington and R. Hoffmann (eds), *Trade Unions in Europe*, Brussels: European Trade Union Institute (ETUI).

Lubanski, N., J. Due, J.S. Madsen and C.S. Jensen (2001), 'Denmark – Towards multi-level regulation', in G. Széll (ed.), *European Labour Relations, vol. 2, Selected Country Studies*, Aldershot: Gower.

Mjøset, L., Å. Cappelen, J. Fagerberg and B. Tranøy (2000), 'Norway changing the model', in J. Waddington and R. Hoffmann (eds), *Trade Unions in Europe*, Brussels: European Trade Union Institute (ETUI).

Murphy, K.J. (1999), 'Executive compensation', in O. Ashenfelter and D. Card (eds), *Handbook of Labour Economics*, vol. 3, pp. 2485–566, Amsterdam: North Holland.

Nedström, C. (2000), 'Sweden in Europe', in R. Crane (ed.), *European Business Cultures*, Harlow: Pearson Education.

Nordic Statistics (2001), Copenhagen: Nordic Council of Ministers.

OECD (2001–02), *Economic Survey of Sweden*.

OECD (2003a), *Economic Survey of Denmark*.

OECD (2003b), *Labour Market Statistics*.

OECD (2003c), *Reviews of Regulatory Reforms*, 'Norway – preparing for the future now', OECD June.

Schramm-Nielsen, J. and P. Lawrence (1998), 'Scandinavian management. A cultural homogeneity beyond the nation state', in *Entreprises et Histoire*, no. 18, Paris: ESKA.

Sivesind, K.H. (1996), 'Norwegian wage-bargaining in the nineties. The oscillation between centralisation and decentralisation', *Finnish Work Research Bulletin*, 7, 11–16.

SOU 1990:94 (1990), SOU 1990:94, *Demokrati och makt i Sverige*: Maktutredningens huvudrapport, Stockholm: Allmänna förlaget.

World Economic Forum, *Global Competitiveness Report 2003–2004*, www.weforum online 03-11-2003.

# 3. Breweries

This is the first of several industry-specific chapters in which we look at three breweries, one in each of the three countries. The purpose is not industry analysis in the conventional sense, but rather to use these matched-by-industry companies to test out the idea of Scandinavian homogeneity in matters of business culture and management behaviour. The three companies are Brewery Group Denmark (BGD), Falcon Brewery in Sweden, and Hansa Borg in Norway.

In this and in subsequent industry chapters we are concerned with two broad questions. First, when we hold industry constant do these matched companies offer evidence of shared Scandinavian culture and practice? And second, is it in fact possible to tease out any differences?

## INDUSTRY DEVELOPMENTS

Before moving into brewing in Scandinavia, however, a word on developments in the industry may be helpful.

Probably the first general thing one would say about brewing is that it is a mature industry. Beer brewing is centuries old, with most of the breweries we know today having been founded in the nineteenth century or earlier, or at least having their corporate origins in this period even if there have been name and ownership changes.

This leads to the next consideration, namely that beer consumption in traditional beer-drinking countries – Northern Europe, North America and Australia – is stagnant or gently declining in part due to competition from wine. This in turn leads brewing companies to seek sales outside their domestic markets, in areas where consumption may be growing. Earlier studies have noted a mild upswing in beer consumption in the traditional wine-drinking countries of Southern Europe (Calori and Lawrence, 1991), but much more important are opportunities for market growth in Central and Eastern Europe, in Southeast Asia, and indeed in developing countries generally. These market opportunities arise from the fact of increasing affluence in some of these areas, often supported by rising aspirations, when consuming some internationally known European brand carries overtones of enviable Western lifestyle. This last point has been particularly relevant for post-Communist Eastern Europe.

Another aspect of the maturity of the brewing industry is its marked tendency to consolidate. That is to say that merger and acquisition activity is common in this industry. Again an earlier study (Calori and Lawrence, 1991) noted the progressive elimination of regional breweries in several countries, leaving national brewers dominating domestic markets supplemented by a few local and micro breweries serving product market niches.

The conspicuous development since then has been cross-border merger and acquisition, when breweries in one country have acquired brewers in another, a phenomenon that is observable among our three Scandinavian brewers. The epic cross-border acquirer of the last few years (end of 2004), however, is Interbrew, the transformed and renamed Stella Artois of Belgium. Interbrew variously acquired Bass and Whitbread of Britain, Becks of Germany and Labatts of Canada, just to mention the top tier acquisitions, and was again renamed InBev.

Yet the country that best illustrates these two trends – consolidation at national level and internationalization via cross-border acquisition – is Britain. In the early 1990s it was common to speak of 'the big six' in Britain – Bass, Allied-Lyons, Grand Metropolitan, Whitbread, Scottish & Newcastle and Courage – these having an 80 per cent share of the domestic British market. It is quite instructive to ask 'Whatever happened to the big six over the next ten years?' Well, the first four exited the brewing industry, though Bass (renamed Six Continents) and Whitbread still operate chains of branded pub restaurants, while the last two – Scottish & Newcastle and Courage – merged. So that now (2003) the 'big six' have become a rather different 'big three', namely Scottish-Courage (a merged entity that also acquired BSN-Kronenbourg of France along the way), Carlsberg Tetley and Interbrew. That is to say, in place of six British brewers the UK now has one (merged) British with a French acquisition; one Danish brewer, with a British (Yorkshire) acquisition; and one Belgian brewery, holding the European acquisition record!

Finally in this brief look at industry trends one would note that market segmentation has taken place. That is to say, beer is no longer an undifferentiated product, but a consumer good that breaks down into several product markets, namely:

- Beer, the 'general purpose' version, what most people drink most of the time, sometimes described (in Britain) as 'session beer'.
- Speciality beers, for example white beers such as Hoegaarden or the various fruit flavoured beers for which Belgium is renowned.

- Strong beers, anything around 6.5 per cent alcohol or more; the first in the field was probably Carlsberg Special, a 10 per cent alcohol beer.
- Non-alcoholic beers.

Cutting across this notion of segmentation is the importance of brands. These brands are the product of the promotional drive of brewers and the attachment of consumers. If that sounds a little vague, one might urge that we all know a brand when we see one: Miller Genuine Draught is a brand, Bud Light is a brand, Labatt Blue is a brand as is Staropramen, and Ceres Royal and Spendrups Gold in Scandinavia are brands. It gets complicated in that some brands overlap with or become the exemplars of particular segments, for example Hoegaarden as *the* best known white beer or Carlsberg Special as a strong beer or Leffe as a malty-tasting abbey brewed beer. Indeed one can see today breweries expanding, that is, making acquisitions in order to acquire brands and at the same time to be represented in additional segments. Interbrew's acquisition of Abbaye Leffe would be an example, or the acquisition by Anheuser-Busch (American brewers of Budweiser) of Leinenkugel of Chippawa Falls, Wisconsin. In this last example the significance of Leinenkugel is that it is a nineteenth-century small town 'family brewery' with a distinctive tasting, reddish-coloured, imaginatively promoted beer; its value to US market dominating Anheuser Busch is that it *is* 'a bit different'.

Indeed to bring several of these trends together one can often see major brewers seeking to acquire distinctive brands and segment access at the same time.

More broadly, all the developments noted in this brief overview are related and have a common cause, as we try to show diagrammatically in Figure 3.1.

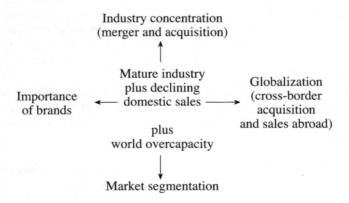

*Figure 3.1   The Scandinavian question*

What we have depicted in Figure 3.1 is common to a number of consumer goods industries in the early twenty-first century, though brewing is a particularly nice example. The story goes like this. An industry is born. Over time demand for produce grows, perhaps massively. Then a time is reached when this demand stops growing, or at least in what are regarded as the core markets, and there is overcapacity on the supply side. The industry is now mature. Companies in this industry are faced with declining demand and thus declining revenues, or at least with the threat of these developments. This typically triggers a number of responses in the industry, all of which we have seen in the brewing:

• Companies merge or acquire each other, at first within particular countries; this reduces the number of competitors and should reduce costs.
• Then companies globalize, typically acquiring companies in other countries, hopefully countries where demand is more buoyant, as with the Interbrew-AMBEV example given earlier; this should compensate for sluggish demand in core markets.
• In mature industries demand tends to segment, different groups want different versions of the product, not just any old beer but say strong beer, or speciality beer; producers diversify the product range to serve and exploit these emerging segments.
• Branding becomes more important in this more competitive business environment as a way of attaching customer loyalty to particular products, so that the customer asks for Carlsberg Special rather than taking the first strong beer they find on the supermarket shelf.

Finally the importance of brands intersects with the desire to serve the range of market segments, in that brewers may acquire another brewery, capturing a brand and having something to sell to a particular market segment, as with Anheuser Busch-Leinenkugel example offered earlier.

While one may to choose to emphasize the elements of homogeneity – the intertwined history of the three countries, their Lutheran heritage, the closeness of their languages and widespread English speaking ability, the values of egalitarianism and pragmatism, together with high welfare levels and general decency – we are in this chapter going to begin with the second question, namely, are there any perceptible differences? In this it is only fair to cast the net wide, going beyond management behaviour and the strategic posture and also the operational dynamics of the companies to consider also any possible effects of national differences of a geo-political kind.

## DIFFERENCES OF CONTEXT

Our ability to appreciate detail and thus to recognize difference is in part a function of distance. While other countries tend to view Scandinavia as something of a 'seamless garment' because of the values noted in the previous paragraph, Scandinavians themselves see differences, particularly as between Sweden and the other two countries. So as differences between these countries that may conceivably impact on the brewing industry, consider that:

- As noted in the previous chapter two of these countries are members of the European Union (EU), Denmark having joined in 1973 and Sweden in 1995, whereas the citizens of Norway twice rejected EU membership in plebiscites in 1972 and 1994.
- In Norway and Sweden alcohol retailing is a (near) government monopoly with sales taking place through the Systembolaget or state liquor store chain in Sweden or the Vinmonopolet in Norway; there is no such limitation in Denmark.
- While Norway and Sweden have a common land border, and both have a border with Finland, only Denmark has a land border with a major non-Nordic country, namely with Germany.
- Denmark is seen in the wider world as a traditional beer-drinking and beer-brewing country, like say Britain and Germany, but Norway and Sweden do not have this reputational advantage; reputation is supported here by consumption – data from the 1990s shows per capita beer consumption in Denmark to be 126 litres, the corresponding figure for Sweden being 64 litres and for Norway 53 litres.
- Only Denmark hosts one of the world's top 20 brewers by output and sales, namely Carlsberg; though this distinction has become a little blurred by the fact that Carlsberg is 40 per cent owned by branded consumer goods company Orkla of Norway that also owns Ringnes, Norway's biggest brewery (Ringnes in turn owns Pripps of Sweden).

To which one might add that Norway is largely mountainous, while Denmark and the inhabited areas of Sweden are mostly flat. Nothing to do with brewing? Read on.

So how do these broad national differences play out?

First of all there is *a different degree of market liberalization* vis-à-vis alcohol in the three countries, with Denmark as the most liberalized and Norway as the least liberalized. The two factors that give us these different degrees of liberalization are the presence or absence of the state in the regulation of the sale of alcohol via the Systembolaget and Vinmonopolet, the state liquor store systems on the one hand and the variable fact of EU membership on the other.

So in Denmark there is no Systembolaget or Vinmonopolet; retailers can sell what they wish and source it anyway they like. But Sweden and Norway do have such a state liquor store chain, with its implicit controls. On this issue non-Scandinavian readers might appreciate a bit of elaboration. As a British national working in Sweden in the 1980s these Systembolaget retail outlets made a big impression on me in that they were:

- Generally rather dreary places, far from enticing.
- Their windows were typically filled with anti-alcohol propaganda, with pictures of glowingly healthy Swedish families cycling off into the sunset (with their bicycle mounted baskets filled with orange juice).
- These retail outlets had restricted opening hours, falling far short of those of say a British off-licence, never mind a British supermarket; Sunday opening? Dream on. They were not even open on Saturdays!
- Once inside you could not simply pick up an item, take it to the till and pay for it; you had to order via a catalogue, and wait for 'the offending item' to be brought to the point of sale by an employee.
- The prices were horrendous; at a time when a pint of beer in Britain cost about 40–50 pence, a half litre in Sweden cost around £1.70.

That was in the 1980s. From the late-1990s onwards one was intrigued to see how the Systembolaget outlets had come on: more attractive, more customer oriented, better choice, more foreign (non-Swedish) produce, less horrendous prices. How is the difference to be explained? By Sweden joining the EU in 1995, and having to come into line, after some opt-out period, with EU competition policies. The ultimate test that EU membership has 'made a difference'? Norwegians now talk even more about going to Sweden to buy 'cheap drink'!

On either side of Sweden as the mid-point in market liberalization we have:

- Denmark, which does not have a state-owned chain of liquor stores, and joined the EU in 1973 (at the same time as Britain and Ireland), has been long subject to EU competition policy, and has a land border with Germany, the world's legendary beer drinking country; and on the other side:
- Norway, with its Vinmonopolet, rejection of EU membership, and incredible oil wealth which means it can do anything it likes (pursue any policy) because it can pay for it.

Norway, it should be added, has a strong teetotal or anti-alcohol tradition, especially in the western coastal districts, whereas in Sweden the control of alcohol is more a matter of government policy, though there is some substance to the view that the introduction of the Systembolaget in Sweden helped to head off a demand for prohibition from the anti-alcohol lobby. Indeed Norway actually had a period of prohibition, like Prohibition in the United States, from 1920 to 1933. Revealingly in the case of Norway the decision to prohibit the sale of spirits and fortified wines was the subject of a nationwide referendum in 1919 winning a 61.6 per cent majority in favour of the ban. Norwegian prohibition was actually introduced in 1921 and banned the sale of fortified wines and spirits; the ban on fortified wines was lifted in 1923 (French lobbying) and that on spirits in 1926.

Meanwhile the Vinmonopolet had been set up as a private company under government control in 1922 to import and sell wine, and this organization took over the sale of fortified wines and spirits when these were de-prohibited. The official status of the Vinmonopolet has changed over time in that it has become wholly state-owned (as of 1939) and, like the Systembolaget in Sweden, by the end of the last century it had become a pure retail organization, not concerned with production.

The Swedish and Norwegian systems also differ in having a different break point. In Sweden beer up to 3.5 per cent alcohol can be sold in other outlets – supermarkets, corner stores and so on, but *starköl* (strong beer) over 3.5 per cent is only available through the Systembolaget. In Norway the breakpoint is 4.5 per cent alcohol, so that the Vinmonopolet is not so important for the sale of beer and as its name suggests has a wine (and spirits) focus. The Vinmonopolet is a smaller chain than the Systembolaget, with 156 outlets at the end of 2002; this is less than those of the Systembolaget in Sweden, even allowing for the population difference in favour of Sweden.

A variation on this theme of market liberalization is *the relative importance of markets*. Generally in the brewing industry there are two markets, viz:

- retail, that is, shops and typically grocery chains to which the brewer sells, and
- what is called in the trade the HORECA (hotels, restaurants and catering) market.

Now the attractiveness of the retail sector varies with the degree of retail concentration. That is to say, if grocery retailing is dominated by a small number of corporate players, each having a high market share, these grocery chains will be powerful vis-à-vis the breweries, drive hard bargains with them, force thin profit margins onto the breweries, and into the bargain the grocery chains may demand that the breweries produce 'discount beer' (cheap beer for sale in multiple retail outlets) or 'own label' beer, that is, beer to be sold under the supermarket's or grocery chain's name, not that of the brewery.

Against this background one should say that grocery retail concentration in Scandinavia is rather high, higher for instance than in Britain, France or Germany. In Norway, probably the leader, we were told that four supermarket chains had a 99 per cent market share.

All this tends to make the retail sector in Scandinavia a thin margin business for brewers. This in turn increases the attractiveness of the HORECA segment, and all three brewing companies testified to its appeal.

The attractiveness of HORECA is reinforced by two further considerations. First, it is less concentrated than the retail sector and thus unable to drive such hard bargains with the brewers. Second, HORECA does not want to offer its customers discount or own-label beer, but to present customers with quality, branded products that also offer the brewer thicker margins.

So the attraction of HORECA for brewers in Scandinavia is higher than for some other countries, say the United States where concentration among brewers is greater than among retailers. But there is a further twist to this argument regarding the three Scandinavian countries. This is that one of these countries, Denmark, has a pre-eminent brewery. Carlsberg is pre-eminent in several ways, namely:

- its size;
- the lustre of its brands;
- the fact that it has subsidiaries in several other countries, for example, Britain, so it is much less dependent on the Danish domestic market.

Carlsberg is in a stronger position vis-à-vis the supermarket chains than brewers usually are in the domestic market.

But a further consequence of this consideration is that in Denmark the HORECA segment is more attractive, indeed is a salvation, for the secondary brewers, those coming after Carlsberg, including the Danish brewery in our study. And if we look outside Denmark to Norway and Sweden we find that the attraction of the non-supermarket sector is enhanced in that the Systembolaget and Vinmonopolet are bracketed with HORECA as part of a softer market segment.

The *dynamics of distribution* also vary as between the three countries. Denmark is fairly small and reasonably compact. The three main parts – Zealand, Funen, and Jutland – have now all been joined up by road bridges and rail bridges or tunnels, and since 2001 Denmark also has a bridge/tunnel connection with Sweden, the Öresundsbro, linking Copenhagen with the Swedish town of Malmö. There is a sense of regional-cultural difference in

Denmark, but it is probably not very important for beer consumption, especially given the long-term predominance of Carlsberg.

Sweden is rather more of a challenge. It is a bigger country, indeed it is Europe's fifth largest after Russia, Ukraine, France and Spain. It is also less compact, running from south to north. These north–south distances are considerable. Stockholm on the east-facing coast is only about one-third of the way up, and from Stockholm north to say Kiruna in Swedish Lapland, the last inland town of any size, is a 12-hour rail journey.

On the other hand, Sweden does have good rail and road systems, and is home to two of Europe's truck manufacturers – Scania and Volvo. What is more, the population is far from evenly distributed, with the three key towns of Stockholm, Gothenburg and Malmö and most of the country's population in the southern half. Indeed perhaps indicatively Norwegians talk about how you can tell if you have wandered across the rather notional northern frontier between Norway and Sweden because 'there are not any people over there'.

Indeed when it comes to the logistical challenge it is Norway that is the *non plus ultra*. It is the wrong shape, long and narrow. It is mountainous, the west-facing coastline is heavily indented by fjords. Above all the population is sparse and scattered. All this makes it a nightmare for suppliers of fast moving consumer goods (FMCGs). As one of our Hansa Borg interviewees remarked, 'From Bergen to Stavanger is four tolls, three ferries and one tunnel.'

Some countries with a mountainous terrain are rendered more manageable by the railway network (Switzerland would be a good example), but Norway is not one of them. The network in Norway is not very dense. It was also constructed fairly late. The connection from Oslo to Bergen, the second city, was only completed in 1909; the line from Oslo to Stavanger, the third business city, was only completed in 1944. Narvik on the north-west coast of Norway, well inside the Arctic Circle, is connected by rail only to Stockholm but not to Oslo. The comparison with Britain here is instructive: in Britain pretty much the whole rail network was constructed between 1840 and 1870. Again a lot of the Norwegian lines are only single track, for example the north–south line from Oslo to Trondheim running through the Gudbrandsdal valley.

All this, of course, is a matter of geography (Derry, 1957). Just consider that:

- four-fifths of Norway lies more than 165 metres above sea level;
- on average Norway is nearly twice as high as the rest of Europe;
- one-third of the west coast is inside the Arctic Circle.

The scattered nature of the Norwegian population is given further impetus by the government's Utkantspolitikk, or policy of supporting the periphery.

This in turn gives rise to agricultural subsidies and infrastructural support for remote communities. Indeed Norwegians line up for the pleasure of giving foreigners entertaining examples of this policy in action. An example we gleaned while interviewing at the Norwegian brewery was of an island community in the north for whom the government had built a bridge at a cost of more than a million pounds: the community consisted of five people, the youngest was 56, and none of them had cars! Another indicative reference was to a brewing outpost operated by the Norwegian brewery that was 300 kilometres and five ferries north of the main production site. The chief operating officer underlined this issue, remarking: 'And they have a broad product range up there, including a local cola!'

Again, as with Norway's Prohibition period, the Utkantspolitikk is a case of policy at least traditionally supported by sentiment. There is a conviction in Norway that 'the good life' is lived in the regions, in communities however small or remote, rather than in the nation's capital. One of the authors who spent time in Sweden was never aware of this sentiment. Sweden's small and remote communities have a vacational significance, nice places to get away to in the summer time, but not inspirational.

But there is a silver lining for hard-pressed Norwegian producers. This is that the trucking industry is very fragmented in Norway (and to a lesser extent in Denmark, though it matters less). Or to put it the other way round, there are few national carriers in Norway like say Christian Salvesen in Britain or Willi Betz in Germany. Instead there is a myriad of small trucking firms, all competing fiercely with each other and their existence also serves to hold down the price scales of the few national carriers that do exist. So road transportation is cheap for producers, and helps to off-set the mountainous terrain-scattered population problem.

Finally, in this brief review of national context factors we might mention the *effect of government taxation on alcohol*. Such taxes are high across Scandinavia, but at their worst in Norway. But this is not entirely bad news for the Norwegian brewing industry. It works like this: taxes are so high that producers' price rises will hardly show! It does something to make up for retail concentration, thin margins and a dispersed population.

Nor are these government taxes without effect in Sweden and Denmark. Most obviously it increases the incentive to make tax-free or duty-free purchases. Since Norway is not in the EU, Norwegian citizens (still) enjoy duty-free purchase opportunities travelling to any other country. They also, as noted, visit Sweden where they can buy alcohol more cheaply in the Systembolaget than at home in the Vinmonopolet. The Swedes too welcome the opportunity to make duty-free purchases when travelling to destinations outside the EU. Or to offer a more folksy example, anyone who thinks the booze cruise is a peculiarly British degeneracy should try the Saturday morning ferry from Grisslehamn, some 80 miles north of Stockholm, to Eckerö in the Åland Islands. The latter, while linguistically and culturally Swedish, in fact belong to Finland but managed to negotiate an opt-out clause when Finland joined the EU in 1995. Few of the Swedish passengers seem to feel the need to actually disembark when the ferry reaches Eckerö!

In Denmark the phenomenon has a different manifestation. Especially in Jutland, Danes relish the opportunity to drive across the border into Germany to fill their tanks with cheaper German petrol and to buy beer taxed much more modestly than at home. But the beer they buy, at retail outlets conveniently placed just over the border, is not German beer but Danish beer, thoughtfully made available by the likes of Carlsberg.

In short, the effect of taxation and other controls is that:

- the Norwegians go to Sweden (or anywhere!);
- the Swedes go on booze cruises and to Denmark (Elsinor of Hamlet fame is a favourite beer-buying destination for Swedes); and
- the Danes go to Germany.

Lest Scandinavian readers at this point feel a little shy, it should be said that the eternal search for cheap drink is not peculiar to north-west Europe. The American state of New Hampshire has as its motto 'Live free or die'. In practice this seems to betoken the absence of any tax on alcohol. When one crosses the border from Massachusetts into New Hampshire a truly enormous duty-free facility awaits.

One is reminded of Margaret Thatcher's remark that if you try to buck the market you may find the market bucks you.


## CORPORATE HISTORIES IN BRIEF

Moving now from the national context to the three breweries themselves, there are certainly some differences of corporate history or formation.

Our Danish brewery is Brewery Group Denmark (BGD); this is the way it titles itself in the English edition of the annual reports, though Danish people probably think of it as Faxe-Jyske. BGD is the second largest Danish brewing corporation after Carlsberg, and it was formed through a merger between the Jyske and Faxe breweries in 1989, these two being approximate equals at the time of the merger.

Jyske Breweries was traditionally strong in eastern and northern Jutland. This company was formed over the years through a number of mergers and local breweries. Today the company has breweries in among others Horsens,

Århus (Ceres) and Randers (Thor) – these are all towns in Jutland, and Århus is the second city after Copenhagen.

Faxe Breweries used to be the Danish brewing industry's *enfant terrible*. It was not a member of the Danish Association of Brewers, and did not accept many of this body's recommendations. Some of Faxe's products were in bottles of non-standard size, and one of these is still on sale via supermarkets. Back in the 1980s there was a famous Faxe advert showing one of these stumpy, non-standard Faxe bottles in a cartoon picture, side by side with standard-size bottles of other Danish brewers: the Faxe bottle says something like 'How surprised I am to find myself in such company'.

Our Swedish brewery is Falcon Brewery in the town of Falkenberg on the west-facing coast of Sweden, south of Gothenberg, the second city after Stockholm. Falcon, originally a family firm founded in 1896 by one John L. Skanze, thereafter had a somewhat chequered career, at one time being part of the British-Dutch multinational Unilever and ending up by the close of the last century being owned by Carlsberg of Denmark.

*En passant* it is worth noting that of what Swedes would think of as their three big breweries – Pripps, Falcon and Spendrups – only the last is still Swedish. Falcon is Danish-owned as noted, and Pripps is owned by Orkla of Norway. Sweden's fourth brewery is not really in the same league as the 'big three', it is Åbro, in the town of Vimmerby in the province of Småland, and Åbro is owned by the Dunge family. In fact with only one exception the whole sample of Swedish companies in our study were in foreign ownership – British, Danish, German, Norwegian and latterly Finnish.

Our Norwegian brewery is Hansa Borg, again the result of a merger and Norway's second largest brewing company. If we start with Hansa, this is a Bergen-based brewery, Bergen being Norway's second city after Oslo. Hansa was bought by Pripps of Sweden. Then Pripps itself was acquired by the Norwegian consumer goods conglomerate Orkla, which owns Ringnes, Norway's largest brewery. This Orkla acquisition of Pripps gave it such a large market share in Norway that it was obliged by the EU Commission (even though Norway is not an EU member) to demerge Hansa. Then 1997 Hansa merged with Borg, also Norwegian, based in Sarpsborg, about 100 kilometres south east of Oslo and about 100 kilometres from the border with Sweden. Then just before the end of the twentieth century the merged entity Hansa Borg acquired the Christiansand Brewery (at that time owned by Spendrups of Sweden!) in the south of Norway. More acquisitions by Hansa Borg may have occurred by the time this book is published.

Clearly these corporate histories are complicated stuff, but it is fair to add that the intertwined histories of Norway, Sweden and Denmark noted in Chapter 2 do have this corporate parallel. That is to say, much of the merger and acquisition (M&A) activity outlined in the last three paragraphs is cross-border M&A within Scandinavia. Furthermore, the whole brewing industry has seen a high level of cross-border M&A through the 1990s and into the present century, as noted in the earlier section on industry developments.

## THE BIG PICTURE: STRATEGY AND COMPETITIVE ADVANTAGE

Next we will try to characterize the three brewing companies in broad brush stroke terms. What do they concentrate on, what is or was their espoused or inferred strategy, what did they see as their competitive advantage? Perhaps a word of warning is desirable here. This is that we did not attempt to 'check them out' on a finite list of goals and strategies, but rather sought to get an insight into these matters by asking open-ended questions and letting interviewees respond in their own way, picking out what they thought was distinctive or important. The breweries in Sweden and Denmark both had a clear vision on strategic positioning, and we will start with the latter.

BGD in Denmark had a nice portfolio of discriminatingly positioned brands, and exports accounted for 65 per cent of its turnover. The proportion of exports had been rising steadily since the late 1980s merger (above) that brought the company into existence in more or less its present form. This export focus was facilitated by the reputational factor mentioned earlier in this chapter, that there is a commonly accepted conviction that 'the Danes know how to brew beer', that Denmark, like its European neighbours Germany and Britain, is a traditional beer-drinking and beer-making country.

Exports, however, are not the same as produce sold in other countries. Breweries bigger than BGD, especially where they dominate the domestic market, tend to service overseas markets by means of overseas subsidiaries or local brewers that they have acquired. Examples here would include Heineken of Holland, Interbrew (Stella Artois plus products and brands deriving from other acquired breweries) of Belgium, and of course Carlsberg of Denmark, service overseas markets by a mix of subsidiaries as noted, and brewing under licence deals where a brewer in an overseas territory brews for its master. In Britain Whitbread, for example, before it exited brewing, brewed under licence for Stella Artois and for Heineken, and staying with the British example, Carlsberg services the entire British market from its own single brewery in Northampton, conveniently located alongside the M1 London to Leeds motorway. We have sketched in this bigger brewery picture to highlight what BGD does, namely:

- It is going for exports, not overseas subsidiaries.

- This enables it to exploit Denmark's status as a beer country, whereby 'brewed in Denmark' is a plus.
- It also differentiates it from Carlsberg (if you cannot beat them, do something different).

In fact BGD is the industry leader in exports in Denmark. What is more, the company has recognized what we noted earlier that for over ten years beer consumption in the traditional beer-drinking countries of Northern Europe is stagnant or gently declining and has exploited more adventurous markets, namely Russia, the Baltic States, Hong Kong, China and even Brazil (there is a further advantage with Brazil that as it is mostly south of the equator its summertime peak occurs in Denmark's winter and helps to even-out production volume). BGD is not alone in having come to terms with the declining consumption in traditional beer drinking countries, but it is still to its credit.

So export focus, exploiting 'brewed in Denmark' as a reputational strength, and an adventurous approach to overseas markets is the main plank, but is there more? Yes, there are three related industry considerations.

First, BGD does not do discount (own-label) beer for the retail chains. Discount beer is a highly competitive thin-margin business, and one which favours big brewing companies with bargaining muscle and a huge marketing budget to promote their brands. Second, in the domestic market BGD has given priority to the HORECA (hotels, restaurants and catering) segment. Here not only are they not disadvantaged by not being the biggest brewer, but their relative smallness may facilitate a more personal engagement. For the domestic market they have a standard brand, a speciality beer and a regional beer. They are also engaged in some business process re-engineering (BPR) initiatives to enhance service quality in the segment, including central invoicing for beer supplied to multiple outlets having the same owner. Third, they also supply an ensemble of non-alcoholic drinks, variously sourced, to provide a one-stop service for customers; this last is an interesting point of contrast with our Swedish brewery.

Falcon Brewery in Sweden is significantly different from its Danish counterpart, while at the same time having a clear strategy and self-image. First of all Falcon is active in supplying all three market segments, namely retail chains, HORECA and the Systembolaget, the 400 or so state liquor stores in Sweden.

Second, Falcon does not export. In the interviews this was treated as a self-evident result of the company being foreign (non-Swedish) owned. Yet that was probably not a sufficient explanation. After all it sold its own beer in Sweden, not that of its foreign parent Carlsberg. And if one argues that any exporting by Falcon would undermine or cannibalize the export or overseas sales of its parent, this would leave unexplored the possibility of parent and subsidiary putting together a portfolio of products/brands that would be complementary abroad rather than compete with each other. It is more than 30 years since Carlsberg and Tuborg merged in Denmark, but they still have distinct Tuborg and Carlsberg brands, both contributing to its overseas sales. So it may simply be that 'one does not expect' Swedish breweries to export except within the Nordic group of countries, that is, Scandinavia, plus Finland and Iceland. If one takes Britain as a test-case of Swedish 'exportability', since in Britain virtually all the lager (lighter coloured, bottom fermented) beer is imported or produced under licence, then there is very little on sale that comes from Sweden apart from Spendrups, which is sold at IKEA mega stores.

Third, Falcon at the time of our interviews had been increasing its sales in all three segments – retail, HORECA and Systembolaget – while admitting that the last two were less cut-throat than the retail sector. The Systembolaget cannot refuse to take your beer or they would violate EU competition rules, and the supplier sets the price at which the Systembolaget will sell it. And the HORECA sector is not 'heavily chained' (compare grocery retailing) in Sweden or in Denmark, as we have seen.

Fourth, Falcon is set on a broad strategy of differentiation, which has specialization and professionalism as its key planks. Part of the professionalism is a recognition that 'times have changed'. In 'the old days' brewers tended to act as preferred suppliers, where the customer purchased a set amount, the brewer provided soft drinks as well, gave the customer a low price for these soft drinks but kept them as a small portion of the total range supplied. These arrangements used to be rather cosy. Now it is recognized, certainly by Falcon, that customers may want, as lots of suppliers, to give a better range and choice. As one interviewee at Falcon put it: 'We don't tell the shops to throw out Pripps Blå (a premium brand) because we know it is a market leader. We have to be realistic.'

Or to put it another way, the breweries are now seen to be more in competition with each other as well as ranged against the (sometimes concentrated) power of buyers.

Another part of this differentiation is being seen as specializing in beer, playing down and running down the traditional obligation to provide soft drinks as well. The purpose here is to crystallize the image.

As with BGD, there is also a move to change practice to suit customers. One initiative that was highlighted was the development of a personal computer (PC) tool that enables sales reps to do instant deals with customers, factoring in any volume discounts and giving the customer an instant printout. Traditionally in this industry, we were told, the sales deal tended to be a rather slower and iterative process, with the sales person going back to base to discuss customer needs and demands with a hierarchical superior and then returning to the customer to close the deal. To put this development into context it would be fair to say that in the months that followed our interviews at Falcon, we heard the same testimony about PC-based instant sales deals in several different industries in Britain and the United States. Now broadly speaking it is clear that the traditional role of the manufacturers representative is being changed by IT, both by Internet buying portals operated by large organizations and by PC-based deals of the type discussed here. Nonetheless, these things have a local context and it was clear from the telling that this development was a significant break with the past in the Swedish drinks industry at the time.

Finally, and this is an observation on the part of the authors rather than something that was told to us, it was obvious that there was a newish group of able top managers driving these changes and implementing these policies. One manifestation was an attempt to put in a proper supply chain management system that would integrate materials–brewing–dispatch. Another change was separate sales divisions treated as profit centres.

In short Falcon was marked by:

- Involvement in all market sectors.
- Growth in all of them.
- Specialization in beer.
- Greater professionalism.
- Streamlining the selling operation.
- Organizational change.
- Foreign (non-Swedish) ownership and no exporting.

A policy of growth and differentiation, but still a contrast with BGD where much of the growth came from a resourceful exploitation of export opportunities. Perhaps our strongest impression at Falcon was of top management's appreciation of external change and the need to adapt to it. As the CEO remarked, 'There is a joke that you have 100 days as CEO in Sweden in which you decide what you want to change, otherwise you carry on as before.'

Turning to the third country, it is not as easy to offer the same broad characterization of Hansa Borg regarding strategy and strengths as we have done with the Danish and Swedish breweries. This is for largely for circumstantial reasons. Our visit was less than two years after it had assumed its present corporate form, a merger of two separate companies in different parts of the country following the demerger of one of them from a larger entity. What is more, the company had made the acquisition of the Kristiansand Brewery only the day before our visit began. All this gave a rather provisional nature to Hansa Borg's strategy and operations at the time we were privileged to be given a view of these issues.

With this qualification the main lines of the Hansa Borg strategy seem to us to start with growth. First, it is the number two brewery in Norway, its existence is based on merger, there is recent acquisition, and further acquisition was anticipated. Second, Hansa Borg is well positioned to ex- ploit the demographic unevenness of Norway. Although there is a political and ethical commitment to support the regions, that is, enshrined in Utkantspolitikk, the population is still unevenly distributed. So a brewery positioned in Sarpsborg from which it can service the Greater Oslo market, in Bergen, Norway's second city, and in Kristiansand, in the south, is accessing a major portion of the Norwegian market. Third, Hansa Borg, unlike Falcon, does have export aspirations, and indeed some overseas sales to cruise ships operating out of Florida. The barrier is that at the time of our interviews Hansa Borg faced an intellectual property/trademark problem, Hansa being a brand name for both a German and a South African brewery. Nonetheless, Hansa's espoused policy is to export. Fourth, again in contrast to Falcon, and BGD, Hansa is brewing a Danish beer and bottling a non-alcoholic German beer under licence to enrich their range. Fifth, Hansa were profiting from the favourable balance of power between themselves and the trucking industry, noted in an earlier section.

Against this background some of what surfaced in the interviews were issues to be addressed and possible solutions to problems. These included:

- Difficulty in checking stock, which was done manually (counting the crates in the warehouse).
- Recognizing that the production section under-report their output, as a departmental buffer.
- Problem of maintaining an adequate supply of returned-washed bottles; these have to be sorted and cleaned, one of those jobs for which it is difficult to recruit in contemporary Norway.
- A recognition that operational considerations predominated strategic ones; as a senior executive remarked, 'Firefighting? Yes, I am not sitting in my office and planning. You have no time for that.'
- A pending decision about where (in which of the three constituent companies) to put the new canning line.
- The challenge of rationalization given the mergers.
- Some delivery failures.
- The challenge of an over-staffed maintenance department: 'We have 40 people in maintenance, we don't need them. The size of maintenance is correlated with the extent of down time!'

In addition one might mention a possibly over-large product range, embracing some 50 beer products: 'We cannot have dedicated bottling lines because the scale is too small. So we get caught with frequent product changes on a single bottling line.'

All this is probably a product of timing and circumstance. Talking to people outside the company it was clear that this Norwegian brewery was decently profitable. Talking to its executives we got the impression that further expansion was likely.

Before moving on to other issues it is worth underlining the demographic-size-terrain peculiarities of Scandinavia. All these countries discussed in this book, together with Iceland and Finland, have an unusually high proportion of the population living in the metropolitan area of their capital city. Denmark is the leader with 34 per cent of the population living in Greater Copenhagen: just consider, if this principle applied to Britain, London would have a population of 20 million. This proportion is lower for Norway (22 per cent), but the non-metropolitan population is more scattered, over a very difficult terrain, with this dispersal favoured by public policy in the form of the Utkantspolitikk.

This is bound to impact on any manufacturing company in Norway, and this impact will be at its most challenging for a fast-moving consumer goods company facing the 'get it to market' imperative. To put it round the other way, these geo-demographic considerations are a clue to the fact that Norway has excelled in a number of 'off-shore' activities – fishing, ship-owning, ship-building, oil exploration and extraction. It gets you away from the tunnels and tolls!

So far we have sought to play up some of the differences between these three brewing companies. Beginning with features of the national context that might impact on the industry, we moved to the actual choices made by the three companies in both strategic and operational terms. But these differences are far from being the whole story.

## MANAGEMENT CULTURE AND MANAGEMENT–WORKFORCE RELATIONS

When it comes to management culture, similarities across the three countries are immediately perceptible, and we discuss some of these here under the headings of egalitarianism, participation, workforce and decency. This miscellany is in fact revealing in that it is quite difficult to distinguish between management culture and management–worker relations. This is because management is in no small way defined by its attitude to other groups and by the way it handles authority, as we hope will be clear.

**Egalitarianism**

In all sorts of ways the people we talked to showed their egalitarian leanings, or perhaps more properly their recognition of the constraint imposed by Scandinavian egalitarianism. No one wants to depict themselves as superior to or even different from others. All are scared by the exercise of formal authority. No one wants to give anyone else orders, still less to be seen to do so. As one of the Norwegian managers put it, 'My opinions are clear, but I am a hell of a diplomat!'

We asked one of the Swedish executives whether decision making in his company was democratic or authoritarian. His replies were indicative: 'As a Swede it is very hard to give an order.' And later: 'I take a lot of the decisions, but we have a discussion first.'

Another manifestation of this egalitarian leaning is the wish to depict oneself as having easy and realistic communication with rank-and-file employees. The Danish brewmaster observed: 'I like to talk *directly* to the workforce, and am sometimes criticized for bypassing my own subordinate managers.'

On this theme of 'the top' communicating directly with the rank and file, we heard the view expressed in Sweden that two one-time high-profile executives, Pehr Gyllenhammar at Volvo and Jan Carlzon of SAS, had actually fallen foul of their middle management for this act of bypassing. The same Danish manager, referring to his role in wage negotiation, continued: 'I can talk their language, and keep my feet on the ground, not to keep a distance.'

In some later interviews at companies in Norway, outside the core sample, this theme of managers being able to communicate with workers was universal. A number of these Norweigian managers speaking English used exactly the same phrase 'I can talk to anyone'.

Given this anti-authority culture the role of the foreman poses a particular problem. Not only is the foreman supposed to exercise authority over subordinates, but the whole thing is made worse by the fact that these subordinates are workers, whose sensibilities must be respected, not other managerial employees. It would be even worse if the foreman's position were based on some external, formal qualification, as with German foremen and their *Meisterbrief*. With relief, we thought, one of the Danish managers noted for us that their foremen were 'internally promoted' and had 'no formal qualifications'.

On the same theme at Falcon we were told by the human resources manager that there was 'no foreman', but on say the bottling line there were technicians who would be able to fix things that ordinary workers could not. The point is that they are seen to have technical know-how rather than authority. In the same company trade union representatives acknowledged that there were 'team leaders', no doubt what would be seen as foremen outside Scandinavia, but a trade union representative insisted: 'They are just like workers!'

We asked if they were paid more than the workers, and received the rather reluctant reply: 'Well, yes, a little.'

This problematic was made even more explicit at Hansa Borg – more aware of its problems, more concerned with the need for change – where they had dismissed all the foremen from their posts on the grounds that they were not sufficiently target driven. But this brewery had not, of course, dismissed them from the company itself (unthinkable).

Another twist to this anti-authority orientation was a tendency to distrust the bases of authority, including personal charisma. One of the directors at the BGD in recounting his prior career mentioned that he had worked for a number of forceful and charismatic bosses. One of us asked if these charismatic bosses were respected and accepted. The director was slow to answer, and then said thoughtfully of one of them: 'I respected him at the start, but came to realize he was crazy.'

Moral: you can lead a Scandinavian astray at the start, but sooner or later he will get a grip on reality!

**Participation**

Overlapping with the value of egalitarianism is the practice of participation. First of all participation is there in a formal way in that all these countries have a system of industrial democracy, based on legislation, and giving rise to works council. While Scandinavians may take this for granted, it is not common in the other countries of the West: Holland and Germany have it, but the United States emphatically does not, and the closest Britain got was commissioning a report on it in the 1970s by Alan Bullock, a famous historian and the master of an Oxford College, but the report's recommendations were never implemented. Our impression is that these works councils are at their most significant in Sweden, certainly by tradition, and probably have least impact in Denmark.

It is, however, probably the informal dimension of participation that is more pervasive and perhaps more important. We have already noted in the previous section how managers like to consult, or at least feel the need to be seen to consult. Another manifestation is the response of management interviewees to a question asking what they thought were the most important decisions they had taken in their present management role. The Scandinavians, even if they end up divulging something interesting, always want to tell you first that it was not really their decision, that it was a group thing, that they had simply been party to it, and so on.

Another way in which this consensual participativeness surfaces is in the prevalence of meetings. All managers everywhere go to meetings of course, so we are talking here about a difference of degree. With that qualification, whenever we asked management interviewees about the meetings which they chaired or which they regularly attended there were always a lot of them. At the same time respondents would often stress the informal and non-hierarchical nature of these meetings. Something else that struck us was that Scandinavian respondents seldom spoke of these meetings with the dismissive cynicism that is common in Britain. Nor would the Scandinavians have a meeting (of the real powerholders) before the meeting in order to fix the meeting. Interestingly one of the Swedish executives complained in anguished tones about the British tendency to do this, though it is fair to say that it is probably the Scandinavians who are the exception.

An observation outside of our study may help to underline the point. The Swedish crime fiction writer Henning Mankell has become something of a cult figure in Britain where four or five of the novels are already available in English translation. One of the things that strikes British readers is how the hero, Inspector Kurt Wallander, has almost daily meetings with all colleagues working on the case of the moment, these meetings being a serious affair, lasting an hour or more. The British equivalent would be a snappy and directive briefing from a forceful commander, who will then glower in silence while his (it is occasionally her) second-in-command hands out assignments to subordinates.

## Workforce

In all these breweries a stable workforce was the norm. At BGD we were told: 'People stay a long time, 20- and 40-year anniversaries are common; whole families work here.'

At Hansa Borg we heard: 'Workers are not mobile; they will change company but not city.'

And if downsizing occurs it will be on the LIFO (last in, first out) principle. Indeed it was admitted at this company that there was over-manning and that management faced a change-resistant culture.

At Falcon we probed the question of workforce flexibility. Was it a problem, we asked? No, not in terms of people's attitudes, according to the HR manager, but yes in the sense that one was bound by past agreements, so that every change ended up costing more than what you had before. Workforce flexibility was still constrained by deals from the mid-1980s when even unskilled workers were in demand.

Yet even when managers are concerned about possible over-manning or lack of flexible working, Scandinavian managers are reluctant to resort to the measures that would be common in Britain never mind the United States.

Again at Falcon the argument was that they would not contemplate downsizing because they needed workforce goodwill to do overtime working in the summer to meet demand (breweries peak in the summer, and have a mini-peak at Christmas). As a practical argument it is not very convincing: in the town where the brewery was located immigrant and/or refugee labour was available for work. But this is not the way you solve workforce flexibility problems in Sweden.

## Decency

Running through a lot of these testimonies is a strain of what one might think of as Scandinavian decency and restraint. It is very clear in the way the workforce is viewed and treated.

These companies were proud of the fact that they did not have to advertise for workers. At BGD, for instance, we were told that they got workers:

- on the *internal* labour market, that is, existing employees introducing relatives, friends or neighbours;
- from a backlog of applications, that is, people just write in on the off-chance;
- and from people giving up other jobs to come and work for the brewery in the summer time.

From this last category they keep on 20 per cent or so to make up for natural wastage, and we were told what positive qualities they looked for, how the lucky 20 per cent were picked, how their integration with the existing workforce was a key criterion and so on.

Just after these interviews at BGD one of the present authors went to Australia for the first time and seized the opportunity to visit some companies, including a brewery, SA Brewing in Adelaide. With Denmark ringing in our ears we raised the question of how they staffed-up for the summer peak, and received the laconic answer: 'We get them from a temp agency.'

The contrast is instructive. In the Australian case it is a purely market-driven transaction, with no commitment. Yet all these Scandinavian breweries were scrupulous about how they hired, and also how it would be viewed in the community. As one of the Danish managers put it, 'We want to be seen as a fair employer ...'

Or again, as a barometer of enduring trade union influence, we were told at Falcon that workers were paid for time on the job rather than measured output. Management may not have been euphoric about this, but it was recognized as the status quo, something you would not find much of in Britain after the 1980s.

Another story from Falcon concerned the practice whereby the company gave a crate of beer a week to employees. This would be beer up to 3.5 per cent alcohol; above this level such beer could only be bought at the Systembolaget. The HR manager was working towards substituting vouchers which employees could cash in at supermarkets. Engagingly, such a voucher system would solve the problem of staff not on site, for whom there is no distribution point, and allow them to 'let go' the employee who does the distribution. This is downsizing, Swedish style!

What we have termed 'Scandinavian decency' also surfaces in concern for the environment. We asked all the breweries about relations with the community, and they invariably flagged up environmental concern; indeed, this was common to all the companies, not just to the breweries. Perhaps more significant, environmentalism was not seen just as a matter of compliance but rather as an internalized obligation.

This mind-set was nicely caught at Falcon, where the PR manager remarked: 'We meet the requirements, but we want to do more.'

This was given a further thrust in a later interview with the CEO. On the subject of environmentalism he observed that the brewery had no problems: 'But we don't profile ourselves as a green company, but we try to be in line with or ahead of the environmental legislation.'

It seemed only natural to ask why, if they did all this, they did not profile themselves as green. The substance of his answer was that environmentalism was too valuable to be a marketing gimmick.

Another dimension of this decency is that no one wants to impose their will on others, or even impose a negative judgement on them. So if negative decisions have to be taken, it is best done by someone else. In this spirit one of the Danish interviewees explained that the organizational culture had previously been somewhat patriarchal, and then added 'but not centralized'. So that unpleasant decisions could always be decentralized, that is, given to someone else.

One situation when this need to make such choices and judgements surfaces is of course rationalization. BGD were in the process of integrating IT and finance systems as between two merged component companies, and they were doing this many years after the merger. Gently we queried the delay and was told: 'No one wants to make these judgements, it is not very nice to say to another company that our finance systems are better than yours so we will make that the system for the enlarged company.'

The same problem surfaced at Hansa Borg with its earlier merger and then very recent acquisition. Again in a gentle way we raised the question of rationalization, which evoked from the commercial director the response: 'We'll have to think about it.' It did not sound as though it was a prospect which they relished.

# REVIEW

In this chapter we began by posing the research question, the issue of homogeneity or difference. Before proceeding we offered an introduction to trends and issues in the brewing industry at a general level. Then after introducing the three breweries we examined the national content in which each of the three operates and then gave a broad brush stroke account of their position and strategy, noting the differences. This was followed by a discussion of various elements of the 'management' culture and of management–worker relations where we saw a variety of similarities. We would like to conclude with an anticipatory glance at the impact of global developments on Scandinavia.

# GLOBALIZATION

Somewhere above this discussion of aspects of sameness and difference is the impact of a bundle of turn-of-the-century developments (Lawrence, 2002) that is being flagged up here with the single word 'globalization'.

This brings a new dimension into the discussion of difference and change. We could see in the discussions that we had with staff at these breweries the seeds of change, which were taking them away from their own 'typical Scandinavian' past. And because they were subject to the same heightened competition that has marked more than a decade in the (Western) business world, these intimations of change are moving them gently in similar directions. Consider that all three breweries:

- were the product of merger and acquisition (M&A);
- with the exception of Denmark, this M&A had involved a cross-border element (though BGD had also made a minor acquisition in Britain);
- are coping, trying to find ways of dealing with being in a number two slot in the domestic market, variously being over-shadowed by Ringnes, Pripps and Carlsberg;
- are executing business process re-engineering (BPR), or agonising over it!;
- are engaged in rationalization or organizational structure change, or at least recognize the need; and
- have managers that look with some reservations on working practices, accrued employee rights and sometimes on change resistance cultures, even though they are reluctant to engage in macho human resource management solutions of an Anglo-American kind in the sense of forced downsizing and changes in working conditions imposed from above.

In their sum these are not minor developments, and they cast a shadow over the debate about Scandinavian homogeneity. This theme is likely to recur.

## REFERENCES

Calori, R. and P. Lawrence (1991), *The Business of Europe*, London: Sage.
Derry, T.K. (1957), *A Short History of Norway*, London: George Allen & Unwin.
Lawrence, P. (2002), *The Change Game*, London: Kogan Page.

# 4. Furniture

One of our reasons for choosing the furniture industry is that it is a Scandinavian strength. Another reason is that it satisfies one of our criteria in being an old industry, local in origin and therefore likely to reveal differences between the countries. It did in fact reveal differences, but not in the sense that we had anticipated. The differences that we found were in furniture style, rather than in management style. Finally, the furniture industry represents a nice contrast to some of the big unit size or volume industries like shipyards and breweries, and it gives us a chance of presenting medium sized companies that are the most common in the industry structure of Norway and Denmark.

In this chapter you will meet three companies that we consider among the best examples of Scandinavian management. The three companies are different in product markets, that is they specialize in different segments, but they have a similar management philosophy and they each excel in their speciality. The first, the Danish company Fritz Hansen, excels in sophisticated design; the second, Ekornes of Norway, excels in its marketing concept; the third, Swedwood, a supplier to IKEA, excels in lean management and cost-efficient production. We can therefore show interesting linkages between producer and the retail business, between producer and massive production outsourcing, and between producer and designers.

In terms of segments, the industry may be divided into:

- high end design products;
- standard for retail; and
- cash-and-carry.

Our three companies are found in each of these segments. But first we will have a look at the industry in the wider context.

## PROFILE OF THE FURNITURE INDUSTRY

At this point it might be helpful to clarify what is meant by the furniture industry: apart from furniture as such – chairs, tables, sofas, beds and cabinets – it also includes the production of doors, windows and kitchens.

The furniture industry is one of those industries that is traditionally artisanal in character, based on craft tradition and on trained skilled workers. It is also characterized by being local, originally dependent on easy access to wood and to local manpower and therefore in most cases located in the countryside, outside big towns. As far as manpower is concerned the industry could for a long time in the post-Second World War period benefit from the exodus from agriculture by farm hands and their sons, and in recent years the shop floor personnel of the furniture industry has been supplemented by immigrants, both men and women. It is also local in the sense that as long as costs prohibited transportation over long distances, this industry served the local market and responded to local needs. One of the effects of this is still perceptible in the styles that developed and our three case companies are clear examples of this phenomenon. Already at this stage, however, we can point to an interesting difference in style between Northern and Southern Europe, according to one of our CEOs, in that in countries like Denmark and Sweden everything in a room has to go together, whereas in Latin countries people have a relationship with individual items and these do not necessarily have to fit together in style. One consequence of this is that in Southern Europe it is easier to sell unit pieces and more difficult to sell whole series. Another, and perhaps more important difference is that interior decoration and furniture is less of a priority in Latin countries, in part for reasons of climate.

Since the furniture industry is craft based, industrial manufacturing is relatively recent, but over the last decade technology has moved the industry towards more automated manufacturing processes, and developments in information technology in particular have helped leading manufacturers to face increased international competition. However, the production is still relatively labour intensive, and for technical and market-related reasons, a high degree of specialization is also required.

Another recent development in the industry is the increased concentration of the distribution sector and the associated increase in the market power of retailers (Eurostat, 2002). An obvious example is IKEA, which is big enough to have its own net of large retail stores.

Now let us turn to the larger picture: of the top 20 furniture exporting countries in the world in 1993, ten were European; Germany was the leader with 28 per cent of the total, followed by Italy with 24 per cent, and here, surprisingly, we find little Denmark, with its just over 5 million inhabitants, among the top ten world exporters. In 2000 the cover ratios – the ratio between exports and imports – was 258.7 for Denmark and 142.1 for Sweden; only Italy was significantly higher (Eurostat, 2000). This is the more surprising since while forests cover 68 per cent of Sweden and 39 per cent of Norway, they amount to only 10 per cent in Denmark.

This shows that depending on what kind of production you have, easy access to wood may no longer be crucial nor even necessary, provided that the producers turn to new materials such as steel, plastics and fabrics instead of solid wood, which has become very expensive. Wood can of course be imported from overseas suppliers in South-east Asia and South America, or production can be transferred to Eastern or Central Europe, which is the solution chosen by our Swedish company Swedwood. The production of new types of furniture is known to be more difficult, and as such it has become a competitive advantage for the Scandinavian countries that have not only kept the old craft traditions, but which also have a high level of general knowledge and skills. The classical career path in a craft tradition is apprentice, journeyman and later foreman; the next natural step would then be to set up one's own business (Henriksen, 1999), typical in the case of Denmark. This pattern has three important implications: one is that Denmark gets a forest of small businesses, of which some may in turn become medium sized companies big enough to access the international market. The second, and perhaps more important implication is that the entrepreneur-owner-manager knows his trade in detail. And the third one is that he will be inclined to hire people like himself, craft trained journeymen for the more important and sensitive parts of the production process, and likely to take on apprentices, thereby continuing the tradition.

It is no coincidence that ten of the top exporting countries are European. First, furniture is normally not considered a primary need, but in countries with a cold climate, you cannot sleep on straw mattresses or sit on the floor, and so since ancient times furniture has been among the primary needs. Second, it takes a middle class of a certain size to form a home market that can function as a springboard for an export industry. Third, in many countries the middle classes are only now emerging or beginning to grow in purchasing power, and such new middle classes tend to copy the Western style of living. In that sense the prospects are good for the furniture industry in general, and consequently we may say that the industry still has a large growth potential.

In 1997, furniture production in Scandinavia represented roughly 8 per cent of the total production of the EU, of which Denmark produced 41 per cent, Sweden 29 per cent, while Norway provided a smaller share (Csil, 1998). The three countries have all followed a major growth trend over recent years, with Denmark recording the highest production specialization in the EU of 216.6 per cent in 1998 (Eurostat, 2002). Indeed over a ten-year period from 1987 to 1997, the Danish production increased on average each year by 7.3 per cent (Eurostat, 2000). If we consider the period 1993–97 alone, the growth was about 6 per cent annually in Scandinavia (Csil, 1998). In 2000 furniture accounted for 4.4 per cent of value added in manufacturing in Denmark, far ahead of all other EU member countries (Eurostat, 2003).

The industry is composed mainly of small and medium sized, family-controlled businesses, and in spite of the limited size of the businesses Denmark and Sweden have highly competitive industries. Other characteristics of the Scandinavian furniture industry include:

- the owner of the business is often also the manager;
- cooperation between manufacturers and distributors/retailers is particularly strong in Scandinavia as opposed to the franchise system which is common in say France;
- producers are extremely conscious of environmental issues, such as process problems and/or the use of specific materials, resulting in emissions of different kinds;
- safety problems are taken very seriously; and
- protection of design is a major issue.

All in all, the furniture industry is dynamic and yet one that lives a quiet life and does not often make headlines in the press in the way that shipbuilding and breweries do.

As examples of what has been said above in the industry overview, our three companies are similar in being family owned or formerly family owned, they are all export oriented, their style of furniture is functionalist and, notably, for all of them what drove changes in production and organization was not fiercer competition, but the fact that demands exceeded capacity.

However, our three furniture companies are also clearly different, in:

- *size*, ranging from 350 to 9000 employees;
- *turnover*, from 325 million to 3500 million Danish kroner (DKK);
- *company age*, from 10 to 130 years;
- *range of products*, from single unit niche products to mass, from sophisticated design to flat-packed components;
- *target groups*, organizations and institutions; private homes; cash-and-carry retail;
- *competitive advantages*, in different areas of the process (conception/design, production processes or distribution);
- *strategy*, branding, dealer relations, expanding production capacity; and
- *production*, Swedwood is exceptional in being a traditional furniture maker integrating the entire production chain from cutting the wood, through sawing, milling and processing to the finished product.

As will be seen, there are a number of parameters in which our three case companies all differ from one another. We will now turn to a more substantial description of our case companies.

# FRITZ HANSEN

Fritz Hansen is situated at Allerød, a small township north-west of Copenhagen in a pleasant landscape of woods, farmland and small lakes. It now largely serves as residential area for people working in greater Copenhagen or in the nearby city of Hillerød.

This is one of the oldest furniture companies in the country, established in 1872, and family owned for three generations until 1979 when it was taken over by a holding company. It was founded by cabinetmaker Fritz Hansen, and the second-generation owner, also a cabinetmaker, took up working with architects and designers in the 1930s. This turned out to be a brilliant idea. Among the best-known architects working for Fritz Hansen for many years we find Arne Jacobsen from the mid 1930s; he designed the Ant, the Egg, and the Swan chairs, which are still sold as classic Danish Design furniture. In the 1960s, Piet Hein designed the super-elliptic table, and by then the concept of Danish Design had established its reputation far outside Denmark's borders. From 1982 the furniture of Poul Kjærholm was added to the collection. The style adopted by the company from the early 1930s relates back to the Bauhaus philosophy, stressing functionalism, simplicity and timelessness.

The cooperation with good designers and architects is crucial for the company, and according to its manager quite an emotional business since this is the creation process. It is not programmable, but is the very *raison d'être* of the company and drives itself as a virtuous circle, so long as they do well. The power of taste and what is considered fine taste is enormous. If you have the right reputation in the field, the architects and designers will be there for you. Almost every day the company is approached by people who want to propose a product, and 99.9 per cent are turned down. The company has become practically a cultural institution in Denmark and well-known abroad for its aesthetics in design. It used to employ only local designers and architects, but has now turned international in this respect. The designers work with Fritz Hansen on a temporary basis.

In order to position the company for readers to whom the name of Fritz Hansen rings no bell, we would place it in a group of producers of luxury products such as B&O high-tech audio-visual equipment, Louis Vuitton, Cartier and Dior.

The company has a flexible collection of furniture within a certain design pattern in four areas of application: conference rooms, canteens or dining areas, lounge or reception areas and office (but not desking), each with at least two alternatives.

## Competitive Advantage and Strategy

The competitive advantage of Fritz Hansen is that it has created a niche for itself in top end sophisticated design furniture of high quality for private homes as well as for the contract market. Whereas there will always be a small market for expensive single unit furniture for private customers who are beyond the ups and downs of the international economy, the contract market is much more sensitive to international trade conditions. In other words in this market the company is more dependent on client power in the shape of, for instance, hotels, institutions such as ministries and big organizations and of course companies.

The company strategy is two-fold: one is external and the other one internal. In the past, the Fritz Hansen strategy was to market their furniture as individual series carrying the name of the designer, such as Arne Jacobsen or Poul Kjærholm. The strategy is now to build a strong brand around the name of the producer Fritz Hansen and only in second position the name of the designer. The other strategy is to make internal changes and adjustments in order to cope with future demands, which they believe will be much bigger than now. For this the organization needed to change from a traditionally family owned, owner managed and entrepreneurial company to a more flexible and better-structured organization with several power centres. At the time of our visit, they were in the midst of this process.

Market expansion is expected to be in Western European markets, representing countries with high and growing purchasing power, and in South-eastern Asia in places like Hong Kong, Singapore and Taiwan, countries where large international corporations have gained or will gain a foothold. Japan is already an important market; the Danish minimalistic design seems to correspond very well to Japanese taste. The US market is also expected to grow. The home market has always been important, representing one-third of the production, not least private homes, and on the export side Germany is the biggest single market followed by Japan, Sweden, the United Kingdom and the United States. The distribution between the private market and the institutional market is 20/80, and the strategy is now to raise the private market to 40 per cent.

## Production and Organization

Since 1996 there has been ongoing development in the production processes with implementation of new technology, construction of a new production unit, and in recent years outsourcing of part of the production; in fact the entire production culture has greatly changed over the past seven or eight years, as will be seen below.

As already mentioned, Fritz Hansen does both mass production and single handcrafted units for both the contract market and the private market, and the balance between the two types of production may be difficult to strike. In certain periods the company lacked production capacity, and in such situations delivery performance becomes a crucial problem. Another big problem is managing the transition from the prototype for a piece of furniture to mass production. Should this process fail, there may be massive problems with satisfying customer demand. So the procedure is that first you have to choose the innovative and brilliant designers, then adapt the production to coping with the challenges that a new design and/or new materials may present. For this reason not only design but also production rank high in status with Fritz Hansen in contrast to companies that have more standardized products.

At the time of our visit, the company was in a state of reorganization from traditional divisions such as sales, production and finance to a product-marketing concept, meaning that after having created the product, the task is to sell it under the brand name strategy, bringing the product and the marketing together, rather than the traditional way, where marketing will figure out what the market wants, and then ask production to perform.

The same kind of change was taking place with product development. This is the part where you need creative and technically innovative people on the one hand, and production/logistics capability on the other, characterized by a structured and systematic approach. Therefore Fritz Hansen had formed a group composed of specialists in product development and engineers specializing in furniture production.

The production was then split into four production centres, one for each application area (conference rooms, canteens, reception areas and office). Each centre was responsible for delivery performance as well as efficiency and productivity, including planning and purchasing. Above the production centres, there was a strategic purchasing unit that had to coordinate purchase, labour and machinery for all the centres, and to which the centres might turn for advice on costs, tools and so on.

The new organization, which also included a customer service and logistics function was not implemented without problems. One of them was the IT system, which was new and which met a certain amount of resistance from the factory floor personnel, who wanted to rely on old-fashioned memory and on the way they used to do things. In the beginning of this chapter we praised the industry generally for having preserved its craft tradition and skills, but here we see one of the drawbacks of using craft trained personnel who want to do it the traditional craft way. Another explanation of the resistance might be that the turnover of personnel was very low, so that many of the foremen and workers had experience and a powerful memory of how to do things. Finally, resistance to use new technology also came from trade union people, who saw it as control, and this perception was aggravated by an external regional union boss, an old-fashioned hardliner.

This point about control may need some further clarification for non-Scandinavian readers. Indeed, in most countries outside Scandinavia shop floor personnel as well as office employees are used to and expect control of their work, but independent minded and self-reliant Scandinavians dislike control, which they see as lack of trust in their professionalism and good judgement. For the trade unions it is of course also a question of maintaining power over their members' freedom of action.

As we have said already, this was a transition period from a craft oriented entrepreneurial and centralized management system in the family ownership tradition to the reverse of all that, including the empowerment of each centre. The whole management philosophy was that each centre should be responsible for getting things done according to the targets defined for each of them, and consequently the team had to do what was needed to meet the targets. As an example of the new style, the strategic purchasing manager would tell the production people not to wait for internal maintenance to come round but to hire external service if the internal service could not deliver within an appropriate time schedule. It would then become clear that internal maintenance could not deliver and it would show in financial loss, since that service would have to bear the costs of external service. This was the new spirit that management wanted to induce.

This complete turn-around of the production process was possible because not only Danes but Scandinavians in general:

- have a high level of general education;
- are used to and prepared to work in efficient teams;
- are also used to working independently and making their own judgement of the situation at hand;
- are used to being given responsibilities; and
- know that they are expected to live up to such responsibilities.

As we have seen, the change was certainly not without problems, but at the time of writing the problems have been overcome and shop floor personnel as well as employees have adopted the new technology and no longer see it as a threat to their professionalism or integrity.

The future challenge is how to be a cost-effective industrial producer and at the same time maintain the craft image and high-quality work.

### Management *Esprit de Corps* and Management–Workforce Relations

Next we will look at some distinctive aspects of management culture and relations between management and the workforce, blue-collar as well as white-collar people. The first thing that we want to mention is that top management in Fritz Hansen was composed of two people, not just one person as would be customary in most companies, unless you have a matrix organization and that was not the case here. For such a structure to function effectively without the eternal competition, rivalries and quest for power that would be normal in say France, a spirit of cooperation and loyalty to one another as well as to the company is required. Below top management there were 11 middle managers and some office clerks, in all some 15 people in the administration out of a total workforce of 350. This is indeed a 'top-light' management hierarchy for a company known worldwide in its industry with a turnover of DKK425 million (about US$55 million) at the time of our visit. The next interesting thing is that this pattern was repeated in Norway and Sweden where the low management/staff to worker ratio was even more pronounced (Ekornes 50/1000; Swedwood 10/180 at headquarters, 9000 workers in all).

En passant a word would be appropriate on the apparently high number of middle managers in comparison with office clerks. The explanation here is that the category of secretaries is a more or less distinct species in Denmark, and to some extent that goes for assistants too. They have been replaced by computers, just as workers are being replaced by robots and automation. What secretaries and assistants used to do, managers in Scandinavia must now do themselves. The companies are constantly upgrading their IT systems and continuing education is a lot about being able to handle the new systems and software programs.

In this connection it might be helpful to turn briefly to a recent report called *Digital Access Index* from the International Telecommunications Union (ITU) that has measured the access of the populations of 178 countries to IT. Apart from the question of access the survey also included the level of education in IT and the costs, and here all the Nordic countries including Finland and Iceland came out among the ten best. Highest on the index was Sweden followed closely by Denmark and Iceland that shared the position with South Korea; Norway came in fifth and Finland seventh.

This is only another testimony of what we know already, namely that the general level of education is high in the Scandinavian countries and the IT example shows that there is a determination to keep it that way. As we have seen above it entails a 'do-it-yourself' culture for all layers of the hierarchy, and at the same time it is an expression of the egalitarian attitude that permeates all relations in Scandinavia. In this case it means: write your own letters or reports, go get what you need, do your own photocopies, make your own coffee.

Now we want to turn to the meso level of relationship with the trade unions. At Fritz Hansen there were four union representatives, each for a different kind of skill. Now while this is normal procedure, the interesting thing here is that in the formal meetings every second month between management and union representative no decisions could be made, we were told; it was more an occasion for the exchange of information. This fact leads us to suggest that the Danish word *samarbejdsudvalg*, which is normally translated as 'co-determination committee', should perhaps rather be called the 'cooperation committee' since what happens is that management listens to the workers' point of view as well as trying to 'sell' up-coming changes and convince workers of the benefits of changes already made. Management cannot be sure what the union representatives tell their members after such meetings, but this uncertainty was being somewhat levelled out by the fact that the responsible manager was in the factory every day to discuss things with workers and thereby got a feeling of what was going on among them. On the other hand the factory manager trusted the union representatives to give fair information, and he believed that loyalty to the company was relatively high. In this connection we should remember that worker turnover was very low and the average age fairly high. Fritz Hansen was known as an attractive place to work; they always had a list of applicants looking for job opportunities and it was not uncommon to have several generations from the same families. So in general people were proud to work for the company and took an interest in it doing well.

However, not everything in the garden was lovely. As already noted, the company was in a state of change; a new IT system had been installed which met with some resistance from the shop floor. On top of all that, management also wanted to change the pay system which had up till then been based purely on quantity. Management now wanted to have a quality aspect attached to remuneration, to have it tied to personal qualifications and results, in other words a change from a standardized system to a more individualized system. The purpose was to make workers feel more responsible and to tie their performance to the overall results of the company in line with the new organization and philosophy. All of this, the new organization, work in production groups, the IT system meaning in fact a new planning system, and the new pay system met with some resistance that was a challenge to management.

The entire process of the delegation of authority and the empowerment of the production centres and production groups was nicely encapsulated by one manager who said that before the attitude was 'I do what I have been told to do', and the new attitude that they wanted was 'I have some targets, I will find out what to do, and I will do it'.

From the above it will be clear that cooperation is a keyword in the organization, cooperation between different levels as well as across different groups and units in order to coordinate and disseminate information. But even if the willingness is there, it is not something that just happens. It needs some formalization in the shape of a meeting schedule, and at Fritz Hansen it looked like this:

- Weekly meetings between logistics and the four factory managers on delivery performance, quality problems, future large orders and sales forecasts.
- A monthly logistics meeting with the four factory managers, plus the information system manager, the accountant, strategic purchase, sales and overall production planning.
- Every six weeks a market meeting (sales, marketing, production development and logistics).
- A four-times-a-year meeting between top management and the 11 people each having a departmental responsibility, called the management group; this meeting is about strategy.
- Four times a year an information meeting where all staff are invited and the situation of the company is explained, lasting 30–45 minutes.
- Product committee meetings ad hoc between the two top managers, the head of development, designers and architects to discuss products that are being suggested by external people for manufacture.
- The committee also discusses future products for a two-year plan and a ten-year plan.
- Management and trade union representatives every second month.

There is a document describing all the formal meetings, who calls them, who is responsible for writing up the minutes, their distribution and so on. Invariably there is an agenda, which is followed. On top of this there are all the informal meetings that people might need to have. The atmosphere is informal and relaxed, everybody can speak his or her mind and ask questions, including critical ones. In most cases people come to an agreement on what action is needed and who does what when. There is no voting. As one manager put it, 'people are quite engaged, but disciplined'. The attitude is to allow time for discussion, and only if this does not lead to consensus, the manager or whoever is heading the meeting will decide.

The drawback of all this meeting activity is of course that it is time consuming and for some it means listening to a lot of information they do not need, because some people participate in all or most meetings. But it is only fair to say that these meetings were expected to diminish as the new organization became established.

The high meeting activity is something that frustrates foreigners working in Scandinavia; as they see it, Scandinavians cannot decide on anything without having sat in meetings first. And they are right, this is what democracy at the workplace entails.

## EKORNES

Ekornes is one of the most dynamic Scandinavian furniture companies, recording steady increases in sales. The company headquarters and one production unit out of five are situated on the shore of one of the numerous narrow Norwegian fjords on the west coast, south of the town Ålesund in mid-Norway in one of the seemingly impossible landscapes of mountains, deep fjords and rock islands, all of which makes it very complicated to get around, and yet the entire area is bustling with activity. The main production unit has direct access to the fjord from a small harbour. The company name is the name of the founding family.

Ekornes was started in 1934 by Jens Ekornes, with the production of springs for mattresses, which soon led to the production of the mattresses themselves, called the Swan. After the Second World War, the owner went to the United States to learn more and came back with expert help and new machinery. This helped to launch the production of sofas and box mattresses. The founder died childless, but by then his brothers had joined the firm. In 1971 the family took out a patent for a recliner chair (the still popular Stressless) with a mechanism invented by one of the nephews, and this was destined to be the start of an extremely expansive period during which the family bought a large number of other factories and firms, among them a big Swedish company in difficulties, almost the size of Ekornes. However, by the mid-1980s sales had gone down and the company had serious financial difficulties due to mismanagement and the wrong strategy. For instance the company failed to establish itself in the US market and had to withdraw. Another problem was that management was torn by internal rivalries among second generation family members who filled all key positions. The managing director at the time, a member of the family, gave up in 1987, but was asked back in 1990, and in 1992, when a new top manager was appointed, he was made president of the group of companies. In 1990 a new and improved patent was taken out, which increased sales again. Financially the company was saved by the local bank on condition that the company was restructured and a new managing director chosen by the restructuring committee, Nils-Fredrik Drabløs. The other family members, apart from the one mentioned above, were neutralized and the new managing director implemented a complete turn around in management culture as well as in strategy and organization. This was to be the beginning of a new brilliant era of what has rightly been termed one of the finest industrial successes in Norway since the Second World War.

On the organization chart and among the staff we still find a number of people carrying the family name Ekornes, but it is no longer a prerequisite for making a career in the company; members of the Ekornes family have to compete on equal terms with people coming from outside the family circle.

What has also helped to neutralize family power is that the company is now quoted on the stock exchange, and today the family owns just 13 per cent of the shares, enough to prevent hostile takeovers, but not enough to control the business.

## Competitive Advantage and Strategy

Ekornes now produces furniture for private homes: recliners, sitting-room furniture and mattresses in the medium market range for retail. The patented chair (the Stressless) was introduced in Norway in 1971.

The company philosophy is a belief in products for the individual: each person his or her chair, each person his or her mattress, to be chosen within a variety of thickness, length or softness. It is like the children's story where Father Bear has a big chair, Mother Bear a smaller chair and the Baby Bear his own tiny chair and so on. Actually, in Norway at the time of our visit they had sold more than one million recliners, in a country which has only 1.2 million households! And the astonishing thing was that the recliners still sold on the home market, where sales went up by 25 per cent a year three years in a row. The Norwegians certainly like their comfortable Stressless chair, and the Swan mattresses are just as popular.

The style is far from the sophisticated minimalistic Fritz Hansen furniture, but then the Ekornes furniture does not sell on design, rather on comfort and function, and yet it was described to us as more simple in style than the big upholstered sitting-room furniture that customers normally preferred in the big furniture producing countries like Germany and the United States. Since sales increased in those countries too, it was interpreted as a change in trend towards the more simple Scandinavian style.

So comfort and function is one competitive edge. Another one is the brand name of the recliner, which is patented. Competitors try to copy the name as well as the recliner construction, but they cannot compete, for two reasons. The first one is low costs, making the products price competitive. This in itself is quite an achievement for a country known for its high wage level. The second reason is the marketing concept. The company works closely with selected dealers (retailers) only, and consequently it becomes prestigious to be among those selected. Then the dealers are tied to Ekornes by a contract of mutual obligation. The marketing department promises to deliver a certain number of units per year according to previous sales, they deliver a shop-in-the-shop exhibition set, which the dealers buy, and advertising costs are split between the company and the dealer. The parties decide together in which media to advertise, when and how, and Ekornes delivers the advertising material.

This model has a number of obvious advantages for the company. First, they can monitor outputs at their production units. Second, they know their dealers so well that the risk of bad debts is limited, and third, it is difficult for the dealers to switch to another supplier. The dealer on his part knows well in advance what his quota will be next year, and since demand exceeds capacity, this is an important assurance for the dealer.

Competitors try to copy this marketing concept, but they are far behind and thus the close link between producer and dealers is an important entry barrier for competition.

Future expansion was expected to be in European markets, the United States and Japan, and it was planned to double the chair production from 900 to 2000 pieces a day.

We would like to make a small and perhaps unusual digression here by reverting to the location of the company, Ålesund, to say that it may be a competitive *dis*advantage in terms of recruitment, especially for management positions. Indeed it is a problem to get people to move to that part of the country, which is on the west coast, away from any big towns, and far from the main education centres, even for Norwegians coming from say the Oslo area. The experience is that they miss their friends and relationships back home and do not stay long. Here we should remember the difficult terrain and long distances, which makes it impossible to just pop in for a cup of coffee or to get grandparents to babysit, even if the air service from Ålesund is frequent. Fortunately, as already mentioned the general level of education is high, also in the provinces, and although Norway has had formal business education for at least 60 years, Norway has a long tradition of young people going abroad to get a higher education. In the company's marketing department we met examples of local people who had been educated in the Oslo area and then gone abroad; one had studied graphic design in London and another had part of his education in France. Another one had his degree from Oslo Business School that runs an MBA programme designed by the Arizona State University with American professors.

Whereas they had a lot of unsolicited blue-collar applications, they still had a problem getting skilled workers. They tried to compensate for these difficulties by having wages at the upper end of the spectrum to which can be added a bonus system related to profits that could give from 50 to 80 per cent extra per month. In spite of this wage policy the products are price competitive, as we have seen.

## Production and Organization

At the time of our visit Ekornes had five production units in the Ålesund area and one in the Oslo area for mattresses. The main product and cash cow is the recliner, next come sofas, which also come as recliners at the time of writing, and third are mattresses. Ekornes is continually renewing technology and the production is just-in-time and computer assisted, which has made it possible over the past few years to reduce greatly production time.

Labour is local and, claimed one manager, well educated compared to, for instance, US labour. As explained in the beginning of this chapter, their journeymen have a craft technical education of three to four years on top of compulsory education lasting ten years.

When the company entered the new era of expansion, management looked around to see where they could find rational production methods. They found them in the car industry and copied the flow of materials and data information in a sophisticated computer system. The various factories are all organized along those lines. There are goals for every day's production, say 750 pieces of a certain product. At all times screens will show everybody how much has been done so far.

However, as at Fritz Hansen, there is also some handicraft: leather has to be carefully chosen, the direction of the leather must be decided, and there is one hour of sewing for each chair. Average production time for each unit has been greatly reduced and is now down to approximately 2.6 hours.

At the unit we visited there were three production lines for furniture (steel, wood and foam), a sewing department and one for assembling. They had three sizes and ten models in each size, making 30 models in all, but since the components are the same they can still do mass production. This is in spite of the additional fact that the base comes in different woods and the leather in different colours. They use the Japanese CanBan system, where production is sucked through the factory according to orders. The flow is as follows: since steel and wood are standardized materials, an order would go to the sewing department for the cutting of the hide and for the sewing and from there to assembling, and that is it. The sewing is time consuming, it cannot be standardized because there are so many different models, and for the same reason robots cannot be used. This is the tension between flexibility and standardization. At the time of our visit, they had a ten-day delivery goal for incoming orders, but it was in fact three to four weeks.

Asked about status of production we were told that probably marketing and customer service had more status, but the gap was now less pronounced.

Marketing and sales are divided into separate geographical areas (Scandinavia, the United Kingdom and Ireland, the rest of Europe, and the United States and Canada). Marketing was organized in projects for each geographical area, and there was more interesting information on the relationship with dealers. We were told that they had a turnover on their investment in sales material of 20 times per year, whereas the industry norm was three to four times. They have a guaranteed turnover per square metre of display in the store. The company wants dealers to make money. The basic rationale is that what is good for the dealers is good for the company. It seems to work in all markets. Only in one case (out of 180) did a dealer not meet the minimum turnover and in that case Ekornes refunded all the sales material. Ekornes trains the dealer's sales people in how to sell the products (on comfort and function). The company has made a marketing package consisting of display equipment, which is a studio system in the store, the so-called Stressless studio, and a training school at the head office in Norway, where sales personnel from all markets were flown in to learn how to sell the products.

Since they could sell more than they could produce, Ekornes had been compelled to set up a quota system, where each customer country was guaranteed a certain number of units; this was built into the budgets a year ahead. Marketing efforts were regulated according to this. If a dealer/country did not use the allotted quota within three weeks ahead of production, that lot would go to other markets. Successful planning is the key to all this.

In the previous section on Fritz Hansen we described 'the do-it-yourself' culture, where the computer had replaced the secretaries and assistants of former days. At Ekornes this culture has been taken one step further in that it has done away with the personnel department. What was formerly done by that department had been split between a lady who took care of the more technical side, such as salary questions, wage payments, holidays questions and the like, and the individual manager, to whom the personnel would have to turn directly, even on the factory floor. Should a problem arise that had to be taken further up the hierarchy, the person in question would do so together with the manager. To give an example, the department manager would have to take care of alcohol problems. If the person needed treatment and agreed to it, the company would pay half the costs and the other half would be paid by the person concerned in order to ensure commitment. In the case of sensitive problems that the person did not want to talk about to the manager, he or she could go to the lady taking care of the more technical side, and she would handle the problem.

All this was not entirely without difficulties. In the old days, and this means some ten years ago, what a production manager had to do was to ensure production, and that was pretty clear cut. Now as a result of the profound decentralization the manager has become a multi-task person responsible for production, for coordination between departments, for the direct contact with dealers whenever they are about quotas, as well as for personnel matters from recruitment to delays. As one production manager put it, 'working with people is the most difficult thing'. Put differently, working with a computer is not a big problem – it does not complain.

## Management *Esprit de Corps* and Management–Workforce Relations

Everybody we spoke to at Ekornes attributed the turn-around of the company to the new managing director who had taken over in 1992. They were also very clear about the key concepts in play, which were:

- cooperation;
- participation;
- decentralized responsibility;
- self-dependency; and
- caring for others, be they colleagues, dealers or suppliers.

To give an example of caring: at one point they had a person who would not cooperate and who did not accept his manager's decisions. He was moved to another job in another department. No question of sacking him just because he had different opinions. The aim was a good balance between having influence and respecting management decisions.

Now we would like to come back to the bonus system mentioned before. It started as a kind of Christmas present the first year that the company had a substantially profitable result, and it then became part of the official policy. The remarkable thing here is that it is not an arrangement for top management to divide the cake, in some cases, as we have seen, a cake which is not even there; it is the same percentage for everyone from top to bottom. For the year prior to our visit it was 70 per cent of one month's pay. This is yet another example of the egalitarian attitude.

The relationship with union representatives seemed to pose no problem. Management took the system very seriously and adhered to all rules regulations, and in contrast to what we heard in Denmark, meetings between the parties were not just to give information; they were about cooperation and also co-determination, and here attitudes to change and to the new technology were positive on the shop floor. But we should bear in mind that the shift had taken place years before and people had seen the positive effects, including the fact that new technology did not mean the restriction of the workforce, but rather the opposite.

The two people responsible for this success story are the new managing director and the president; the latter, Jens Petter Ekornes, is a management hero in Norway like Ingvar Kamprad, founder of the IKEA company, in Sweden.

## SWEDWOOD

We will now turn to a company which is somewhat different from the two previous ones. Swedwood is different in that:

- it is a young company, founded in 1991;
- it produces ready-made flat-packed furniture;
- it integrates the entire production chain right from cutting the wood in Eastern and Central Europe, through saw milling and all the other steps in the processing to the finished pieces of furniture;
- it has only one customer, which is IKEA, for which reason
- it has no marketing department nor sales department; and
- it is investing heavily in Central and Eastern Europe; where it has
- 35+ production units; and finally
- it is expanding extremely rapidly.

The most interesting things about this company is its lean management and efficient production organization.

But let us start at the beginning. The headquarter is situated at Ängelholm, a small township in south-western Sweden, south of the second-largest city, Gothenburg, in an area characterized by agriculture and light industry.

The company was established to provide production capacity in Eastern Europe for the mother company, IKEA, which is the owner. For decades IKEA had suppliers in Eastern Europe, and due to the changes in Eastern Europe at the end of the 1980s it feared discontinuity in production and wanted to ensure external supplies at reasonable and stable prices. This is why Swedwood was born in 1991. The first factory started producing in the spring of 1992. By 2001 it had more than 30 production units in 10 Eastern European countries. So its *raison d'être* is to establish production in places where it would be difficult for the mother company to obtain supplies at reasonable and stable prices. On top of some 30 production units in Eastern European countries, the company has five units in Sweden, one in Germany and one in Canada. The total workforce is about 9000 people. Swedwood also provides industry related production expertise to the IKEA group. The company is expanding extremely fast, doubling its total size every two and a half years.

## Competitive Advantage and Strategy

The key success factor of Swedwood is that production is technically advanced and efficient and takes place mainly in low-cost countries, all of which makes it a low-cost producer. One of the advanced techniques is a lightweight 'sandwich' construction, which is technically difficult.

The strategy can be explained just as briefly as competitive advantage. It has two elements:

- continual expansion in order to satisfy the demands of its one and only customer; and
- continual technical improvements to production.

The next production units were planned to be in Russia, White Russia, Romania, Latvia and Slovakia, and the existing ones would be expanded. In order better to serve the mother company, Swedwood was also considering North America, and possibly to follow the trend to move production from Eastern European countries to Asia, especially to China.

Regarding strategy, it should be mentioned that the company was considering its role as a supplier to IKEA in terms of the way it negotiates prices, quantities and conditions, and at what level this is done in the mother organization.

## Production and Organization

Swedwood's production units are organized in functional divisions starting with machine operation, colouring, assembling, packaging and storing. Each division is based on a flow process with minimum waste of time and space. The span of control of the first line manager (foreman) is 30 to 60 workers in Sweden, and somewhat narrower in the Eastern European units, where the workforce need more direction and expect tighter control.

The management has adopted the IKEA way of organization right from the start in 1991, not because it had to, but because that is what it prefers. The philosophy is to create big results with limited resources, that is:

- with simplicity;
- by avoiding bureaucracy;
- by having minimal hierarchy; and
- by extensive delegation and empowerment.

As at IKEA, managers right down to foremen have big responsibilities and decision-making authority at a very young age. The spirit was to rely on people, to trust them to be able to make the right decisions.

Here again cooperation is a key word. People are being judged on their ability to cooperate and function as a team, at the same time allowing for different opinions. Cooperation means discussions leading to consensus on major decisions most of the time. There is no voting. If discussions do not lead to consensus, the manager will decide, and from there on loyalty to the decision taken is expected. To give an example, the top manager of Swedwood had experienced the need to step in less than five times during the past six years.

Apart from mere production there were cross functional teams organized in projects, for instance environmental questions, improvements in technology, cost reduction and so on. All units are organized the same way, and we were told that some Eastern European units were more efficient than the Swedish ones, probably due to a well-educated workforce with high motivation. The hierarchy at the production units was quite simply: managing director, functional managers, supervisors (foremen), then workers.

To put the management style into perspective, in their East European plants Swedwood had adopted a more local style, more traditional, with direct orders and clear instructions. Most Scandinavian expatriates had managed to change from their usual democratic and consensus seeking style to a more authoritarian one. Production and organization are the same as in Sweden, but managing people is different.

At the corporate office in Sweden the administrative hierarchy is: CEO, sector managers, business area managers then factory managers.

Here again, as at Fritz Hansen and at Ekornes, managers have no secretaries, it is the 'do-it-yourself' culture, and again, as at Ekornes, this includes human resource functions such as recruitment, taking care of individual development, plans for education and salary negotiations. There is a person taking care of the technical side as well.

The style also includes little differentiation between people, egalitarianism being a credo along with unpretentiousness and modesty in personal behaviour whatever a person's rank.

Some readers may be wondering what it is like to have manufacturing facilities in Eastern Europe. The first answer is that the local authorities pose no problem to the company. On the contrary, Swedwood is welcomed in the host countries because it provides production facilities, the latest technology, employment and export incomes. Some 95 per cent of the production is exported to IKEA stores all around the world, the rest is sold locally. The company has good support from the top level of local authorities. From time to time, according to the chief executive officer, it has problems at the middle level, where there is still a lot of bureaucracy and in some regions a bit of corruption. In such cases Swedwood unit managers will go up a level to complain. There is also from time to time demands from criminal organizations in the classical two-step fashion: first they want to impose their 'protection' on the company, which management invariably refuses to accept, and next there are threats, something might happen to the plant or to people, but management never gave in, we were told, and nothing has ever happened. Another type of difficulty might be corruption in the local bureaucracy. It could be refusal to reimburse value added tax (VAT) for exports unless a certain amount of money is paid to a civil servant. Swedwood systematically refuses; instead the person responsible at the next level is approached, or the next, or the next.

The company wants to be a model of good behaviour in Eastern Europe, not only in terms of its ethics, but also in areas such as organization, efficient production, human resource management and environment. In short, the company quite consciously wants to export the Swedish way of doing things.

## Management *Esprit de Corps* and Management–Workforce Relations

Swedwood's main concern is getting the right people for management. So far it has managed to get the people needed, but it can be a problem finding project managers for overseas operations. Not many Swedes are prepared to go to say Ukraine for four years to establish a new factory. But middle managers in the Eastern European factories are gaining experience and they will soon be ready for management positions. The expatriates sent out are mostly Swedes and Danes, but also Finns, Germans and other North-west Europeans. The recruitment base needs to be expanded: Swedes are not very mobile, but it turns out that neither are East Europeans. They prefer to stay where they are, globalization or not.

Managers are paid according to the industry norm while expatriate managers are paid above average. Managers may have up to two months extra salary as a bonus per year. On top of that they get a free car and telephone. In each unit this is four to five people. According to one manager, Swedish managers have about 70–75 per cent of a German salary and 50 per cent of an American one.

We will now turn to the Swedish unit that we visited at Ängelholm.

Operators for the factory may be hard to get because unemployment is low in Sweden and this type of job is not very attractive. Operators have to be able to handle computers. The company invests heavily in new technology, which means that fewer but better skilled people are needed. Swedwood sends people on courses if they are not sufficiently qualified.

All workers are paid a fixed salary. They used to have piecework pay, but now the pay is equal for people with similar training and experience. The question of lowering wages in return for a bonus arrangement had been discussed in the co-determination committee with workers' representatives. However, the union members preferred to stay with the higher salary instead of reducing pay in order to have bonus on top. Unions will not accept individual pay.

Cooperation between management and the factory floor was considered satisfactory by managers as well as by the union representative, who testified that the level of information was very good and transparent, with figures about production results, orders, future plans and changes. Any changes in production are discussed with all parties involved up front. The union representatives are also members of the board, where they can speak their mind. The union representative appreciated the personnel policy in rehabilitation schemes in case of illness, the fact that they have a gym for training and an employees' club that organizes excursions and other activities.

## Potential Conflicts

In their ten years of existence, Swedwood had never had a strike, although there had been disagreements on wages from time to time, in which case the workers might go slow, refuse to work overtime and so on. The production manager was of the opinion that work discipline, punctuality and production efficiency were lagging in the Swedish units; management had communicated their discontent in this respect to the workers but no changes in behaviour were seen. The union representatives agreed with management but did nothing. This is an example of the difficult balance between clear direction and empowerment with which follows responsibility. According to management workers this method had not lived up to expectations. Some of the personnel had even been sent to sister companies in Poland to see how things worked there, but that did not lead to improvements in the Swedish factories. Shortly before our visit the production manager had told workers in so many words: the reaction was silence, stony faces.

The question here is why did they all judge the situation to be harmonious when in fact there were major disagreements? Nobody wanted to call them conflicts. Several explanations are possible:

- The workers, including the union representative, used silence as a strategy for not changing anything.
- The workers were embarrassed at being criticized and the non-reaction meant 'we do not agree, but we do not want to stir up a conflict', Swedes being more conflict avoiding than most.
- The union representative has no real power over his members and cannot make them do what they do not want to do.
- As long as management does not use sanctions against unwilling and undisciplined workers, it is easier not to change behaviour.
- In Sweden the relationship between the parties on the labour market is by definition harmonious and non-confrontational.

This is a principle that was set down in the so-called Saltsjöbaden agreement in 1938. It is an agreement between the Swedish Employers' Confederation (SAF) and the Swedish Trade Union Confederation regulating the treatment of conflicts and giving rules for cooperation and negotiations between the parties. A major goal was the elimination of conflicts that could be a threat to society. It became the very model for orderly negotiations and positive cooperation on the labour market, and the spirit of that important agreement has become a principle, almost a doctrine, that is generally not violated. The result is that apparently nobody will admit to there being conflicts between the parties from time to time.

It is only fair to say that open conflicts on the Swedish labour market have occurred and that today decentralized wage negotiations may prevent some of the classical worker–employer conflicts, but this also goes for Denmark and Norway, where our respondents did not deny altogether having conflicts from time to time.

Whatever the explanation, this attitude, we found, was particularly pronounced in Sweden. In the Danish company, the parties admitted that the relationship between management and unions was tense and conflictual over the changes that management wanted to implement, but mostly the attitude in all three countries between the parties was one of 'we are in the same boat'. In other words the former 'them and us' opposition has changed to an 'us versus the market' attitude.

## CONCLUSION

In conclusion the management *esprit de corps* in all three companies was characterized by delegation of decision-making authority to all levels according to their experience and expertise, which is a manifestation of trust in the sound judgement of people and on their being able to take initiatives; it is further based on cooperation in teams and between teams and levels. A prerequisite for all this is low barriers to communication, hence the meeting activity. A way of illustrating this openness would be to cite the president of Norwegian Ekornes: 'The employees need to feel safe, to know management's motives, they need to be able to accept and respect management for what they do. They need to be informed at all times. Then there are no conflicts. Management must listen to people and give honest answers. Since there is a constant dialogue, management knows what people think before they make decisions', and he continues, 'For the sake of all kinds of relations don't do anything dishonest, be straightforward and say what your motives are.'

## REFERENCES

Centro Studi Industria Leggera (Csil) (1998), *The Furniture Industry in the European Union*, High Point, NC; Oakville, Canada and Milan: Aktrin Research Institute and Csil.
Eurostat (2000), *Panorama of European Business*, theme 4, Luxembourg: European Commission.

Eurostat (2002), *European Business*, facts and figures data 1990–2000, theme 4, Luxembourg: European Commission.
Eurostat (2003), *European Business*, facts and figures data 1991–2001, theme 4, Luxembourg: European Commission.
Henriksen, L.B. (1999), 'The Danish furniture industry: a case of tradition and change', in P. Karnøe, P. Hull Kristensen and P. Houman Andersen (eds), *Mobilizing Resources and Generating Competences*, Copenhagen: Copenhagen Business School Press.

# 5. Confectionery and food production

Food and confectionery businesses in Scandinavia are influenced by differences in the countries' relations to the EU and the effects of this on taxation and competition. Since Norway is part of the European Economic Area (EEA), most processed food is tax free, but there are mutual quotas with no tax or reduced tax as for instance for chocolate. Most food related raw materials are more expensive in Norway than in the EU, with the exception of sugar, condensed milk and butter. However, chocolate and confectionery products are subject to a special tax in the Norwegian consumer market.

The prospect of new and growing markets in Eastern Europe and Russia has been recognized by some producers. In all three countries there has been an increasing number of mergers and acquisitions (M&As), some of them cross-border both within and outside Scandinavia. Despite these changes, food and confectionery markets are to some extent stabilized by traditionalism in customers' preferences, tastes and brand recognition. This stability, however, seems to be stronger in Sweden and Norway than in Denmark. The expanding parts of the confectionery and the food industry reflect social changes in the late twentieth century: more leisure, youth with buying power, changed family patterns and tighter schedules have promoted snacks and ready-made foods. The Scandinavians' spending in restaurants, cafés and so on is increasing.

The retail chains have increased their market shares in grocery as well as in petrol stations and kiosks. The producers respond to this strengthened market power with branding, while the retail chains, on their side, have no scruples about selling advertised, branded products at prices that just cover their costs in order to draw customers, and at the same time weaken the producers' ability to command premium prices in the future. So, producers use advertising to build the producers' brands, and retail chains try to trash them. At the same time, the in-house brands of the retail chains are getting more shelf space, and in some cases such products have been upgraded from mediocre to premium. The difference in pricing between the brands is narrowing. Although an increasing segment of consumers are expected to be willing to pay more for high quality and fresh food, the retail chains mainly compete on volumes and prices.

Concentration on the retail side is met by concentration on the producer side as well, an example of counter-concentration (Lawrence, 2002). In this way, the Nordic markets are becoming increasingly integrated.

Despite the fact that the Scandinavian cases we have studied in confectionery and food production are quite dissimilar in terms of products, organization structure and markets, they are all influenced by similar dynamics, whether these are generated by market forces or by fads and fashions.

## BRIEF CASE HISTORIES

Nidar is a result of a merger in 1980 between Bergene, a family owned company established in 1906 with the strongest position in southern Norway, and Nidar, a shareholder company established in 1912 with the strongest position in the middle and northern parts of Norway. Nidar was bought by the food company Nora, which was merged with Orkla in 1991. The production facilities and corporate office are located in Trondheim, while the marketing is located in Oslo, to be close to the retail chain headquarters. At the time of our interviews, Nidar was Norway's second largest producer of confectionery. Nidar's market share is almost equal to Freia, which also used to be a family company, but is now owned by Kraft General Foods and ultimately by Philip Morris. Between them Freia and Nidar have a 70 per cent share of the Norwegian market, which is said to be stable, and split equally between chocolate and sugar confectionery.

Procordia Food is the result of the merger of three Swedish companies, Felix, Ekströms and Önos, within Volvo Procordia. In 1995, Procordia Food was bought by the Norwegian Orkla group, which had acquired Bob, a fourth Swedish food producer in 1993. Orkla was originally a small Norwegian mining company that has gradually expanded to become the largest supplier of branded consumer goods in the Nordic region. From 1983 to 2002, the stock price increased at an average annual rate of 29.5 per cent, faster than General Electric and Coca-Cola share prices. The branded consumer goods comprise foods, beverages (40 per cent of Carlsberg Breweries since 2000), Orkla brands and media. In addition, the Orkla group has a footing in chemicals and financial investments. The latter comprises 25 per cent of the Orkla group's value, which gives it one of the largest market capitalizations in Norway. The acquisition of Procordia Food is part of Orkla's long-term strategy to expand in the Nordic countries, the Baltic and in Eastern Europe.

Procordia Food's factories in Sweden deliver products in three areas: snacking, pizza and taste enhancers, such as sauces and dressings, mainly to grocery retail chains, but also to the catering and fast-food market. When we gathered data in 2001, the ambition was to grow in the Nordic countries and Eastern Europe within these product areas. Orkla does not manufacture for other brands. The expansion therefore involves takeovers or cooperation with producers of established brands, and intense marketing and brand-building efforts. For Procordia the first steps have been to launch products jointly in Norway and Sweden, and to acquire companies in the Baltic and Eastern Europe in order to expand manufacturing capacity. The result was that Orkla had 42 production units in Europe, some of which produced the same products. Consequently, rationalization strategies involve fewer factories, increased utilization levels, fewer product types and slimmer organizations.

The Danish company Dandy was the third largest producer of chewing-gum in the world, next to the US-based companies Wrigley and Warner Lambert. Dandy has its corporate office and largest facilities in Vejle on the east coast of Jutland. It was founded by a husband and wife team in 1915 and was a family-owned company until 2002, when Cadbury Schweppes acquired the sales, marketing and production of Dandy's own brands and the factory established in 1998 in Russia. In 2002 the name of the company was changed to Gumlink. However, since our visit was prior to 2002, the following will all be about the former Dandy. The family keeps full ownership of Fertin Pharma, a company acquired in 1978, in view of producing functional chewing gum, or medical chewing gum, such as nicotine gum. It also kept 75 per cent of Danish business-to-business production (that is, private labels) and 50 per cent of research and development activities in Dandy. While sweets traditionally are associated with fun and luxury, chewing-gum has also become related to dental care and pharmaceutical products through added functions such as caries (cavity)-protection, teeth whitening and vitamin C, and thereby gained appeal in increasingly health-conscious market segments.

Dandy made an attempt to establish its products in the Polish markets. However, when Wrigley introduced sugar-free chewing-gum, the market turned against them in a matter of months. The lesson learnt from this was used to conquer Russia. Advertising on national television, which was extremely cheap at the time of this initiative, was used to create a surge of demand even before the products were available on the market. Russian business entrepreneurs then contacted Dandy after seeing their request for dealers in newspapers. Eventually, this led to a successful market establishment. This was later followed by the building of a packaging plant in Novgorod, staffed by well-educated employees and supported by the municipal government for creating much needed employment and economic activity in the community. This situation also put pressure on the Danish factory. First, it would have to double production to meet the new demands, and later, compete with the packing done by Russian low-cost labour. The next step was a Russian production facility that after a while took over all production. Consequently, activities in Vejle, which had provided employment for around 1000 people at the time of our visit, were reduced mainly to headquarters function with 90 employees as of 2003.

# NIDAR

## Strategy

The confectionery market is very traditional, in particular in chocolates, but also to a large extent based on impulse shopping. Strong brands, campaigns and availability are therefore key success factors. People may like to try new products, but very few new products have actually permanently established themselves since the 1960s, except for sugar-free chewing-gums. Nidar sells and distributes Wrigley, which has almost 75 per cent of the Norwegian chewing-gum market. The production has a large Christmas season and a smaller Easter season. Due to a large number of seasonal workers, 900 employees only put in the equivalent of 650 full-time workers per year. Campaigns and product innovations have an increasing importance. A market driven, process oriented organization is put in place to handle this. Since the middle of the 1990s, the distribution is handed over to grocery chains and other distributors, but Nidar still has a sales force of 130–140 employees. However, one of the major customers, a retail chain, does not want to see any sales representatives any more, a change that has been identified in other industries by one of the present authors (Lawrence, 2002), so further changes can be expected. Nidar's exports are minor after some attempts that failed because of consumer conservatism and the inability to find established distributors that were willing to cooperate. However, as a part of the Orkla group, the strategy for the next decade would be to get access to the Nordic countries and to the Baltic and Eastern Europe. Learning from previous failures, this would involve acquisitions or distribution agreements, for instance in Finland or Sweden. Organic growth in these conservative markets would be too slow. Expansion should begin with entry to the Nordic market, it was planned, or else the Nordic market would enter Norway first through integrated grocery chains. Nidar did not make a profit in the early 1990s. Orkla and the new management initiated a turnaround process in 1994 that brought the bottom-line back into the black. To cope with increasingly sales driven operations, an organization structure strongly resembling the business process re-engineering (BPR) concept and new production technology had been implemented, and product innovations and campaigns generated an increasing share of Nidar's sales and income.

## Management

In Nidar, top and middle managers are recruited mainly from the Orkla group. All of them are male and have university level education in engineering, business administration or economics and so on. To break the trend, the new managing director is a 35-year-old woman, but she also came from within Orkla. While there are plenty of engineering graduates in Trondheim due to its technical university, it is difficult to find people with sufficient competence in marketing and finance there. This is one of the reasons that marketing was moved to Oslo a few years before our study, plus the fact that the retail chain headquarters and Orkla headquarters are also located in Oslo.

After the Orkla takeover, a turnaround process was initiated at Nidar. To make the company earn money again, a BPR-inspired process-based organization structure with stronger customer focus, new technology, delayering and downsizing was initiated. The organization units would be process areas, not functions as they used to be, and new technology replaced many tasks. Most managers would have to apply for new jobs because their old jobs did not exist any more. Several lost their titles and were put on the same level as people they used to manage. In addition, many managers were not comfortable with the chaotic transition period when design of the new organization and operation of the old one took place at the same time. Some realized that their competence was more needed elsewhere. In the end, perhaps as much as 80 per cent of the middle management left the company. This was indicated as one of the reasons Nidar succeeded in establishing the new structure. Leaders on lower levels and operators were given more interesting and skill-demanding work, so they, for the most part, enjoyed the change.

The new process organization flattened out Nidar's hierarchy from 12–15 levels to just five, from the managing director to the operators. This created some confusion among the career minded white-collar rank and file, in particular in sales and marketing who expected to be promoted every few years. In marketing, for instance, there is a marketing director, four marketing managers and then the rest of the team. Few people would stay there longer than five years, but a high level of turnover was not unwanted in such a dynamic organization. Wages for middle management and staff are in practice decided by their superiors. There were few incentives other than wages, since fringe benefits such as free cars and phones were largely taken for granted by those eligible for them. There were, however, many opportunities for taking courses and further education. Within the Orkla system, it was even possible to get scholarships to go abroad to follow MBA courses.

The Orkla culture implied more presentations at meetings, analysis and documentation before decisions were taken. Decisions about launching new products, or taking projects to new major steps had to be backed by the management group. However, many decisions were not taken at meetings, but in projects or between managers at a lower level. 'Because of the way we are working, we are always checking everybody in the project group or people concerned with the decisions', one manager claimed. There were few examples of managers making important decisions without a previous information and discussion process. 'It takes a long time to do things, but when you take decisions, everybody has had an opportunity to say their opinion at least.' *The important thing is to make sure that everybody understands every side of the problem when a decision is made.* In this way they can secure loyalty to the decision and ensure that it will be implemented. Lack of information to the right people at the right time would cause problems because of the frequent changes, launches and relaunches of products. The monthly management meeting was described in this way: 'It has an agenda sent out a week before and all cases to be discussed have to be included. Then we have ten minutes to one hour to make the decision, and it is a discussion; we all know how it is going to end, how it is going to be.' The preceding information process and discussions are often more important than the formal decisions.

**Subcultures and Potential Conflicts**

Marketing has become the most prestigious department at Nidar, and the marketing culture with its focus on the consumer has become more important than typical production values, with high pride in products and capabilities. Campaigns account for an increasing share of the sales, and this may cause strains on other departments. To avoid this, coordination between production, distribution and sales is essential. This is done in more or less permanent projects, which means that Nidar has implemented a matrix-like structure.

'Meetings are frequent', too frequent in some managers' opinion, and they are formally structured by an agenda. In the production, some meetings had a fixed agenda over several years. However, the meetings are used not only to give instructions, or for the coordination of activities, but also to make subordinates take responsibility. Middle managers were not supposed to attend all meetings, and in some cases they forced their subordinates to make decisions on their own. 'Some of the decisions I refuse to make, I won't make them because I force them to make them all by themselves. It is a kind of educational point in it. So it is more like the situation decides what I have to do.' There seems to be a consciousness of the need for variation in the leader's role between autocracy, coordination and delegation.

In the cross-functional project environment, the production and marketing cultures are brought together. Due to stronger focus on markets and earnings, concerns for production had increasingly to come before people, several managers explained. 'If we do not survive in an effective production environment, then we don't have anything at all, so production comes before people.' Management by walking around was another measure used by managers to reduce barriers between the marketing and production cultures.

'You get a closer relationship with the people and they discover that you are a normal person and that is a discovery for them too, that it is possible to speak both ways in a very open and informal way.' Middle managers on a lower level use the word 'lobbying' to describe how they influence decision making.

Conflicts between individuals and departments are generally handled without making them too explicit. Different opinions and discussions are considered necessary to improve the organization. Problems with personal chemistry or prestige, however, would create problems for this process. One manager explained that if he had problems with a person in marketing, he would go to the marketing manager and tell him about it. Instead of confronting that person directly, interpersonal skills and problems would be put on the agenda in the next meeting. In that way it would be possible to make people work together on a professional level, even if they would not go together personally.

Similarly, interdepartmental conflicts are dealt with without hurting the pride of others by proving them wrong:

> It is easier to handle those problems when you are organized as we are with very many cross-functional relationships, because we do not have a department here and another department here working on separate levels. ... We always come together and discuss things. And that is a tool to speak up and to lay it out open. When it comes to conflicts, you get aware of them very early, and you get to know rumours very early because people are talking very much to you cross-functionally.

Deep and lasting interdepartmental conflicts are pre-empted by early warnings and discussions, which is a part of the process-oriented organization structure combined with the projects, and the discussion-before-decision culture.

## Management–Workforce Relations

Nidar's organization structure in production is based on goal driven groups, mostly with between seven and ten people responsible for one machine or a physical area. The groups are collectively responsible for production according to plans decided by the manager and worked out by the planners. There are several such groups under each process leader. Since the mid-1990s there have been no foremen or shift-leaders. This means that the span of control could be anything from 60 to 150 persons depending on department and seasonal variations. There is a meeting for all operators at 10 o'clock every day to coordinate production and allocate personnel, based on 24-hour plans made by the planners. The operators in the goal-directed groups can just check the computers to see what needs to be done. Within one goal-driven group, predefined tasks rotate at least once a year, including the group coordinator task, which entails responsibility for the psycho-social environment in the group. If that task gets too tough, however, the process leader is brought in. In some groups one or two persons may grow informally into the role of coordinator, while in other groups work runs smoothly without one. This can be seen as a further development of the self-governing groups that were introduced in Sweden and Norway in the 1970s to make industrial work more meaningful and pleasant. The main reasons for using goal driven groups today, however, have to do with flexibility and advances in planning and production technology. Upskilling, work-enlargement and autonomy are the results.

One process leader claims that he really wants the groups to make decisions themselves about what to produce when. In spite of this, they call him to check if it is all right, although he always says yes because so far they had never made the wrong decision. It takes several years to give people the confidence to make the decisions they have to take, he explains. He does not show up at the planning meetings any more, which is accepted after some initial resistance. He still gets all the information he needs from the planners about what is going on at all times.

There is a wage scale with four levels for non-management in production. Only US$1500 (NOK10000) a year separates semi-skilled and skilled workers. Technicians are on the next level. There is no extra payment for the group coordinator task, only for skills. There is no wish to turn them into foremen, which is a category that lacks any firm base for authority in Norway, such as formal education on a higher level than the operators. Instead they must avoid creating hierarchical distance, and they tend to fall in the trap between friendship and leadership (Sivesind, 1995).

In production there is an informal hierarchy of functions. Maintenance workers come above operators, and below the operators are the cleaners. There are implicit conflicts between production, symbolized by workers in white clothing, and maintenance, symbolized by blue clothing. There was an attempt to solve this by putting some people from central maintenance into the production groups, but the attitudes and views still remained. The maintenance people also had to be allowed to put on their blue clothes again, after a while. Conflicts between maintenance and production could for example be about planned versus unplanned maintenance. The maintenance department has plans for jobs that need to be done, and informs affected parts of the production. However, the maintenance staff are often approached by people in production to do other things, for instance to fix a production line that has stopped. This means that their maintenance projects will be delayed, which causes complaints from others in the production expecting planned maintenance. However, the production leader, with long experience and knowledge of all the rules of the old organization as well as business strategy, is a discussion partner for everyone. Being a problem solver is an important part of his role.

In addition, there is a cultural clash between white- and blue-collar workers; a leader in production claimed: 'Sometimes people in the office think that the operators are just a piece of meat, you can offer them anything, their human worth is not as big as on that side.' Despite efforts to level out many social differences in Scandinavia, cultural distinctions between white- and blue-collar employees, deeply rooted in industrial history, are very much present.

## Participation and Relationship with the Trade Union

Internal communication is very open and direct in Nidar, so much so that the investor relations people in Orkla complain because some of the information could upset the stock market. There are 'team briefs' once a month in each department where economy, social issues and market situation are presented by department leaders, and every four months there is a meeting for all employees headed by the managing director. After some initial problems with financial data that used business terminology, the employees appreciate these presentations. Some of the information is considered so sensitive that there are no handouts. However, this is in line with the Orkla culture. Orkla's former CEO, Jens P. Heyerdahl Jr., is famous for informing the trade unions before the management. He was the president of Orkla from 1979 to 2001 when the company grew from a small mining company to a Nordic giant. He is still a member of the blue-collar trade union LO and the Labour Party, despite coming from a very rich family. He attended meetings with top politicians wearing a knitted jacket and sneakers, and could be seen driving around in his Citroën 2CV. His credibility in the labour movement meant too much to him to be jeopardized by flamboyant behaviour. One of the Nidar managers says that union representatives coming back from national union meetings may have news to tell that management does not yet know.

When this new information strategy began in the early 1990s, a very ugly economic picture was painted, and people were angry because they thought it was unfair. One hundred and fifty employees, including trade union representatives, were invited to start working with a new business idea and vision. In the design of the new process oriented organization in Nidar, the need for personnel and skills was mapped, and 20 people with the lowest skills and seniority were put on a list of 'leftovers'. The unions were invited to take part in this process. The operators and the unions had seen the problems before management, so they were keen to cooperate. They made sure that the operators got their skills upgraded, with apprenticeship certificates and courses to enable them to do the new jobs before the process organization was introduced. There were many arguments and no written agreement, but there was a common understanding of the underlying problems, based on good information, and both parties told us this. In 1999 a new project initiated by the board was set up to reduce the number of employees in production from 320 to 210 in five years. Although this was hard to swallow, the union realized they had to take part in the changes to save the company and the rest of the jobs. The proportion of female operators at Nidar is 60 per cent, and there are few alternative industrial jobs, particularly for women, in Trondheim.

Meetings prescribed by law and wage negotiations with the unions are very formalistic. Informal consultations with the production and personnel managers, however, are very important. The trade union representatives have asked the top management to allow time for these processes, which they have done. In addition, the management also invites the union representatives to take part in projects from the start instead of informing them afterwards. In any case the unions have people on the board, so they will know what is going on.

One manager explains the reasons for the openness in this way:

> The goal is that people should know the situation Nidar is in, so they can take the right decisions in their work ..., we don't give this out because we are nice or as a benefit, we do this because we want people to make the right decisions in their daily work.

In conclusion, Nidar has been able to turn around the company by implementing a BPR-inspired rationalization strategy. The result is that profits increased from nothing to more than US$10 million (NOK70 million) in five years. This process relied on extensive information to the employees and involvement of the trade unions at early stages in the decision-making process, which seem to have been preconditions for constructive cooperation about upskilling and increased responsibility. However, a planned down-sizing process had only just begun.

## PROCORDIA FOOD

### Strategy

Procordia Food covers three business areas on a cross-national level: snacking, sauces and pizza. The managing director of Procordia is heading snacking products cross-nationally within the Orkla group. The organization structure is process oriented, as we saw in the case of the Norwegian Orkla daughter company Nidar. This means that similar processes should belong to the same part of the organization. In addition, some attempts have been made to make the Procordia organization more customer oriented. These seem to be concepts that Orkla firmly believes in. The major parts of the organizations are: supply, which is purchasing, production and logistics, including seven production plants in Sweden; demand, which is product development, marketing and sales; and support functions such as information systems and finance. Originally, the organization consisted of three business areas in the whole value chain. Through the reorganization, logistics has become less involved in moving materials within the production system and more oriented towards trade, customers' needs and just-in-time delivery. It is the bridge from supply to demand and is not involved in the whole value chain any more. Sales has become more centralized and focused on growth and efficiency.

The major reason for these changes is concentration in the grocery business. Three retail chains cover 90 per cent of this market in Sweden and own-label products, in many cases manufactured outside of Sweden, have gained an increasing share of shelf-space. They put pressure on the producers. Even other markets that Procordia serves, such as petrol stations, catering and fast food, have been concentrated into fewer and larger wholesale and retail chains.

The restructuring of the Procordia organization was also seen as a sign that Orkla had the intention of being an operating company, not just a holding company. Orkla would attempt to take advantage of possible synergies through the coordination of purchasing and the production of similar products in different factories and countries. Procordia's jam factories, for instance, had been reduced from three to one. The goal is also to reduce overheads and increase the utilization level of the factories in the Nordic countries. This level was only about 50 per cent, but due to large seasonal variation some overcapacity was unavoidable. Procordia was also determined to cut down strongly on the product range. Following the mergers that took place from 1993 to 1996, employment was also reduced by 600 employees and the downsizing would continue.

The food industry is not changing very rapidly, although there have been some substantial changes in processing, packaging and conservation techniques. Product innovation for the most part means modification or extension of existing product lines, mainly because consumer tastes can be very conservative, or limited to certain age groups or regions. Some types of Procordia food, such as pickled fruit, are not expected to grow in the Swedish market. In contrast, fast food consumed out of the home, typically between meals, has a more promising potential. Procordia targeted chilled dairy snacks and savoury snacks such as pizza for this market. Not surprisingly, one of the few newly established Procordia products belongs to this food group: Risifrutti consists of fruit purée and creamed rice in two separate chambers of a plastic container. This is food straight from the fridge that easily can be consumed on the run. The product was launched in 1993 by BOB, introduced in Norway, Denmark and Finland in 1996–97, and by year 2000 sales had reached 41 million units in Sweden alone. Functional food is another group with an expected growth potential. It could for instance be yoghurt with added bacteria that improve wellbeing. However, the introduction of such food is not an easy task in Scandinavia. If the products are advertised with health benefits, they would come under the strict production and marketing regulations that apply to pharmaceuticals. The communication of health-related messages would have to be very discreet.

Food quality is also a major issue, concerning packaging, durability and waste reduction, but also animal welfare and gene-modified crops. Procordia is also focusing on integrated farm production which entails control of seeds, timing, fertilizers and pesticides. The goal is better yield and lower prices. Environmental protection also has a high priority, and among other things there is a joint project with the municipality to build a plant to produce bio fuel. There is an understanding among managers that openness was the only possible policy if there were any pollution problems. The public has a right to know about such matters. Our informants were not able to recall any recent examples of pollution, though one of the production plants spread an unpleasant odour in the neighbourhood. The strategy to handle this was to explain the reason for the problem to the public, and to promise that Procordia would do everything they possibly could to solve it, even if that meant investing a lot of money.

## Management

After Procordia was bought by Orkla, the management was quite stunned to discover what they thought was Norwegian business culture. It was a written culture. Decisions should be based on discussions in meetings and written documentation, as one manager described it:

> There is a great difference between Swedish and Norwegian culture in the way you perceive different settings written or said and the way you are working, the meetings and writing. They are writing heavily, much more than we are, and all kinds of decisions are based on good documentation before they decide.

Or again, 'They regard themselves as having a writing culture, so they are aware of it; I think it is good. But then of course it is a little contradictory to fast decision making and speed and tempo doing business.'

Based on our study of Orkla-owned Nidar, and compared to other Norwegian companies, however, this seems to have more to do with Orkla than with Norwegian culture as such. It is also in line with the image Orkla has created of themselves in the Norwegian media. Major decisions should be based on documentation, analysis and discussions on several levels of the organization. It was pointed out that the former Procordia owner Volvo also had emphasized systematic thinking and planning, but Volvo did not know the food industry very well. Orkla in contrast was more involved in the management of its subsidiaries. This in particular applied to marketing, as one manager explains:

> Orkla is a very serious company and rather theoretically oriented in some way, I think. It is on the front line with the marketing areas, they have a very good reputation there, but I think we in Sweden are more practical, and the Norwegians are more theoretical.

The 'theoretical' approach is probably also a feature of Orkla rather than of Norway; it does not necessarily characterize other Norwegian companies. Since Orkla also has a financial investment division and managers rotate within the group, they have people with special experience and competence in investment analysis based on documentation. It seems like they use similar procedures to decide on investments in production as well.

Insisting on well-founded decision-making processes involving many levels and functions meant that they could take a rather long time, as one Procordia manager explained:

> There were still others between us and the board meeting that you would have to pass, kind of sub-boards, or pre-boards, so it was a rather long distance for an investment of 70 million Swedish kronor (US$10 million). I remember dragging a new factory of 75 million through the system. I think there were about seven decision points. ... and on every board they had some suggestions for change. It is not just a matter of sending a paper through the system.

This thoroughness could be a plus point if it helped the company avoid bad investments. However, in some situations business opportunities could be lost if decision making was too slow and complicated. It could also discourage managers from initiating new investments. However, the Orkla culture was not equally present in all areas of the company as in marketing and investment. In personnel issues, for instance, Procordia did not receive many directives from Orkla.

The emphasis on a thorough decision-making process can also be observed in the middle management of Procordia. In one process area, there are monthly management meetings with an almost fixed agenda. Items are presented, discussed, there are questions and answers, and decisions taken and written down. However, the emphasis is not just on making decisions, but ensuring that they are followed up with results. It is therefore important that people feel they are involved in the decision making and thereby made responsible for the outcome. Thus joint decisions or delegation to the subordinates are preferable. However, as the manager points out: 'If they can't take it jointly, then I take the decision.' This means that there is a consciousness of using different styles of management in different situations, as we saw in Nidar as well.

Managers are recruited through information meetings at universities and university colleges (högskolor), in Sweden, through the Internet, recruitment firms, and from Procordia or elsewhere in the Orkla group. The company can easily get new employees, since it has a good reputation, in particular in marketing, and it could get 200–300 applications for a product management position. Wages for management and for white-collar employees are individually determined, and fringe benefits include pension schemes and cars for some managers, a heavily taxed benefit. This is not so different from what can be found in similar companies. However, the turnover of white-collar employees is just 2–3 per cent in Procordia, either because it is professional work in a high-profile, expanding group, or because of lack of alternative opportunities. Consequently, the largest group of managers were those between 50 and 60 years old. There was also, however, a large group between 30 and 40. In an increasingly competence-based industry, recruiting more and highly and recently educated people is a priority.

Even in management, Swedes may underplay hierarchical distinctions. One of the researchers asked what the overall number of management personnel is. The manager answered 140.

'And you said half is top management, and the rest is …?'

'We are all top leaders,' the manager answered, and emphasized similarity in management quality. This remark resembles the famous quote from George Orwell's Animal Farm: 'We are all equal, but some are more equal than others.'

## Subcultures and Potential Conflicts

In every company there are potential conflicts between different parts of the organization over unavoidable decisions that will have to be unpopular for at least one of the parties. Procordia deals with this by letting the people involved come up with suggestions. They are encouraged to come up with a solution they can live with, or else the result might be worse still. A major decision may be prepared by letting those involved take a few days to gather relevant information, and then free them from normal tasks in order to focus all their energy on the discussion. By encouraging different opinions to be expressed many positive spin-offs can occur. But more importantly, in this way the decisions are more likely to be respected and followed up. One manager pointed out that although such processes may take some time, it is much more time consuming to find out who is working against a decision. Such negative dynamics may even spread to other parts of the organization and be very counter-productive. Although a lot of energy is tied up by the process of decision making, many conflicts die out when the decision is taken and people adapt to the new situation, one manager claimed.

A merger always implies the possibility that there will be winners and losers. Even if the four old companies in Procordia Food had been acquired by the same owner, it was felt by some of the merged companies that they were the losers in the process of merger and integration. They all had their own culture that underwent changes in the process of merger and integration. Earlier, the different parts of the company saw Procordia as 'the enemy'. Now Orkla had become the 'enemy' they could unite against, but after a while more consciously planned cultural changes took place, and Orkla, on their side, no longer expected everything to be their way. Still, there are people who 'close their eyes and hope the nightmare will be over when they wake up'. The problem may not be so much related to the Orkla group as such, as to that of being subordinated, and if that was not enough, it is subordination to a foreign group from 'little brother' Norway. However, the trade union was positive about the acquisition by Orkla, since Orkla is a Scandinavian company and owners from other countries might not be so understanding of Swedish work relations.

## Management–Workforce Relations

The food industry with its many simple tasks together with a high proportion of female workers in general means low pay. Despite this, there did not seem to be a shortage of workers, since Procordia Food has a list of people that want to come to work there. Workers are in many cases recruited from the ranks of one-time seasonal workers or by recommendation from other workers. Vacant positions are first advertised internally to encourage rotation, while people with special skills are recruited through newspaper advertisements. Turnover is down to 5 per cent for blue-collar employees, which is extremely low.

The production is to a large extent based on task-oriented groups, as we saw in Nidar, but in Procordia the team leader function does not rotate and it is better paid. Increased utilization of capacity and downsizing are important strategies for Procordia. There are large seasonal fluctuations in the production and they use a large share of temporary staff in the busy seasons. However, the number of core workers cannot be reduced below a certain limit. It is essential to keep a skilled basic staff at a certain proportion in relation to the seasonal workers, or else it may prove difficult to put them all to work in an optimal way.

Human resources is a big issue in Swedish management. It is really important to cooperate, listen to each other and get people motivated. Procordia has a system for organized annual talks with the supervisor. The process started at the top of the company, but so far it had only reached about 30 per cent of the blue-collar employees. In Eslöv and some other production sites, all employees have access to a gym and there is a leisure centre that arranges swimming, fishing, tennis and so on, and the company celebrates a harvest festival. This Swedish company really tries to take care of its employees.

## Participation and Relationship with the Trade Union

Procordia management describes the relationship with the trade union as less formal than it used to be, except for wage negotiations. There are not many other issues that are negotiated any more. The atmosphere is characterized as straightforward and honest. Quite often the union representatives could agree with the management about what to do about problems that were brought up and discussed. Management, on its side, is glad to have a system for handling labour relations, since it means that there are rules and therefore they know how to handle things. The system is functional if it doesn't become too formal, one manager claims. There had been no strikes or major conflicts in recent years.

Unions in Sweden have much to say on downsizing. Procordia therefore had involved them at an early stage in such processes: 'You work very close with the unions in this situation, so they are inside every decision.' The logic is, claims a manager, the more they know, the better the chance that they will end up with the same decision. The union will defend every person that is left without a job. It is therefore essential that the company puts money and effort into finding new jobs or other alternatives for them. One manager claimed: 'We have laid off 600 people through these five years; maybe 50 did not get a new job.'

Blue-collar wages are differentiated in six steps, from about US$1850 to US$3000 (SEK15000 to SEK25000) per month, depending on job and responsibility. In addition to wages, there is a bonus system that includes all levels of the hierarchy in Procordia. The bonus level is based on a combination of three different target areas: Profit, results of the department and personal results. Bonus systems are quite common in Swedish industry, for the most part based on collective results. Procordia had attempted to increase the wage differences, but the union resisted this. One manager ascribed this to 'old traditions among the blue collars that there should be no differences between people'.

## DANDY

### Strategy

Dandy put large resources into development of chewing-gum to make it a more functional product. The dental segment grew fast. As a specialized company, Dandy made a more focused effort on chewing-gum than can confectionery producers with a broad product range. In addition, Dandy had some brands with a rather broad coverage in Europe. It is important to make them available in kiosks, petrol stations, sportswear shops and other places where people may get an impulse to buy chewing-gum. Dandy also produced private labels for third parties to reduce the dominance of Wrigley in certain markets. By such deals, Dandy received help to enter those markets. Production was exchanged for distribution, or distribution in one market for distribution in another. As the third largest producer in the world, Dandy wanted to be open to negotiations. After the successful entering of the Russian market referred to earlier, continued expansion in Eastern Europe and entry to markets even further east was to be attempted.

Because of consumer reactions to campaigns and new products, Dandy experienced large variations in demand, up to 40–50 per cent from one month to the next. To plan production, all subsidiaries made detailed estimates each month of sales for the coming three months and for the next year in more general terms. Concentration in grocery chains required an increased focus on just-in-time delivery. One customer demanded delivery to its warehouses in no more than 18 hours after they put in an order, or they would start buying from another supplier. Supply chain management, restructuring and streamlining the process from raw material to delivery became a priority.

**Management**

To recruit white-collar employees the managers responsible for the unit that needs the new people would make a description of the job and what kind of person and qualifications they were looking for. The human resource department acted as a consultant in the process. Dandy received applications for management positions all the time, and these applications were filed. The human resource department checked the files before advertising in newspapers or professional magazines. Dandy also attended recruitment days at business schools, and took in trainees from the technical university.

In some parts of the factory a meeting was held every morning to discuss the day's production. For support staff monthly department meetings were common, but in addition there were many meetings to discuss planning, statistics and results. Some managers found there were too many meetings. However, discussions on e-mail and distant work locations reduced the number of meetings for parts of the administrative personnel.

Discussions did not necessarily result in any formal decisions. One manager claimed: 'Sometimes we go back to a situation and say "who decided that?", and actually it was nobody that really took this formal decision, and we can't find the paper where someone is signing that.' Or again, 'Sometimes we just know what is right to do.' Once more we see that the discussion process can be more important than formal decision making. The point is to create a common understanding of the situation, and then everybody knows what the right thing to do is.

## Subcultures and Potential Conflicts

Some managers claimed that no department in Dandy was inferior to the others, while others pointed to the sales department as the most important. However, there is a difference in perspective between those who work with strategies and those who work with day-to-day business. A management committee was supposed to sort out such problems, and according to one of the members: 'When we have finished the fight we say: we have to go on, and no hard feelings.' In addition, new projects were being created around innovations involving marketing, production and other business units. The point was to reorganize this kind of work frequently to harness energy. Some conflicts created new energy and possibilities: 'If there is no conflict, we die,' as one interviewee put it. However, if there were too many non-business-creating conflicts, or if they could not find a solution, the boss decided.

There can also be conflicts among the blue-collar workers. In one instance there was a shift where the teams did not get on well together and they split up into different cliques. When the manager did not succeed in making them talk together, a psychologist was brought in. However, the problems had gone too far and the solutions were too hard to face. The workers were unable to solve the problems even with external help, and in the end many of them left the company. The human resource personnel was called on to initiate talks when they heard about such problems. Since they were not part of the conflict, they could function as mediators.

Dandy's culture was shaped by its history as a family owned company. This had created a certain atmosphere; people knew how to behave and what was expected from them. At the time of the interviews, the company slogan at Dandy was 'Something for something'. Its meaning was that by not doing anything, you don't get anything; you have to offer something or make an effort; you have to go to work and do a good job and be responsible every day. But the company also saw itself as caring for people and creating a spirit of long-term cooperation. To promote a feeling of community, employees were encouraged to become members of the company's sports centre, and about 500 employees and their families used this facility. Each department from time to time conducted weekend events where the employees' families were invited.

However, it was not all tradition. Management also tried to create among the employees an image of Dandy as a very dynamic company, and to promote an understanding of the need for adaptation to changing markets.

## Management–Workforce Relations

At the time, Dandy was the largest employer in Vejle and had a good reputation, so there was no need to advertise for unskilled workers. People initiated contact by themselves, and in fact, Dandy had a bank of people to choose from. However, there was a lack of skilled workers, so Dandy advertised to 'steal' them from other companies. Workers can be attracted by good wages, but if they are not satisfied, they will leave. That is also the case if they don't get along with their co-workers or manager. To keep useful workers from moving on, the Dandy management tried to make them feel good about their work, their relationships with other people, and gave them responsibility and let them make decisions on their own. The workers also got the possibility to change jobs at Dandy from time to time.

There were no temporary or seasonal employees at Dandy. To bridge variations in demand, the production used stocks as a buffer. In addition, management was more reluctant to replace people if production forecasts had a negative trend. Normally, skilled workers were expected to put in 37 hours and unskilled workers 39 hours a week. The operators worked two hours extra each week to get more holiday. Unskilled workers earned US$16.50 (DKK100) and skilled workers US$20.50 (DKK125) per hour. The pay difference was slightly larger than in Nidar, but on the same level as in Procordia.

A new arrangement Dandy used to improve flexibility was to pay 14 workers full wages to work only four days or 32 hours a week, but in return they had to be available whenever they were needed. The trade union immediately supported the deal. This flexible workforce meant that Dandy could reduce its overtime and stocks, and thereby save money. Although its products have long durability, production flexibility was essential since there were frequent campaigns and changes in the products' taste, colour, consistency, packaging and so on. Some brands are very old, but the products change on average every ninth month. In addition, changeovers in production were necessary since the tastes and contents of even the same brand of chewing-gum may differ between some countries.

Co-determination is prescribed by law in certain matters. The works council (*samarbejdsudvalg*) discussed the reason why people working in one area frequently got headaches. It also made an inquiry into the need for a child care during the evening shift, but found that there was little demand for it. Another theme was improvement of teamwork in the factory. One manager said he wanted to delegate certain decisions to subordinates, but decisions had to be made. There has to be someone controlling this process, or responsibility will be pulverized. However, some decisions can be left to subordinates, because it is their responsibility. In parts of Dandy's production, for instance, there was a leader on the day shift only, while on the other shifts, the workers had to decide for themselves what to do in line with production plans. To make the staff more flexible, more self-governed groups were planned.

Once a year Dandy's managers had talks with their employees individually about job development and the need for training or education, and both parties raised problems and evaluated each other's performance. There were training programmes in the factory together with the AMU-school (Arbejdsmarkedsuddannelse), for instance on how to operate a packaging machine. The workers were allowed two weeks away from work to follow such courses. Some young people with only secondary school and a few years' experience in the factory had embarked on education programmes to earn apprenticeship certificates. Skilled workers could get further education at technical schools to be updated in their field. For administrative personnel, there were many in-house courses available and human skills were increasingly being put on the programme.

Discussions were actively used by Dandy management in questions about development of the factory. The aim was to give information and 'give people a feeling that they can influence the decisions before they are made', as one manager put it. The phrasing 'feeling of influence' was not necessarily just a slip of the tongue. When it was decided to build the new factory in Novgorod, it was kept secret at first. When it was opened, the in-house magazine wrote about the plant from the workers' point of view and the Danish workers who were involved in training employees in Novgorod were interviewed about their experience. The employees were told that the planning of a new production facility in Novgorod had started and were given information so that they could prepare for the new situation and discuss how to handle it. They were not, however, involved before the decision had been made. There seems to be no co-determination in such major strategic questions. In general, there seemed to be different management styles in relation to different questions and in different situations at Dandy, as we saw in the other Scandinavian food and confectionery producers. However, Dandy had not gone so far in the direction of goal-directed groups, as we saw in the case of Nidar.

## Participation and Relationship with the Trade Union

Management at Dandy had tried to establish a long-term cooperation with the union. They attempted to discuss the wage structure and related issues before the trade union representatives found problems. To avoid friction, it was considered important to make sure that the wage differences between groups did not change too much. To encourage dialogue the management introduced new ideas and said: 'We would like to try this.' They aimed to discuss changes before a crisis developed or before the other party had set its mind on a particular outcome. In that way Dandy management and workers could both achieve some of their goals and major conflicts were avoided.

The overall level of wages was set according to national agreements and in comparison with other work places. Dandy's wages for blue-collar employees were almost at the top of the nationally negotiated tables for the industry. The agreements also contained a personal performance-related part of the salary, which meant that some would get lower pay if they did not reach their target.

At the time, human resource issues were more important than wages in management's encounters with the trade union representatives at Dandy. The trade union representatives were informed when there were to be redundancies. They could object to which employees were affected, but not how many. Performance seemed to be the most important criterion. The new demands from the grocery market made the union more cooperative, according to managers: 'We have the same target to keep the company running.' Competition from the more flexible and lower staffed packaging unit in Novgorod was another reason for less antagonism. One manager put it this way:

> Every time I have the chance, I say: what I'm fighting for, and I am hopefully fighting with you, is to keep labour in Vejle. In order to keep labour in Vejle, we have to be competitive. If you don't come along with me to do that, then we won't do it.

Internal competition was increased by measuring efficiency at each plant. After several changes in working time in one month, one manager said 'I wonder why it is so easy?' It seemed that the trade union had taken the seriousness of the situation into account. The union representatives also accepted that redundant skilled maintenance personnel preferred working in packaging at wages for unskilled workers rather than to remain unemployed. The local union and company level representatives realized that Dandy had to be a competitive company.

Despite this cooperative spirit, one manager said: 'Dandy in the long term wants to get out of the employers' union, and we want to get rid of the unions. ... *Jyllandsposten* [one of Denmark's national newspapers] has done it. So that is our ultimate goal – how far we can go, I don't know.' The reason was that the central levels of the trade union and employers' union had too many rules and were too much into politics: 'We think we can do it better both for Dandy and the workers.'

## CONCLUSION

All in all, there seems to be a common understanding that the food and confectionery business has become more market-driven and dynamic, and on the producer side a common response has been rationalization strategies inspired by BPR, involving reduced stocks, simplified product flow and a process orientated organization with projects, delayering and downsizing, and an increased demand for young people with university level education. Procordia and Dandy have been involved in a cross border M&A, and they also had strategies for production, distribution and marketing in other countries. Nidar was bought by Orkla, and was thus involved in strategies for branded consumer goods in the Nordic and Baltic countries, but did so far not have any significant exports. They did, however, distribute Wrigley's products in Norway.

In terms of management, a common feature of the three factories is that, when strategic choices are imminent, discussion in the management group comes before decisions, and the importance of giving this process sufficient time was underlined by several of our informants from all three companies. The reasons for this, they explained, is to enable everyone to get sufficient information, come up with suggestions, understand the necessity of change and the reasons for the decision they eventually make. This will ensure that they participate in its implementation and not work against it. In addition, new ideas may emerge through the discussion. Thus even if meetings are commonly structured by an agenda and decisions are written down, the decision-making process in many cases is more important than the formal decision itself. After a while everybody knows what the right thing to do is. This type of decision making in management seems to be more frequent in Scandinavia than elsewhere.

It is important, however, to underline the fact that this is not the *only* option. Another important quality of Scandinavian management is that there is a repertoire of decision-making modes to choose from. Sometimes, when the group of managers are unable to come to a conclusion, the superior makes a decision. Important investment decisions in a factory may require a lengthy process of presentations for different groups of management at higher levels. At least this was reported to be the case in the Orkla group. In other questions, the superior may force the subordinates to make a decision. This seems to be most common in the relationship between second- and first-line leaders, such as process leaders forcing the coordinators of goal directed groups to decide for themselves what to produce by not showing up at planning meetings or by having a leader only on the dayshift.

Project groups and management meetings and discussions-before-decisions are also important ways of discovering problems and potential conflicts between departments at an early stage. Such measures have become more common and important because of the increasing priority put on consumer focus, process orientation and product innovations and campaigns.

There is variation in the style of management. There can be discussions before decisions involving higher and/or lower levels of management, autocracy, coordination and delegation. The style is chosen according to hierarchical level and what type of decisions is pending. Unfortunately that does not mean that the right mode of decision making is chosen every time. There can be a tendency to avoid controversial decisions by diluting the responsibility or by delegating to others. It is therefore important for managers in Scandinavia to strike a balance between group discussions and having decisions made; going too far in either direction will unquestionably cause problems. Managers coming from other countries to work in Scandinavia need to be aware of this.

Moving production to other countries, coordinating production, closing factories and downsizing seem to have become common in the food and confectionery industries. This means a radical break with the sheltered paternalism which used to exist in many of the old companies in this sector. Relations with the employees and unions are thereby put to a severe test. It seems as though power has shifted to the employer side. The unions must either work together with management in keeping up production and employment, or they may lose everything. The unions and shop stewards are deeply involved in the personnel policy in questions like rationalization, work force flexibility, downsizing and upskilling. For the trade union, this is the opportunity to secure the employees' interests, but increasingly this is done with a knife at their throat. As mentioned earlier, one manager said after negotiating several such changes to working time in one month: 'I wonder why it is so easy?' However, there may be a thin line between cooperation and cooptation that the union people need to be aware of, or they will lose their credibility. For management the reason for cooperation is to make the rationalization processes run smoothly, and they want to be proactive and have solutions to discuss with the trade union before there is too much friction.

However, management at Dandy thought the company would be better off without a union, primarily because of agreements between the trade union and the employer's federation at national level. This has not been common in Scandinavia, in particular in Sweden and Norway, where the advantages of a good cooperation usually are underlined by managers as well as by the trade union representatives. The company meetings at Nidar which frequently included information that could alarm the stock market illustrate this. The reason was not to be nice, but to make the people able to make the right decisions in their daily work. If there is comparative strength in management–workforce relations in Scandinavia, it is the belief in the mutual benefits of delegation of authority even down to the operator level by means of information, training and responsibility. However, the operators may not be very skilled in the first place and may need experience and confidence to be able to handle this authority.

## REFERENCES

Sivesind, K.H. (1995), 'The indispensable role of culture. Explaining different understandings of work through a comparison of German and Norwegian factories', *Comparative Social Research. A Research Annual*, 15, 35–101.
Lawrence, P.A. (2002), *The Change Game*, London: Kogan Page.

# 6.   Shipbuilding and more besides

The slightly twee chapter title flags up the fact that we have departed somewhat from the industry chapter formula of comparing companies from the same industry, one from each of the three countries. While everyone connects Scandinavia with the sea and shipping, getting a sample of matched shipbuilders is not so easy.

In Norway the shipbuilding industry is represented by Ulstein Verft on the west coast; Denmark has what is probably Europe's leading commercial shipbuilder, Odense Lindø, part of the A.P. Møller group of companies; and in Sweden Kockums, in the southern town of Malmö, on the coast opposite Copenhagen. But these three are not as nicely comparable as say the three breweries discussed in an earlier chapter, as will be clear by the report findings. In particular Kockums has massively downsized since its heyday, and reduced the scale and range of its output. Also our visit came just after Kockums had been acquired by a German shipbuilder, and we were simply granted an interview with Kockums' public relations manager. This meeting was exceptionally interesting, as it always is when one comes to a company at a time of critical change, but this experience did not match the raft of interviews we were able to conduct at the other companies in the sample. Also we were told that there was no other substantial shipbuilding company in Sweden which might have been a match for Ulstein and Odense Lindø.

So to add to the representation of heavy industry in Sweden we have included the steelmaker Sheffield Avesta in the study, from what one might call a neighbouring industry, and it is discussed in this chapter alongside the shipyards. At this company we did the full range of interviews, both at one of the leading plants, in fact the one at the town of Avesta itself, and at the head office in Stockholm.

## INDUSTRY DEVELOPMENTS

The issues explored in this sector relate to shipbuilding, though a number of them apply to the steel industry as well. The first consideration is that shipbuilding is an industry marked by long-term overcapacity, going back to the mid-twentieth century. Traditionally shipbuilding was an industry that most countries wanted to have: it is macho, has served as a benchmark of industrial development and national pride, has implications for defence, trade and even for imperial ambitions. Rulers have loved shipbuilding, from Russia's Peter the Great to Germany's Kaiser Wilhelm II.

This long-term overcapacity has several further implications:

- It has induced many governments to subsidize the industry.
- This in turn eventually produced a concerted effort from super-national organizations such as OECD and the EU to have subsidies removed and capacity taken out.
- As with other industries, overcapacity crossed with subsidy removal has led to enhanced competition, merger and acquisitions, rationalization, downsizing and specialization.

Incidentally the idea of subsidies has become ingrained – perhaps 'embrained' would be the right word – and has meant that countries endlessly denounce each other as 'subsidy junkies'. The year 1997 saw the biggest order book for shipbuilders in that decade, and also saw South Korea push Japan from the top position. Japanese shipyards responded with the claim that Korean state-owned shipping companies had placed orders domestically without opening bidding to overseas yards, and that Korean steel firms have supplied domestic shipyards with subsidized steel plate. On the other hand, other countries in the region, for instance Australia, have claimed that only a couple of Japan's numerous shipyards are genuinely profitable, the rest being cross-subsidized by other companies in their conglomerate groups. This is what happens when there is overcapacity in a nationally prestigious industry. It is also perhaps surprising how much unvarnished national self-interest there is in an age of globalization. But with these references to South-east Asian countries we are getting ahead of ourselves.

A key development in the shipbuilding industry has been its migration from Europe to South-east Asia, as the data in Table 6.1 indicates. This is a truly

*Table 6.1   World shipbuilding deliveries: percentage proportion of total*

|        | Europe | Far East |
|--------|--------|----------|
| 1964   | 50.8   | 38.7     |
| 1974   | 37.5   | 51.8     |
| 1984   | 20.0   | 67.3     |
| 1994   | 16.0   | 74.1     |
| 2002   | 10.2   | 83.2     |

*Source*:   Lloyd's Register (2003).

staggering switch of capacity location, and one which requires further comment.

In one way we are used to seeing European manufacturing capacity migrate to Asia. Hardly a week goes by without being able to read in the business press of some company – British in the first place, but sometimes French, German, Dutch or even Scandinavian companies – that is closing plant in Europe and transferring capacity to Asia to benefit from lower labour costs. But the shipbuilding story does not exactly fit this model.

After all the two shipbuilding stars in South-east Asia are Japan and Korea. Japan is not low wage, certainly not regarding its front line companies as opposed to tiered suppliers. And South Korea is high wage by the standards of developing countries. So clearly there is another cause.

It is most clear in the case of Japan. Here is a country that has no raw materials, is a major manufacturing country, and has pegged its economic destiny to export-led growth. Japan needs reasonably cheap and very reliable shipping, and feels it needs to control the industry.

This control is in part effected by Japan's ability to mildly bully South Korea, forever cast in the role of 'little sister' to Japan. An interesting manifestation of this relationship occurred as a result of the 1973–74 oil crisis which plunged the world into recession. To stabilize ship prices, the Japanese reduced world capacity by closing some of their production sites. The Koreans obligingly followed suit while pitching their prices some 5 per cent behind those of the Japanese. This Japanese initiative succeeded in its objective. We should probably add that the case made for Japan here, an island dependent on raw material imports and on the export of manufactured goods, applies also, though less obviously, to South Korea. Not for nothing was South Korea identified in the mid-1990s as one of the 'Asian tigers', also pursuing a policy of export-led growth. What is more South Korea is best considered as an island: its only land border is the 38th parallel dividing it from a hostile North Korea, and this is the world's most ferociously guarded land border.

None of this argument concerning Japan and South Korea is to say that there is not *also* a trend for shipbuilding to move to lower wage areas as well. Examples here would include shipyards in Brazil, Croatia, perhaps Taiwan, and above all China. This trend, of course, sometimes produces a counter response. To give this argument a Scandinavian twist, the company Maersk Container Industri located in Tinglev, Jutland, was founded in 1991 to make 'dry boxes', that is, non-refrigerated containers. Maersk Container is part of the A.P. Møller group, like Odense Lindø, our Danish shipbuilder. By 1996 Maersk Container gave up dry boxes because of Chinese competition and concentrated on the production of 'reefers' – refrigerated containers – in the Jutland plant. Between 1996 and 2002 Maersk managed to halve the cost of their reefers by means of automation supported by cross-border materials sourcing.

To move to a new consideration, as a mature industry shipbuilding is a segmented industry. That is to say there are several discrete product markets, sometimes having different features and dynamics. Briefly there is:

- A basic distinction between military and commercial shipping.
- From a manufacturer's viewpoint there is segmentation by size of dock; small docks cannot build supertankers.
- Segmentation in the commercial sector by user, namely passenger versus cargo.
- Segmentation by ship type – bulkers, tankers, containers and so on; among our Scandinavian shipbuilders Odense Lindø of Denmark, for example, is a key player in the larger container market.

Having said all this, a country that one does not think of as a traditional shipbuilding country may come to dominate a particular niche segment. Australia, for example, is a key player in the production of fast, lightweight, aluminium-hulled ferries, catamarans and yachts. In the late 1990s something like 90 per cent of Australia's production in this segment was exported.

Finally, while military shipbuilding may be tied to particular countries for security reasons (super-powers do not like other countries building their ships and knowing their specifications and capability), commercial shipbuilding is a global business. It is global in the sense that the same major commercial shipbuilders confront each other as competitors in all markets, geographically defined.

If we put some of these developments together, namely overcapacity, the Asian migration, the progressive withdrawal of subsidies in the West, and of course globalization, then there has to be good reasons for shipyards to survive in Western Europe. This is the issue to which we turn in the next section.

## COMPETITIVE ADVANTAGE AND STRATEGY

### Avesta Sheffield

There is a problem in discussing this company in the context of strategy and competitive advantage because after our research there towards the end of the year 2000 the company experienced a change of ownership. And we cannot research its new situation beyond accessing websites and being alive to references to the change in the business press. Nonetheless our research at Sheffield Avesta does yield another slice of Swedish management and organizational culture, and on the issue of strategy we will make the account true to our understanding at the time.

By way of introduction we might say that the steel industry does share a number of features with shipbuilding, including:

- world overcapacity;
- competition from countries that are not thought of as traditional steel producers;
- downward pressure on prices;
- industry concentration;
- cross-border M&A (well-illustrated in the case in hand); and
- severe trend towards rationalization and downsizing.

It differs from shipbuilding in that there is not the same scope for specialization, so clear in the case of Ulstein Verft; in steel the equivalent is more in the form of a search for new applications.

Avesta Sheffield counts as one of the world's leading suppliers of stainless steel and at the time of our visit was the third largest producer in Europe. There is a long history of first iron smelting and then steel-making in the town of Avesta, where the key plant we visited was located. Avesta Sheffield was formerly Avesta AB, a company whose shares were listed on the Stockholm stock exchange. Then in the 1990s what was British Steel (British Steel changed its name to Corus after merging with Hogoovens of the Netherlands in 1999) started to buy shares in Avesta to the point in 1995 that they had 51 per cent. At that stage Avesta Sheffield became a subsidiary of (the then) British Steel. At the time of our research the company was organized into nine divisions, one geographical (North America) and the rest by product. The Avesta plant produces wide cold- and hot-rolled products in coil form at widths of up to 2 metres.

So how might Avesta Sheffield strategy be characterized as of 2000? First of all the merger with British Steel seemed to have facilitated the emergence of dedicated plants. That is to say that previously all the plants had made a range of products, but by the time of our visit plants dedicated to a particular product or output had become the norm. Second, rationalization and downsizing then occurred: later in the chapter we will give figures for the Avesta plant, which are truly staggering; there is also telling trade union testimony to the increase in work pressure. Third, there was an espoused emphasis on 'moving up the decision chain' and attempting to get a better understanding of customers' needs. This in turn led to a search for new applications; examples we were given included the water pipes in Tokyo and the possibility of using stainless steel for bridge construction in Sweden. Another example we were given is that Sweden's crack, long-distance trains,

the X2000-type, are now made of stainless steel, which is more crash resistant.
Fourth, this search for new applications was often backed by:

- environmental considerations; that is, arguments about stainless steel
  being less damaging than traditional materials; and
- life cycle costing considerations, along the lines of 'steel may be more
  expensive in the first instance' but it will last longer or require less
  maintenance.

Fifth, a more idiosyncratic argument was advanced by the Avesta plant
manager, namely that the management team should include some dissidents,
that there was a need for lateral thinkers and change agents, not just the
conventionally extolled 'good team players'. The idea here is that given overcapacity, heightened competition and the search for new applications, there is
a need for a management mind-set that focuses on adaptation and innovation.
Sixth, it became clear that Avesta Sheffield was alive and responding to a
cyclic problem that besets the steel industry. It goes like this: demand for steel
picks up, steel companies commission massive new plants that take years to
come on stream, by which time there would theoretically be a world recession.
Demand was indeed increasing in the 1999–2000 period, and the Stockholm
head office spoke of controlled investments likely to yield a short-term
capacity increase. Finally, Avesta found a satisfactory partner in British Steel,
financially if not always culturally, which enhanced their economies of scale,
market access and the move to dedicated plants. But after our research at
Avesta Sheffield they were in fact bought by the Finnish steel maker
Outokumpu, creating Avesta Polarit. Thus ended the British connection.

Let us hope that their more recent partner will be as good.

## Kockums

Kockums of Sweden is a legend. In the 1970s, Kockums in Malmö had 10 000
employees. They used to launch a big ship every seven weeks. That was then.

Now at the start of the twenty-first century they employ 250 people in a
design office in Malmö (and some further 800 in a yard in neighbouring
Karlskrona), they specialize in submarines and they are owned by Germans.

Briefly, the story is along these lines. In the mid-1980s a government
decision was taken to close the company because of the cost of subsidies. A
series of changes of name, corporate identity and conglomerate ownership
ensued for Kockums. When commercial shipbuilding was eventually closed
down, naval construction continued. This development was given a further
thrust by the renamed Kockums, now called Celsius, getting a contract to build
submarines for the Australian Ministry of Defence.

Then in 1999 Celsius, the new conglomerate owner of Kockums, sold Kockums to the German shipyard HDW. This does not mean extinction for Kockums; the enlarged HDW has a joint board with equal numbers of Swedish and German members.

If we pause at this point to raise the question 'why did Kockums shrink in this way?', we have a classic combination of factors, namely:

- because of world overcapacity and uncompetitive labour costs in Sweden, government subsidies are necessary;
- in the 1980s when the 30-year post-Second World War boom had ended the government became concerned at the cost of subsidies; and
- the concern over public expenditure was heightened as governments in the West gained control of inflation, meaning that governments could not shrink debt through inflation.

All this occurred in the context of the Asian migration outlined at the start of this chapter.

If we next ask of the Kockums-HDW merger 'what is in it for HDW?', there are a number of answers. First of all Kockums' later specialization in submarines suits HDW – they are in this product market too. Second, still on the subject of submarines, Kockums have been working for decades on the development of the Sterling engine, which in submarine speak is 'an air-independent engine'. If the submarine engine does not need air, it can stay down much longer. Third, and now we are on to surface vessels, Kockums is a leader in stealth technology. This is about enabling vessels to pass undetected through radar screens. In addition to the three Ss – subs, sterling and stealth – the acquisition conferred another advantage upon HDW, namely at the time it had a backlog and needed additional capacity. The acquisition would also enhance the product range capacity of HDW. Finally, it was suggested that the Kockums-HDW merger would not pose problems of cultural integration like those that once haunted the strategic alliance between Renault of France and Volvo of Sweden.

Turning the question around, the benefits to Kockums are:

- release from a Swedish defence conglomerate where it did not sit well;
- survival, part of a bigger and stronger company; and
- access to a larger market in the sense of HDW's existing or expected customers and thus the expectation for Kockums of being able to amortize its R&D spend over larger sales.

And why should HDW be more successful at survival in the hostile world of contemporary shipbuilding than Kockums? Again there are several factors:

- HDW is a bigger company with a bigger market;
- it has powerful backers, in the sense that three-quarters of HDW's equity is in the hands of Deutsche Babcock and Preussag;
- the German government will continue subsidies up to the limit permitted by the EU; and
- HDW is active in more product markets than Kockums and is a leader in non-nuclear submarines; this offers the hope that not all markets will slump at the same time.

To which one should add that HDW has the will to survive and is likely to be given support by the German government.

The Kockum's story is very different from that of Odense Lindø, and in a way it has a certain sadness. Yet the reasons for Kockums' continuation, albeit as part of a merged entity, are no less compelling, namely:

- it withdrew from big ship production, where it was most in competition from Asia;
- it specialized – in submarines;
- it put design and development, rather than construction, in the foreground; and
- it secured strengths in stealth technology and with the air-independent engine.

To which one must add that it appears to have found a suitable partner.

### Ulstein Verft

Ulstein Verft of Norway was founded in 1917 by Martin Ulstein and his brother-in-law Andreas Flø. What they established was a small shipyard that took on repairs for local fishing boats and ferries. It was their descendent 'grand old man' Idar Ulstein who later gave the yard its scale and visibility, and indeed his children are still (2003) managing director (MD) and deputy MD, and the Ulstein family owns some 55.9 per cent of Ulstein Verft A/S.

The core of Ulstein Verft is two yards now merged into one at Ulsteinvik on Norway's west coast, just south of Ålesund. The Ulstein family has been community builders rather than traditional paternalists. The region itself is seen as distinctive by Norwegians, being characterized by rural-coastal solidarity, a strong work ethic and pockets of pietism, outside of the state church, together with the new Norwegian accent – though this last may need a bit of explanation for non-Norwegian readers. As noted in Chapter 2, Norway was united with Denmark under the Danish crown from 1380 to 1814, and then from 1814 to 1905 was, loosely speaking, ruled by Sweden. When the country finally became independent there was a desire to promote national identity via a new language, *nynorsk*, which would be based on the purer accents of these rural areas. Ulsteinvik was determined to have the right dialect. One interesting outcome of this phenomenon is that a lot of people from the Ulsteinvik area work in television, thanks to a quota system representing *nynorsk* speakers. It gives rise to jokes along the lines of: 'Ten people from the area were shipwrecked. When they were rescued five years later on an otherwise deserted island they had founded a shipyard, two furniture factories, and three television stations.'

Until 1974 when they began to make vessels for the oil industry Ulstein's product range had been fairly traditional. From here on, however, they embarked on a process of dynamic and variable specialization designed to neutralize the downside of European shipyards, which as we have seen afflicted Kockums. As Ulstein's strategy and development manager put it:

> The Western European yards have a high skill price, the labour price is higher, so the only way to survive is to go into the special market for special vessels, where there are not so many competitors and the price is consequently higher ... We have about 1 per cent of the worldwide market and all of this is specially made vessels, for special purposes.

In this spirit of revolving specialization Ulstein has worked its way through the miscellany of oil platform supply vessels, ice-breakers, seismic exploration vessels, anchor handling vessels, combination of multi-purpose vessels, cable-layers with a supply capability, ships for diving with an oil and recovery capability and more besides – everything except platforms and big ships. The opportunism is quite conscious, as a remark from the project manager suggests:

> ... in the start we had many fishing boats and trawlers, trawlers for Alaska, we delivered several. Later after that period, we had a time with mainly seismic vessels, six seismic vessels for western geophysical, you would say. And we also built a couple of supply ships in between!

This endless 'raising of the game' through specialization, to neutralize economy of scale and low wage competition, is the key to Ulstein's strategy. It is based on the conviction that Ulstein's strength is design and customization and value added. The company also prides itself on its design database, which facilitates variable-combination customization.

All this enables Ulstein to 'keep ahead of the pack'. But when 'the pack' catch up, Ulstein licence construction and move on to the next game. This again is made clear by the strategy and development manager: 'The philosophy is that in the group the yard is developing the first vessels. When this is quite a known technology, *then we sell the design and the package*.'

One development that Ulstein's specialization has tracked in the oil industry has been the move to exploit ever deeper and more marginal oil fields.

One might add to this account of the virtue of specialization crossed with customization the fact of Ulstein's more international orientation. This is a reference not only to the Ulstein approach to sales, but also to capital markets and finance, having recourse to London as well as to Oslo.

## Odense Lindø

Odense Lindø has a number of advantages, some of them interlocking. But in our view the single most important fact is that Odense Lindø is part of the A.P. Møller group, which is a major commercial shipping operator. For non-Scandinavian readers we should underline the fact that A.P. Møller is a quite exceptional customer. Not only a shipping operator, it is a vastly rich corporation having been given a monopoly by the government in 1972 to exploit and develop Denmark's share of North Sea oil. Odense Lindø supplies about one-third of A.P. Møller's ships. It is thus a major beneficiary of vertical integration in the A.P. Møller group.

This does not mean that Odense Lindø is uncompetitive. Indeed the fact that A.P. Møller gets *only* one-third of the ships it needs from Odense Lindø suggests the opposite. The parent company, that is to say, will be buying ships from other shipyards, and will thus have a built-in standard of comparison. Indeed interviewees at Odense Lindø asserted that the parent company encouraged them to be 'state of the art', an entirely credible claim. One piece of evidence is that Odense Lindø was a leader in double-hull tankers, which are now required by legislation. Odense Lindø also boosts an extensive research network, in the sense of a variety of institutions, typically universities and other engineering colleges, where company related research is being carried out by dedicated personnel. Revealingly interviewees at Odense Lindø spoke discriminatingly of how such institutions were chosen and of how the relevant people were to be motivated. Including these university-based researchers, Odense Lindø's R&D personnel represent some 10 per cent of the total workforce, 300 out of 3000 at the time of our interviews.

There is another consideration, and this is that Odense Lindø is positioned at the big ship end of the spectrum, indeed perhaps one should say at the 'biggest ship' end. The argument goes like this:

- the bigger the ship, the more cargo it can haul;
- increasing the size of the vessel puts up the cost of fuel, but not that much; and
- increases in vessel size may not require any increase in crew numbers.

Therefore in commercial shipping, big really is beautiful, and Odense Lindø is operating in a highly desirable segment and one most likely to confer an operating advantage on its parent.

There is another feature of its parent company which is relevant here. A.P. Møller is one of the richest private companies in Denmark. It is not going to attract any state subsidies. In consequence Odense Lindø has become a ruthless cost-cutter and rationalizer, thereby adding to its efficiency. This is reinforced, of course, by the fact that it is not the only seller of ships to its parent company. So it has to match the prices of competitors (though not beat them) and of course gets to know the bids of these outside rivals – free market information.

Finally, although Odense Lindø only supplies one-third of A.P. Møller's ships this represents some 96–100 per cent of Odense Lindø's capacity. This is an ideal situation, leaving Odense Lindø free to seek additional non-Møller contracts. Yet the importance of the A.P. Møller link is confirmed by a further development. Odense Lindø have a capacity problem; they are hard put to sustain their one-third share of the parent company's shipping purchases. To overcome this, to maintain their ability to satisfy one-third of Møller's needs, they have enlarged their capacity by acquisitions in Eastern Europe.

In this section we have looked at three separate company survival and success stories. Perhaps a significant thing to emerge is that there are some similarities in the stories of Kockum and Ulstein in the sense of expertise, specialization and segment domination. The formula was enforced sooner, broader and deeper by Ulstein, but some common elements remain.

## PRODUCTION AND ORGANIZATION

Next we would like to look at some aspects of production and organization for the four companies. This will overlap a little with what has already been said, but may still help focus the comparison.

### Avesta Sheffield

What had been Avesta AB joined forces with British Steel Stainless, a division of British Steel as it was then known, in 1992. This led to the formation of Avesta Sheffield. British Steel originally owned 40 per cent of the shares, but by 1995 British Steel had increased its holding to 51 per cent, thus making Avesta Sheffield a British Steel subsidiary. This merger enabled Avesta Sheffield to grow, and at the time of our interviews at the company (late 2000) Avesta Sheffield was one of the three largest stainless steel producers in Europe.

The company was organized into nine divisions as noted earlier, one of which was North America, the remaining eight being based on product. At the time of our interviews demand was rising, in part because of the positive state of the world economy but also as a result of exploiting new applications for stainless steel as noted in the previous section. This in turn was matched by increased output. At the plant in Avesta the site manager noted a five-fold increase in output in his 12-year tenure there.

It should be added that increases in output and/or productivity were a common feature of our sample of companies. We have already mentioned the case of Maersk Container Industri in Denmark halving the price of its refrigerated containers between 1996 and 2003, by means of global sourcing of materials together with massive automation. Or the Norsk Hydro aluminium plant in Denmark where the personnel manager spoke of an increase in output from 40 kilos of aluminium per man hour to 200 kilos. In the 1993–98 period the showing on the key performance indicators (KPIs) doubled at this plant, and then it doubled again in the 1998–2000 period. This Norsk Hydro aluminium plant's customers, principally suppliers to the automobile industry, demand annual price reductions of 5–8 per cent. None of this is to diminish the output achievements of Avesta Sheffield, but just to note that they are not isolated.

A general production organization change in Avesta Sheffield is a move away from the practice where all plants make all products to a system of dedicated plants that specialize in a single product or discrete product range. No plants, we were told, had actually been closed, though in some cases the move to 'dedicated plants' was supported by plant upgrading or refurbishment. Even such refurbished plants, however, are disadvantaged in comparison with plants on greenfield sites. The Avesta plant site manager noted:

> Greenfield sites have cost and scale advantages. Ones like ours are handicapped by
> the past, but we have more industry knowledge, more diverse experience and better
> application knowledge. But to cash in on this you need to be imaginative and be
> able to ride with change.

Note this richer Swedish testimony. It is saying, yes, we acknowledge the force of economic rationality – the tribute to greenfield sites and scale economies – but there are other human issues that may also impact on the bottom line.

The same interviewee on being asked where he would place himself on the Blake-Mouton grid responded: 'You can't get good production by being only production centred, this can only be achieved by a people orientation.'

Finally, regarding the organization of sales, we heard further evidence of change. Again the Avesta site manager summed it up: 'Now we have reorganized total sales capacity; the salesman has a dialogue with the customer, the salesman knows from his laptop whether or not he can accept the order, and it is automatically inputted.' Very much along the lines of what we were told at Falcon Brewery as part of professional differentiation strategy.

## Kockums

The more limited research access we enjoyed at Kockums tends to limit what can be added here. In organization and production terms the key developments were:

- descent from the status of national champion in Sweden;
- the end of commercial shipbuilding;
- a contract with the Australian MOD, leading to an involvement that transcended Kockums acquisition;
- the three Ss specialization – submarines, the sterling engine, stealth technology – and the reallocation of resources to support these ventures; and
- the acquisition of Kockums by HDW.

One might express some of this a little differently and say that the major production organization change is a reorientation from construction to design. Most of Kockum's slimmed-down workforce may still be engaged in the construction of surface vessels and submarines in Karlskrona. But the heart of the company, its *raison d'être* and probably its future, is the 250-person office at Malmö doing submarine design, R&D work and development of the sterling engine.

## Ulstein Verft

A key organizational change at Ulstein in the late 1990s was a restructuring away from a traditional hierarchical-functional model to a matrix structure. The vice-president at the start of the interview testified: 'We spent all the year trying to structure all the systems and the teams and procedures that we are using. So quite a bit of work is done it is fair to say. But I would like to move much faster ... it is a matrix structure.' One axis of the matrix would be functions, and the other would be projects. It is likely that the Ulstein matrix structure is similar to what is common in offshore engineering. Indeed the transition to matrix seemed to follow Ulstein's heavy involvement in vessels for the oil industry, and one of our key interviewees at Ulstein was ex-oil industry.

There were also some production organization changes of a more

international nature. First, some of the more labour intensive steelwork had
been transferred to Poland. Second, Ulstein aimed to build more ships in yards
in other countries, for example in Brazil, both in order to be closer to
customers and to bypass protectionism. Finally, Ulstein's ship equipment
division was sold to Vickers of Britain in 1998. As outsiders it seemed to us
that this equipment division had:

- conferred a vertical integration advantage on Ulstein, the advantage of
  having this capability in-house, at cost, under their own control;
- the availability of equipment also facilitated the variable customization
  of Ulstein vessels, identified as a strength earlier in the present chapter;
  and
- the possession of an equipment division also served to differentiate
  Ulstein from other yards.

Nevertheless, the ship equipment division was sold for a good price, and its
loss did not prevent Ulstein from achieving bumper profits in 2001 and 2002.
By the spring of 2003 things did not look so good, a reflection of the world
economic situation, and Ulstein went as far as to warn employees of possible
redundancies. But then the company got an order for two platform supply
vessels, no redundancies occurred, and things do not look so bad (Summer
2003).

**Odense Lindø**

In the chapter on the brewing industry we talked about the problems of
physical distribution given the uneven distribution of population in Norway
and Sweden particularly, compounded by the difficulties of terrain in the case
of Norway. The challenge of physical distribution is an issue characteristic of
fast moving consumer goods (FMCG) industries. The corresponding
challenge in industrial goods, typically made to order and not for stock, is
getting these made to an agreed deadline, what in German is called
*Termintreue*, literally faithfulness to the promised date. And the more
expensive the unit that is being made and delivered, the more critical
*Termintreue* becomes. After all, whoever ordered it needs it for their business
and aims to make money using it.

Against this background it is of note that Odense Lindø volunteered the fact
that their delivery performance was perfect. This was not a boastful claim. The
reason they gave was that they never make unrealistic promises, and it was
cited in the context of their down-to-earth attitude. In the same spirit one
of their production controllers cited as a key problem getting costs and
timing right when building a new ship, a type/size not previously constructed,

where you have calculations and predictions but not the evidence of past experience.

Another general production issue is the persistent striving for further rationalization and cost efficiencies. As noted in an earlier section, Odense Lindø management explained this in terms of the wealth of the A.P. Møller group of which they were a part and which would preclude any government support. But one should put this into a wider context. Shipbuilding, that is to say, is an industry where nearly every company enjoys government subsidies or is cross-subsidized by other parts of an industrial group. And in the instances where this is not the case, it does not make any difference because competitors will assume it anyway.

All four companies discussed in the chapter have been involved in M&A activity. Two of them, Avesta AB and Kockums, have been at the receiving end of it variously passing into British and then Finnish ownership, and German ownership in the case of Kockums. Of the other two, Odense Lindø has made acquisitions in Central Europe and Ulstein Verft has sub-contracted to Poland. Odense Lindø gave the integration of its Baltic acquisition as a key organization and production problem at the time of our visit. It figured as a real challenge since these acquisitions will serve to lower overall cost and increase capacity.

Finally, no company is an island. Part of its existence is determined by the actions of others. The transfer of shipbuilding activity from Europe to Asia noted at the start of this chapter, and the burgeoning of some of these Korean and Japanese companies, meant that Odense Lindø was no longer among the world's top ten shipbuilders.

## WORKFORCE DYNAMICS

In this broad section it may be appropriate to 'flag up' different things for the several companies. In the case of Avesta Sheffield, for instance, we benefited from a very revealing interview with a trade union representative as well as with other on-site (Avesta plant) interviewees and the HR manager at the corporate office in Stockholm.

### Avesta

In this subsection the references are primarily to the Avesta plant, which we visited, and perhaps the first thing to say is that the workforce was stable – or at least it would like to be!

First, the site manager on this subject: 'Most people here stay to retirement.

So we have a high age profile.' In a later interview we were given as average ages 48–49 for white-collar employees, 46 for blue-collar employees. We also checked on the presence of foreigners (not born in Sweden) in the workforce with the trade union representative and received the laconic answer: 'A few, mostly older Finns who came to Sweden in the 1950s.' This is a common theme across the sample on heavy manufacturing sites where good Swedish speaking is held to be a prerequisite for job safety.

We also inquired as to the recruitment of blue-collar workers and were told by the trade union representative that this operated primarily on a local basis with advertisements on the Internet, in the local press and by making the vacancies known in other towns where Avesta Sheffield has a plant.

The same source, however, said that they do not use the informal network to recruit family members (of existing employees) and that this was rather frowned upon in Sweden, suggesting favouritism with a hint of corruption; outside of Sweden, though, the recruitment of family members did come up, for example at Dandy, Brewery Group Denmark and Fritz Hansen in Denmark and at Ulstein in Norway.

Against this rather stable and familiar background, however, was a diffuse change scenario, of which the most dramatic element was the scale of the downsizing at the Avesta plant. How big the numbers were, of course, depended on how long the informant had been at the plant; it did not sound so bad when articulated by the site manager, but he had only been there 12 years. The record account was given to us by a retired foreman who came in to take us on a tour of the works. When he began his apprenticeship in 1958 the plant employed 3700, which reduced to 900 by the year 2000.

This change in employee numbers, however, was far from being the whole picture, which includes:

- a general change in the nature of the 'manual' work from checking the process to specialization in, as the site manager put it, 'being tuners and managers' of the automatic system;
- this in turn led to greater emphasis on training;
- recruiting from people with a high-school rather than a vocational school background;
- encouraging the over-55s to retire early; and
- a change in the system of blue-collar work supervision, with the abolition of shift foremen and their replacement with rotating worker coordinators.

This last point concerning foremen is a recurrent Scandinavian theme: an egalitarian society does not like to have an occupational stratum (foremen) whose *raison d'être* is telling others what to do.

Our trade union interviewee did not represent the large blue-collar Swedish trade union confederation generally known by its initials LO, but rather the white-collar, supervisory, technician union SALF, though many of its members will be promoted blue-collar workers.

Scandinavians do not like to discuss salary differentials, but this interviewee was prepared to offer a view. There were eight salary grades in operation, but the lowest – one and two – were not filled at this plant. The strongest differential comparison one can therefore make is between three and eight, where the interviewee suggested 'the difference could be SEK6000–7000 a month'. At summer 2003 rates that comes out at a difference of a little over £500 or US$800. To flesh out the difference a little, level three will be cleaners, level seven will be tradesmen (we were given the example of electricians) and level eight was described as 'process engineers'; these no doubt will be the 'tuners and managers' of the automated system. This may be of interest as a concrete example which readers from any country can use to make a rough comparison.

Redundancies came up in this discussion with the SALF representative who referred to an episode two to three years earlier where those who stayed were expected to work harder, and resented it. He added: '... and people are not so open about their grievances in case they get picked out for the next lot of redundancies.' We also asked about conflict, but received a polite denial that there were any violent disagreements, although the qualification was telling: '... this is not the Swedish way, we will ingest grievances rather than have confrontations. Sometimes they will go to the doctor and get a bit of time off, rather than fight it out at work.'

On the subject of bonuses we were told that there was a short-term production bonus, but more interestingly if the company earns 15 per cent return on capital employed (ROCE) employees get a share in relation to their salary. But: 'we don't usually get it; last time was three years ago. We've had this system for five or six years,' that is, since British Steel became the majority shareholder.

This interviewee had another observation of the merger with British Steel. At the time of this merger a lot of British operators came to Avesta to see how the Swedes do it, but 'our operators did not get to go to Sheffield'. There is an interesting contrast here in that the site manager observed that the Swedish part of the company was not big enough to rotate managers to enhance their competence and experience, but that after the merger they could be rotated through the United Kingdom.

At several points in this discussion with the SALF representative one had the feeling of hearing things that would have been inconceivable 20 years ago in Sweden. At the same time this is not exactly a reliable litmus test of Sweden's industrial ethos, since to a large extent Avesta were 'having it done to them' by the British. However, 20 years ago there was little in Sweden that was not in Swedish ownership, yet at the start of the present century nearly our whole company sample in Sweden is foreign-owned.

## Kockums

Again the main lines of development for Kockums can only be simply stated, namely:

- a massive downsizing from 10000 employees in its heyday to 1100 at the start of the present century; and
- a change of focus from construction to design, rendering the design and development staff more central.

Together with a more diffuse change, this is the end of paternalism, of the expectation of lifetime employment by Kockum's workers – as the PR manager remarked, people in Malmö used to say 'You know where you are with Kockum's, they have been there for 300 years'.

That was then.

## Ulstein Verft

The recurrent theme in the interviews on the subject of Ulstein Verft's workforce concerned the difficulty of getting, and sometimes keeping, skilled blue-collar workers.

Several background reasons exist for this. The first and most general is the high level of prosperity in Norway and the country's low overall level of unemployment. But second, and more particularly, Norway has a big offshore sector, and big in relation to a relatively small economy, and of course the offshore sector is a competitor to shipbuilding for many of the same skills, and pays more. The vice-president on this subject: 'When you are investing US$70 billion in the offshore sector that hurts the (shipbuilding) industry because the offshore sector does have a better ability to pay higher wages than the shipyards.' What is more, shipbuilding is somewhat cyclic, and our visits to Ulstein took place in good times.

All this raised the issue of labour turnover. The HR manager had the score off by heart: 'Last year up to the 11th of this month I had hired 165. And I had lost 134.' The search for workers also highlighted the cosmopolitans versus local debate. The traditional view was that local employees were best, and a lot of effort went into local recruitment. With locals you knew what you were getting, existing employees know them, and of course they do not face relocation costs into the area. This last is one more element in the 'they are more likely to stay' dictum that has come up several times, for instance in the Hansa Borg brewery and the Avesta steel plant.

At the same time, needs must. So that they had recruited as well in southern and eastern Norway (Ulstein is west coast, of course) and in Denmark and Sweden, and even further afield as the following piece of dialogue makes clear.

> *Researcher*: Why don't you take workers from further off, from Central Europe, from the Far East, where you can get people?
>
> *HR Manager:* We had a lot of workers from Sri Lanka, they came up about three to five years ago, they started coming in, very good people. Very well liked by people here. They are living for one thing and that is money.
>
> *Researcher*: But they left again?
>
> *HR Manager*: No, they are here and functioning very well in this local area.
>
> *Researcher*: So they are stable?
>
> *HR Manager*: Yes, very stable. We have people here from Iran, Iraq, Bosnia, Serbia. We have a lot, 25 different nations.

Yet in spite of this exemplary internationalism, one is never far from local-regional attachments in Scandinavia. We asked the strategy and development manager about recruitment, where and how, and we were told: 'Advertise, locally. Primarily locally. ... I think we should build up our resources based on local recruitment. Long term it should be like that.'

On the subject of corporate culture, there was a general agreement that Ulstein had one, though they were not always able to specify its values. But the elements which were mentioned were:

- the effects of Ulstein being a family company; and
- pride in the products, in Ulstein's technical virtuosity generally.

And of course Ulstein as an expression and focus of local, community sentiment.

## Odense Lindø

Scandinavian organizations generally distinguish between skilled and unskilled workers, without the intermediate Anglo-Saxon category of semi-skilled. The criterion for being skilled is having done an apprenticeship, so that at Odense Lindø painters for instance were viewed as unskilled because no apprenticeship scheme was needed. Differentials between skilled and unskilled exist (see Chapter 2), though these may be modest by Western standards generally. The hourly differential is DDK10, giving a gross weekly differential of DDK370, about £36 or US$57.

Odense Lindø blue-collar workers do a 37-hour week; only a minority of these do shift work, some 300 out of 2400, and these shift workers do a 35-hour week. Basic wage rates in Danish industry are reached by agreements between a national trade union organization on the one hand and the appropriate industry association on the other. This, however, only sets the base line, and there are local/company deals at a higher rate. Odense Lindø conforms to this model, and in addition there are further bonuses for building a ship in a pre-specified number of hours or indeed beating the target (reference has been made earlier to Odense Lindø's good delivery record).

All this results in high blue-collar wages, above the national industrial average. In consequence the blue-collar workforce is stable and long serving. Though as one manager noted, 'The higher rates attract good people, and make it easy to keep them. But you cannot dismiss the bad ones to make it right.'

Denmark is a country with industrial democracy legislation, which gives rise to a works council, in Danish a Samarbejdsudvalg, and this body will meet at least every three months. Questioning suggested that the Samarbejdsudvalg is rather less powerful vis-à-vis management than the corresponding Swedish MBL committee. Nor does the Samarbejdsudvalg have the ability to appeal to higher company-wide and national level negotiations in the event of some impasse with management.

Trade union membership rates are high in all the Scandinavian countries. Interestingly Odense Lindø had not tried to buy its way out of trade union membership in the way that privately held companies in other Western countries sometimes do, Mars Ltd in the UK, for example. The Danish system also has shop stewards (*Tillidsmand*). There were 13 of them at the time of our visit, all elected by the trade union members, some of them also serving on the Samarbejdsudvalg.

All we heard and saw suggested that labour relations were reasonably good. And it was conceded that management tended to be reactive; that is to say, it would respond, take action, provide information, explain, if and when requested. Indeed looking across several countries management does tend to be reactive where a system is in place and relations are reasonably good. It is countries where labour relations are more adversarial, most obviously the United States and Britain, where management adopts a more proactive posture.

## MANAGEMENT *ESPRIT DE CORPS*

We will use this section in a fairly open-ended way to consider appropriate issues of management style, values or indicative behaviour. Furthermore we are of course interested in anything that tends to link the three Scandinavian countries, or alternatively to differentiate them. Similarly we may use the section to highlight anything of interest regarding corporate culture, and where relevant we may make occasional comparisons between Scandinavia and other areas in matters of business and management.

## Avesta Sheffield

First of all there was evidence of a certain mildness of manner, a lack of individual assertiveness. We asked the Avesta site manager what had been the key decisions in his 12-year period in office as we did with some of the brewery managers reported in Chapter 3. But Swedish executives do not speak of taking key decisions, but of being a part of groups that do so. When pressed this interviewee replied: 'It was not really me, the group, but the site was rebuilt costing billions of SEK. I was pleased to have been part of it.' The site manager again elaborating on the key decisions issue emphasizes the importance of democratic discussion: 'If everyone agrees with me, I have failed.' Also a side tribute to the cult of competence, and trusting colleagues to have it: 'You only take a decision yourself if you cannot rely on others.'

Switching themes gently, the tension between British and Swedish culture serves to illuminate the latter. The view of one of the Swedish managers of the British was that 'They are more individualist and Americanized. It even shows in strategy. You think they are putting the company first, but they may be putting themselves first. This is forbidden in Sweden.'

Another part of this tension revolves around the understanding of what a meeting is all about. Swedes went to joint Anglo-Swedish meetings believing that these were discussion meetings, were open to offering and receiving ideas, were open-minded. But the British saw these as decision meetings; the British had done their thinking in advance, and done their lobbying. As one Swedish manager recalled, 'So they thought we were indecisive, we thought they were manipulative.' A somewhat different spin on the British was offered by the HR vice-president at the corporate office. In a discussion of graduate recruitment he observed that the British were 'broader'. This remark is a recognition of British management generalism in contrast to Swedish *teknik*-driven functional specialism.

Another possible manifestation of this 'differently coloured' view of management is the matter of corporate culture. British managers like the idea of corporate culture. Typically they tell you that their organization has one, that it is strong and distinctive: often they are not as good at telling you what it actually consists of, but this need not undermine their convictions about it.

That is the British response: we tried it out on the Avesta site manager and got a much more conditional answer, including these:

- you don't develop a corporate culture (cannot be fabricated to fit by some over-egoed, charismatic mover and shaker);
- but we may have a site culture (get real, get down to specifics);
- indeed we do have a site culture but I cannot describe it (isn't that the way it should be?) and
- differences between the sites are as big as the differences between Britain and Sweden (*lagom*, meaning 'let's keep a sense of proportion here').

Exactly the same diagnosis was offered by the corporate communications officer at head office. In other words corporate culture is part of fashionable management rhetoric and the British have bought it: the Swedish approach may be more distanced and evaluative. Indeed few of our Scandinavian companies' managers gave the spontaneous and emphatic accounts of corporate culture common among the British and Americans.

At the Avesta site we were told three interesting things about management and especially graduate recruitment. First, when asked about the rival merits of internal or external recruitment the site manager switched the emphasis in his reply to the importance of having divergent thinkers. This idea has surfaced several times in the discussion of Avesta. The essence of it was that in conditions of fast change and severe competition there are still opportunities, but only for the resourceful and imaginative, so you don't want a bunch of yes-men!

The second was in the form of reflections on the change in the way graduate recruits were deployed. The old model was to take people into R&D and then a few years later redeploy some of them in line production management posts or in sales. The new model is that they are recruiting into specific job positions with the expectation that these graduate recruits will move fairly quickly into something else.

It is an interesting issue, though it probably tells us more about the pace of change than about Sweden. In the good old days – when you could sell all you could make, when the world economy was expanding effortlessly, before globalization – the old model was fine. Recruit too many: it doesn't matter, you'll be glad of them one day. Put them into R&D: fine, they won't do any harm and might even do a bit of good. Pick out the few with personality, organizational talent and management aspirations later – sure, what's the hurry. But now that competition has hotted up, the operation has to be more focused.

The third point about graduate recruitment is the regional issue. If Sweden had a Silicon Valley or an M4 corridor, Avesta Sheffield's plants would not be in it; it is to be found in smallish town, provincial locations and north of Stockholm. So the ideal graduate recruit is someone who comes from the region of the plant, who went away for higher education (but not too far) and wants to come home again. So 'local boys' are in, but '... if you hire graduates from Stockholm, they leave if they don't meet local girls here!'

This story is included because it has more than local interest. As the non-Scandinavian author, I have never heard so many people say they would not move out of the capital city for job enhancement or career advancement as in Scandinavia. Nor does one hear anyone in Britain say anything equivalent to 'There are too many old and stupid people here', once heard as a reference to provincial Denmark, or an equivalent of 'No one wants a Tønder address' (Tønder is in south west Jutland, it is the last town before you get to the now unmanned German border). Or, 'People will change company but not town' (provincial Norway).

In short it is being suggested that these regional issues impact more on job mobility and professional recruitment in Scandinavia than in Anglo-Saxon countries. What may be causing the Scandinavian difference is the skewed population distribution and over-concentration of inhabitants in the metropolitan area of the capital cities, discussed in the chapter on brewing in the context of the distribution challenge faced by FMCG producers in Scandinavia.

## Kockums

In spite of our more limited research access to Kockums, there are clearly some broad changes in management orientation.

First of all, Kockums' management has clearly gone from big to small as the company contracted, but perhaps more interestingly its focus will have shifted from a downward organizing one (getting big ships made) to an upward and outward one that relates development capability to market opportunity. But differently one might speak of a phased transition from production management to project management.

Second, Kockums' managers are experiencing integration with a German company, and in a quite tangible way will interact frequently with German colleagues. Our PR manager asserted that the acquisition of Kockums by HDW was not seen as involving a culture clash.

Finally, the changing fortunes of Kockums will lead its managers to a greater concern with external finance and political issues. In no small way the future of the merged entity will be shaped by offset deals and by the power of HDW to provide credit finance for would-be customers.

## Ulstein Verft

One theme running through Ulstein Verft management's account was that of flexibility, which will come as no surprise to readers after the references to restructuring, some production outsourcing, major sell-offs and recruiting from Ulsteinvik to Colombo. This flexibility ethos is caught in several dicta of the vice-president, namely: 'I have claimed for a long time that whatever sells I can build. So whatever they manage to sell, I will build with this organization here or modifications to it.' This flexibility, of course, needs to be supported by resource allocation: 'Then my job becomes one of portfolio management of these various contracts. And certain management of the total yard resources as they have to be divided between these various projects.' A real point about the industry is being made here. This picture is a long way from just-in-time at Toyota City.

It also emerged that there had been some management change in the literal sense of people coming and going:

> I don't think that the problems in the management team as such were the biggest, but of course, we restructured here quite a bit. The procurement manager we had at the time, he quit. The engineering manager ... was given a central position in this new organization. But he was removed as engineering manager. So a few things did take place here on the personnel side.

There is also some outsourcing of professional competence, and the strategy and development manager is explicit on this issue. When asked how many people he had working for him the response was 'I am running the philosophy where we don't, I don't want people on my staff. I want to buy the competence where I can find it. So I am running ten to 12 projects and I have one man with me on a full-time basis and a secretary.'

And again: 'I buy project management, I buy development, I buy facility, but I am writing the specifications.' Again an important point is being made here, not especially about the essence of Scandinavia, but about management change in the West. In some industries at least management is becoming less about the internal dynamics of running the organization and more about the management of interfaces with other entities.

There was an accompanying suggestion in the Ulstein interviews that some change in management recruitment and/or advancement was occurring. That middle management was promoted from within, but higher management came increasingly from outside the company, though from within the industry. A contrast, as far as we can judge, with Odense Lindø and the A.P. Møller empire generally.

Finally, Ulstein offered an illustration of the fact that democracy does not have to lead to indecision. On this the strategy and development manager deserves to be quoted: 'Yes, you have to be democratic before the decision is made, but there will be no democracy after. In my opinion if you try to be somewhat democratic here, it will only be a mess.'

## Odense Lindø

One expects companies that are rich, successful and in family ownership to have a distinct identity, even to be a bit idiosyncratic, and Odense Lindø does not disappoint.

One key plank in this identity is a long-serving, internally promoted management. As the labour relations manager put it, 'People either stay for a few days, or you stay for life.' There are now a few management appointments from outside, but we were told 'we still don't advertise'.

Our impression is of a sober, performance-driven culture, rather meritocratic but stressing loyalty as much as ability. You do not have to have terrific qualifications to get hired. Indeed several managers reported quite modest educational antecedents, but once in impressive qualifications or previous reputation would not help you; only work, performance and loyalty will get you promoted. And both at Odense Lindø and at other A.P. Møller plants visited later, one met plenty of senior people who had come a long way within the company.

Interestingly several management interviewees mentioned humble origins in the sense of an early exit from the education system and of blue-collar starter jobs. At an orientation meeting at the company we were told of people joining A.P. Møller at 17 and ending up as partners (becoming a ship's captain is the obvious route). Again interestingly it is only a few years ago that A.P. Møller embarked upon graduate recruitment. The organization chart at Odense Lindø had bracketed numbers after people's names, signifying their years of service with the group.

As with private companies generally A.P. Møller has a reputation for being private, for being sparing about the information it gives out, and wanting to control publicity. We were told that 1997 was the first time Mr Møller had given the press enough information to enable an attempt at a business analysis.

The family, of course, are always news, always legendary. Like the story of Mr Møller visiting the Prime Minister, driving up in a Ford Escort and making a virtue of economy. Though on re-running this story at another A.P. Møller plant, the impression was that it was a bit of a pose, that was what he kept the Ford Escort for. Perhaps a better one and a quote from one of our interviewees was: 'Mr Møller retired at 80, so he stopped coming to the office on Saturday.' On his 90th birthday he treated all employees to a piece of Danish pastry! It should be noted that he likes to cite his father's motto: 'We should suffer no loss that can be avoided with proper diligence.'

# CONCLUSION

In this chapter we have looked at two industries, shipbuilding and steel, which are both under pressure. This pressure comes from the now familiar sources of world overcapacity and competition from non-traditional producer countries in Asia. Nonetheless, all our four companies have survived, albeit not necessarily under national ownership.

The developments in the four companies also read like a roll call of turn-of-the-century change, including:

- cross border outsourcing or acquisition to enlarge capacity in two cases;
- foreign ownership in the other two;
- pervasive cost-cutting and restructuring;
- massive downsizing of the workforce in two cases

and the march of globalization also has a more novel manifestation at Ulstein in that they are recruiting a significant part of their blue-collar workforce from other countries, ranging from Sweden to Sri Lanka.

There is, broadly, a common dimension to their survival. All four, that is, are studies in adaptability and specialization. This is true for Avesta with its move to dedicated plants, new applications, and the management of capacity. Odense Lindø is focused on the big ship segment, pursues quality and delivery punctuality, and is a progressive cost-cutter. Kockums has survived by making the switch from commercial to military shipping, and succeeded in making itself attractive as a merger partner through its specialization in submarines, air independent engines and stealth technology.

But if there is a prize it should probably go to Ulstein on the basis of the developments reported to us. Their company has not only reconfigured its organization and operations, but has shown a distinctive *elan* in 'chasing the market' and moving capably through a series of products to serve that market's changing needs.

## REFERENCE

*Lloyd's Register* (2003), 'World fleet statistics' London.

# 7. Differences and similarities

In this last but one chapter the purpose is to re-examine the homogeneity thesis, the idea that the three main Scandinavian countries have so much in common that they may be treated as a cluster with regard to management practice and business culture, and to offer some broad conclusions. To put the cluster thesis to a test, we need to see if we can tease out any noteworthy country differences that run across industries.

We will approach this task in various dimensions, first by looking at similarities and differences in the national context between the three countries. Next, we will look at similarities and differences in terms of the organizational dimensions we used in the industry chapters: strategy, management *esprit de corps*, production and organization, company culture and management–workforce relations to which list we also add interpersonal relations.

## NATIONAL CONTEXT

Are there differences in the national context of the Scandinavian countries that would make it reasonable to expect companies in the same industries to have differences in management and organizations? The following is a brief comparison of our three countries in terms of some basic facts in order to see what the differences might be.

As will be seen from Table 7.1, the three countries are very different in terms of geography, especially Norway and Denmark, the first one mountainous, the other only lowlands; in area Denmark is ten times smaller than Sweden, whereas it is by far the most densely populated. In natural resources Norway and Sweden share some things such as minerals, timber and hydro power, but not to the same degree. Denmark has none of those primary resources important for industrialization and only recently has embarked on the extraction of oil and gas. Denmark and Norway are similar in industry structure, whereas Sweden stands out with a surprisingly high number of large-scale companies. Attitudes towards European integration have been vastly different in the three countries, with Denmark joining the community as early as in 1973, Sweden only some 20 years later, and Norway not at all. Norway has a large state-owned business sector, especially in the oil industry, in contrast to Denmark that has practically none. The only thing they really all

*Table 7.1   Bird's-eye comparison of the three countries*

|  | Norway | Sweden | Denmark |
|---|---|---|---|
| Geography | Mountains | Some mountains but mostly lowlands | Lowlands |
| Area per km$^2$ | 306 253 | 450 000 | 43 000 |
| Population per million | 4.3 | 8.9 | 5.3 |
| Population density per km$^2$ | 14 | 20 | 124 |
| Natural resources | oil fish hydro power timber minerals | minerals hydro power timber | oil soil fish |
| Industry structure | SMEs few large firms | many large and small, fewer medium sized | SMEs predominate, few large firms |
| Recent economic crisis | 1980s | 1990s | 1980s |
| EU membership | No, twice rejected | from 1995 | from 1973 |
| A state-owned business sector | yes | some | practically none |

have in common is a recent economic crisis, which they all overcame albeit with different strategies.

Notwithstanding these tangible contrasts we find a surprising number of societal and organizational similarities, including:

- similar philosophy in societal institutions;
- strong trade unionism;
- advanced welfare states;
- social solidarity;
- high level of general education;
- high female participation on the labour market; and
- small wage differentials.

In the following text we will treat some of these in more detail using our findings, and at the end of the chapter we will revert to the country cluster theory.

What we may conclude already at this stage, however, is that *a society does not appear to be formed primarily by a country's geography or natural resources, rather it is formed by the values, attitudes and determination of its people.*

## STRATEGY

First, let us ask if there are any differences between the Scandinavian countries in terms of company strategy and competitive advantage. The a priori view would probably be that strategy and competitive advantage is not going to inform the homogeneity thesis strongly, neither confirming it nor disputing it. That is to say this would probably be the view of most business consultants and managers of international operations. Such a view would be based on the premise that it is the dynamics of particular industries, not particular countries or groups of countries, that determine the parameters of corporate strategy and shape the choices open to particular companies in a given industry.

While such a view is quite widespread and is implicit in much writing on strategy and competitive advantage, we do not have to accept it without debate. We do have the data generated by the present research and this data has a reasonable degree of comparability between the three countries. So let us look at the evidence from this study and run afresh the question of regional homogeneity or its converse. As an introduction to the discussion it may be helpful to offer the reader the data in summarized and tabular form, given in Tables 7.2, 7.3 and 7.4. Whereas in the earlier industry chapters the companies were grouped by industry cross-country, here we will group them by country, cross-industry. And as well as noting what seem to us to be the key points of individual company strategy and competitive advantage, we will include four further columns headed:

- Foreign owned;
- M&A, which will note whether the company is the result of past merger and acquisition or whether it has grown by merger and acquisition subsequently;
- C/B, for cross-border outsourcing of at least some production, typically to lower wage countries in Asia or in Central and Eastern Europe;
- Exports, where we will indicate whether a significant proportion of output is exported.

These four columns will be filled in with a YES or NO.

*Table 7.2  Business strategies in Norwegian firms*

| | Key points | Foreign owned | M&A | C/B | Exports |
|---|---|---|---|---|---|
| Ekornes | Furniture<br>Domestic, mid-market (recliners, sitting-room furniture, mattresses)<br>Strong brand name, especially for recliners<br>Sells on comfort and function<br>Strong distribution, close relations with selected retailers<br>Cost cutting, production time reduced | No | Yes | No | Yes |
| Hansa Borg | Brewing<br>Growth via M&A<br>Acquisitions in demographic centres of gravity<br>Cut-price logistics<br>Work practice reform and restructuring in train | No | Yes<br>Based on mergers | No | No |
| Nidar | Confectionery<br>Strong brands<br>Promotional vigour<br>Distributional effectiveness<br>BPR/rationalization | No | Yes<br>Nidar and Bergene acquired by Orkla | No | No |

| Ulstein Verft | Shipbuilding<br>Revolving specialization<br>Moving on to new types as demand/opportunity changes<br>High value-added<br>Know-how driven<br>Design and customization led | No<br>Except for equipment division sold to Vickers of UK | Yes | Yes | Yes |

*Table 7.3  Business strategies in Swedish firms*

| | Key points | Foreign owned | M&A | C/B | Exports |
|---|---|---|---|---|---|
| Swedwood | Furniture<br>Vertically integrated supplier to IKEA<br>Production efficiency<br>Low cost, most production in CEE<br>Slim central staff | No | Yes | Yes | Yes |
| Falcon Brewery | Brewing<br>Differentiation via specialization and professionalism<br>Supported by restructuring and BPR<br>Streamlined field sales operation<br>Growth in all segments | Yes<br>By Carlsberg (Denmark), in turn by Orkla (Norway) | No | No | No |
| Procordia | Food-processing: snacks, pizzas and taste-enhancers<br>Presence in two markets: retail and catering/fast food<br>Rationalization of plants<br>Cost reduction<br>Concentration on growth segments: snacks and functional food | Yes<br>By Orkla (Norway) | Yes<br>Three merged Swedish companies | Yes | Yes |

| | | | | | |
|---|---|---|---|---|---|
| Kokums | Shipbuilding<br>Focus strategy: submarines, sterling engine, stealth technology<br>Design and development rather than construction | Yes<br>By HDW (Germany) | No | No | Yes |
| Avesta Sheffield | Stainless steel<br>Dedicated plants<br>Vast productivity improvements<br>Customer intimacy: moving up customers' decision-making chain<br>Innovative as to product use | Yes<br>By British Steel, later by Finnish steelmaker | Yes<br>Prior to acquisition by British Steel | No | Yes |

*Table 7.4  Business strategies in Danish firms*

| | Key points | Foreign owned | M&A | C/B | Exports |
|---|---|---|---|---|---|
| Fritz Hansen | Furniture<br>High-end, institutional and domestic<br>Design-led<br>Functionalist/minimalist style<br>Successful relations with high-profile designers<br>Brands itself rather than designers, i.e., departs from industry norm | No | Yes<br>Family company acquired by Danish holding company | No | Yes |
| BGD | Brewing<br>Good brand portfolio, partly achieved via M&A<br>Successful exporter (65% of output)<br>Exploits Denmark's image as a beer country<br>No own label/discount beer which is thin margin<br>Courts HORECA segment | No | Yes<br>Based on merger between Faxe and Jyske | No | Yes |
| Dandy | Confectionery/chewing-gum<br>Taste quality: tablet, not strip form<br>Dominance in dental/functional segment | Yes<br>In sense later most of it acquired by Cadbury Schweppes (Britain) | No | Yes | Yes |

| | No | No | Yes | Yes* |
|---|---|---|---|---|
| Multiple distribution channels | | | | |
| Successful penetration of Russian market | | | | |
| Workforce flexibility improvements | | | | |
| Cost reduction via packaging and manufacture in Russia | | | | |
| Discriminating use of own-label deals | | | | |
| Odense Lindø | No | | | |
| Shipbuilding | | | | |
| Benefits from vertical integration in A.P. Møller group | | | | |
| Cost control, 'runs a tight ship' | | | | |
| Extensive R&D network | | | | |
| Market information via parent company | | | | |
| Technical leadership | | | | |
| At big ship end of market | | | | |

*Note:* *Most of Odense Lindø's output goes to A.P. Møller; the spare capacity does fuel exports, each of which will be high value although only a small proportion of overall revenue.

Probably the main effect of our laying out the key strategic and operating features is to confirm the a priori view alluded to earlier. The data presented in this way do not undermine the Scandinavian homogeneity thesis. With one or two possible exceptions, which we will come to later, this data simply demonstrates the degree of variety, the range of policies and pluses, of corporate antecedents and aspiration which one would expect with a sample of 13 companies taken from four to five industries, never mind the national origin.

Neither do these companies present an image of strategic homogeneity across the three countries, such as to reinforce the idea of a distinctive Scandinavian cluster, differing broadly from other Western countries. The most that could be said is that if one has a good knowledge of business in several other Western countries, and particularly of the developments over the last few years, is that the companies summarily depicted above have gone less far down the road of downsizing, restructuring, imposed workforce flexibility and cross-border outsourcing to achieve cost reduction than is the norm in, most obviously, Britain and the United States. But to make this judgement one needs some knowledge external to Scandinavia: this interpretation is not demonstrated by the companies in our case sample considered in isolation. Also it would have to be said that this possible 'Scandinavia versus the rest of the West' thesis is only a matter of degree, and perhaps also a matter of timing. One can after all see instances of all these 'typical Western' developments in our core sample.

So in all probability the general view that industry is a stronger determinant of strategic choice than is country of origin is quite simply true. This leaves us with the residual question of whether there are any differences between the countries on this strategic/competitive advantage front.

It probably is possible to point to one or two things that derive from economic history and structure. The three countries have experienced different degrees of industrialization, with Sweden the most industrialized and Norway the least. Similarly Sweden has spawned far more big, and big-name, companies than the other two countries, as was argued in Chapter 2.

This is the clue to one of the differences flagged up in Table 7.3, namely the fact that nearly the whole sample of Swedish companies are in foreign ownership. Sweden has an abundant supply of companies big enough to attract foreign corporate predators in an age of aggressive globalization. There is a further manifestation of this phenomenon, albeit not drawn from our core sample. This is that while Sweden does not attract much foreign direct investment (FDI) in the sense of foreign investors wanting to set up manufacturing facilities in Sweden, there is an interest on the part of foreign investors in buying shares in existing Swedish companies. So to take a headline example, it is said that 20–40 per cent of the shares of Sweden's

Ericsson are in the hands of guess who? British and American pension funds! There are large shares of foreign stock-ownership in many major Scandinavian companies. In addition, many Scandinavian companies in high-competence industries such as IT and pharmaceuticals have been taken over by multinationals. Highly-educated but low-paid brain-power, combined with a fact-oriented, patient and equal discussion-style management means a good environment for high-tech innovations in Scandinavia.

The economic history and structure argument may also explain another oddity contained in our summary tables, namely the omnipresence of branded consumer goods conglomerate Orkla of Norway. Orkla owns Nidar and via their stake in Carlsberg of Denmark they may also be said to own Falcon Brewery in Sweden, and they certainly own Sweden's Procordia. In other words, Orkla owns nearly a quarter of our core sample, as well as other substantial entities such as the Pripps and Ringnes breweries in Sweden and Norway respectively. However, Orkla is a rather unique case, being one of the very few large private business owners in Norway; a large share of the stock market is owned by the state. In contrast, Sweden has the Wallenberg dynasty and the banking group Handelsbanken, and Denmark has A.P. Møller and the Carlsberg foundation, in addition to other large private fortunes.

Again taking Norway as an example one might point to certain country effects. The very difficult terrain of Norway has been mentioned earlier. It does not favour agriculture, nor does it favour the domestic transportation of manufactured goods. How congruent then that so many of Norway's strengths were or are off-shore, in the sense of polar exploration, whaling, trading, shipbuilding, ship owning/ship operating, fishing, off-shore oil extraction and processing.

In his excursion into strategy and business advantage in countries other than the United States, Michael Porter (1990) has argued that individual countries do not promote industrial success in general terms, but that they may facilitate or advantage the development of particular industries. Building on the Porter platform Örjan Sölvell and his co-authors (1991) proffer a number of Swedish illustrations. Consider for example the demand conditions, which led Sweden to develop competitive advantage in heavy trucks (Scania and Volvo):

- as the Swedish road system expanded there was a need for trucks which could transport large amounts of stone and gravel, that is, a demand for heavy trucks;
- plus the fact that the railway system is not dense in northern Sweden makes this demand more critical in the north;
- the north in particular needed big trucks to transport pulp and timber;
- the cold climate put a premium on durable trucks; and

- there was a premium on trucks that did not break down, given the relative absence of repair and rescue facilities in the north.

And there we have a national context creating ideal demand conditions.

Now we do have some evidence of this in our core sample, though the forces at work tend to be less tangible and more reputational. We have already drawn attention to Denmark's beer brewing reputation, and to the fact that BGD of Denmark is the only serious exporter among our three Scandinavian breweries.

Or again consider the reputation for stylish design enjoyed by the Scandinavian countries. This is clearly an element in the success of Danish furniture maker Fritz Hansen, both reputationally and in terms of the mutually beneficial relationship the company has with individual designers.

A Norwegian example is Ulstein, which is one of several shipyards on the Norwegian west coast. Its international competitiveness is a result of the fact that the company is part of a strong maritime industrial environment, consisting of suppliers, R&D facilities, classification and insurance companies, all stimulated by demanding customers such as shipping companies, an increasingly technologically advanced fishing industry, and not least oil-related activities (Reve et al. 1992). The increasing input of advanced technology in all kinds of ships and the non-standard design of specialized as well as multi-purpose vessels has created an international market for high value-added ship production. In this niche Ulstein, being a part of a strong industrial environment, can thrive, even on an island on the Norwegian west coast, as long as it can 'keep ahead of the pack' in terms of design.

In summary one can point to some country differences in this consideration of competitive advantage. With the exception of some reputational issues, however, these do tend to be economic and structural rather than socio-cultural and are in consequence rather on the perimeter of our thesis. One could even say that if we find similarities in management and organization between the countries, despite these differences in economic and structural context, it is in line with our argument that the particularities of the Scandinavian cluster have cultural roots. So let us go further with the comparison of organizational dimensions.


## MANAGEMENT *ESPRIT DE CORPS*

What we are going to describe next might be regarded as just ideals, managers' ideas about how things ought to be. However, it is not *just* wishful thinking. In many companies we heard very similar descriptions of decision making, information, delegation and empowerment told by personnel in different departments and at various hierarchical levels. We see this as an indication that these ideals are also put into practice, in many cases to a surprisingly high degree. It is not just rhetoric.

One of the most uniform features of management in the companies we have studied is the emphasis put on information, discussions and suggestions before decision making. This is seen in the many types of management meetings; some are regular, others more ad hoc. For the formal meetings there is a written agenda, which may stay unaltered for years, and in most types of meetings minutes are taken and distributed to whoever might be concerned. This contributes to an open communication flow. Management meetings often involve several departments or several levels of the hierarchy, and this has become more common due to process-oriented organization structures, coordination committees, more or less permanent projects, or even matrix structures.

Another distinctive feature of Scandinavian management, we find, is the importance put on the decision-making process itself. It should in principle be open. Decision-making before the meeting is considered unfair; participants should have reasons to believe that they have a real possibility of influencing the outcome. In this connection we noted earlier Swedish consternation at Avesta of the English habit of having 'a meeting before the meeting'; a meeting, that is, of the inner cabinet, of the real power-holders. This way, it is more likely that they will identify with a decision, even when it is not in their favour. Loyalty to the decision process may in many cases be stronger than loyalty to particular leaders, no matter how charismatic or competent they may be. If the decision-making process is unfair, this loyalty may fail, leaving managers in a rather precarious situation. Another reason for the often lengthy decision-making processes, managers explained, is that people should have information in order to understand the reasons for the decisions. Even if they do not agree with the outcome, or if the outcome is unfavourable to them, it is more likely that they will participate in the implementation of the decision if they are familiar with its grounds. Some managers even say that it is better to have a thorough decision-making process than to try to find out afterwards who works against a decision and spreads confusion in the whole organization. Many underline that they favour democracy before a decision is made, but not afterwards.

In relation to decision making we found a difference among the countries in as much as the Swedes took longer to come to a decision than did the Danes, the process could be lengthy because everybody had to be heard, and once the decision was made they did not want to reconsider it, whereas the Danes would not hesitate changing the decision should new circumstances or facts turn up. This earned the Danes, among Swedes and some Norwegians, the reputation of being unreliable merchants, whereas Danes on their side found the Swedes inflexible and too rule oriented. Indeed the Swedes took rules seriously.

The ideal is to reach a consensus. In many cases everybody knows after a while what the outcome will be. And there is of course a limit to the discussion. If people do not reach a conclusion, the superior must in the end decide. However, a manager should not use this strategy too often when it comes to complicated strategic decisions, since it might undermine his or her credibility in terms of the democratic process.

Allowing discussion before decisions does not mean that management can abdicate. Managers must point out the important strategic choices, highlight the decision factors, and stand or fall by what they believe. But still, participation is the key word.

One of the problems with group decisions is that they may result in weak individual incentives for making a difference, for standing out. That is, this consensus-seeking approach may be in discord with the individual killer-instinct that is sometimes needed in tough, rapidly changing business environments.

## PRODUCTION AND ORGANIZATION

As it will have been seen from the above, many of our case companies had recently changed strategic focus from production to a more customer oriented approach. One of the consequences of this has been a reorganization of the work procedures in administration as well as in production in view of having more flexibility and not least better coordination and cooperation. This meant the creation of cross-functional work groups, project groups and teams that crossed hierarchical divides. It also meant delegation of responsibility from functional leaders to the groups, including decision making and a more active participation in goal attainment.

Delegation of responsibility and authority to the shop floor personnel does not always come easy. In one case the process leader was constantly being asked for direction whenever the operators had to make decisions, and in order to force them to decide on their own the production manager stopped showing up at planning meetings.

By increasing the level of formal education on the shop floor and by using state-of-the-art technology for production planning, the tasks of foremen and shift leaders have been made superfluous in some of our companies. The kind of first-line leader who lacked formal education on a higher level than the operators has always been an ambiguous character in most branches of industry in Scandinavia, since they had to balance between leadership and chumminess. So management, operators and trade unions seemed happy to get rid of them.

Our case companies favoured 'top light' management hierarchies, and this also became evident at the shop floor, where in some of the factories we saw remarkable examples of wide spans of control, with between 60 and 150 operators per process leader. Advanced information technology is used to plan production and distribute tasks, and from the screen each operator can easily see what to do next, so that a foreman is not really needed. In some cases, we learned, the group coordinator task rotated among the operators without extra pay, or simple tasks rotated in order to upgrade skills and promote multi-functionality. These groups may have some similarities with the semi-autonomous work groups of the 1970s, but the reasons for implementation have to do with flexibility rather than with workplace democracy.

In countries where authority is built on hierarchical position or formal education, such differences in levels and types of competence may create difficulties for collaboration in work groups. In Scandinavia, where informal coordination, down-to-earth discussions and emphasis on taking everybody's view into account are the rule, such organizational novelties may be implemented more easily. So the lack of strong traditions of hierarchical authority may eventually prove to be an advantage. This is particularly important, since high value added production based on a well-educated workforce is likely to be the future for Scandinavia.

## COMPANY CULTURE

Most of our respondents instinctively said yes to our question as to whether the company had a specific culture, but very few could tell what it was. Notable exceptions were Norwegian Ekornes, Swedish Swedwood and Danish Odense Lindø.

In other companies that had recently been acquired or merged with other companies, aspects of the former company cultures were revealed at the same time as they were being eroded. This applies in particular to the companies Avesta, Procordia and Nidar. In the latter company about 80 per cent of management left because they felt uncomfortable being part of a company that was redesigned in the middle of normal operations, and because they would have to reapply for their jobs. This was too much of a culture clash. Old practices and values were put aside in one sweep, giving some managers a feeling of the ground disappearing beneath their feet.

Even if people had problems describing company cultures, however, there is no reason to assume that Scandinavian companies in general lack character and well-established values and practices. Most Scandinavian managers do not believe in 'corporate cultures', in the sense of officially approved lists of company goals and values. But to be able to describe the culture in practice, they seem to need particular pegs, such as a founder or an owning family, as a starting point for the story. Nonetheless, takeovers and major restructurings can bring taken-for-granted values and practices to the surface. But this aspect of management and organization seems to be unrelated to national differences or similarities, with the important reservation that company culture cannot of course go against general values and attitudes in its environing society.

## MANAGEMENT–WORKFORCE RELATIONS

Industrial relations in Scandinavia are built on old traditions, agreements, laws and prescriptions. This has ensured a low level of industrial conflict on the national level, and also an atmosphere of cooperation in the companies. In many factories, union representatives are involved in so many decisions related to employment, health, security and social issues that they are almost part of the HR department. Several of the union representatives we interviewed use the same expression to explain their willingness to cooperate: 'We are in the same boat!'

The most striking quality of management–workforce relations we found was the willingness to cooperate on implementing rationalization strategies, certainly in Norway and Sweden, though in Denmark we saw several cases of resistance. Denmark was also the only place where we heard companies express the desire to get rid of trade unions altogether. In Norway and Sweden managers expressed unconditional loyalty to rules in dealing with the trade unions. Still, the general attitude to trade unions in Scandinavia is a far cry from the confrontational style that we see in Southern Europe, say France and Italy, not to mention the United States. Non-Scandinavian managers opposed to union power will find Scandinavian attitudes almost incomprehensible.

In the companies where cooperation worked well, it had a tremendous impact on the future of the company. The success stories include the Norwegian furniture company Ekornes. When the company was on the brink of financial failure, employees contributed to the turnaround by accepting reduced pay for a time to avoid redundancies. Later they were rewarded by production related bonuses. Among the reasons for employee participation was the extensive information they received on the company's situation at all times, and a new organization structure that meant delegation of authority to the lowest possible level. The workers took part in a continuous improvement of the production process that over time resulted in more than 60 per cent reduction of production time per chair within a few years. The result was growth in output and employment, and in 2001 Ekornes was able to open a new factory, which meant further growth in turnover and profits.

Another success story is the confectionery company Nidar. Bad financial results necessitated a complete turnaround. The union representatives had seen the writing on the wall for a long time, thanks to their seat in the board of directors when management involved them in the making of a new strategy.

Downsizing was inevitable, union representatives agreed, and in return they insisted on upgrading the skills of the remaining operators to enable them to handle the increased responsibility required by the new process organization. The reason was not to be nice to people, but to make them able to take the right decisions in their daily work.

These examples show that it is indeed difficult to distinguish between management culture and management–worker relations, since both are characterized by the way authority is handled.

We believe empowerment represents a great potential for creating an offensive organizational flexibility that is related to the Scandinavian business context in general, not to single countries or industries. On the other hand, companies opting for more defensive types of flexibility through cost cutting and downsizing and outsourcing of low-skills/low-cost production may find other environments more conducive.

Increasingly trade unions in Scandinavia are facing tougher negotiations or no negotiations at all. Cross-border outsourcing, closed factories, downsizing and continuous productivity growth have become part of their everyday experience in more and more industries. Concentration of ownership, more active capital owners, often represented by multinational groups, and radical process oriented rationalization concepts mean that Scandinavian trade unions now are confronted with a more dynamic and multinational business environment. There is no doubt that power is slowly shifting to the employers' side when it comes to the more general strategic questions with which a company is faced.


## INTERPERSONAL BEHAVIOUR

Perhaps one of the more surprising elements of management in Scandinavia from the viewpoint of non-Scandinavians is the interpersonal behaviour. Apart from the importance placed on cooperation and consensual decision making already mentioned, this behaviour is marked by low power distance, egalitarianism, informality, direct communication, decency and conflict avoidance. Whereas some of these characteristics may also apply to other cultures, it is their combination that makes Scandinavia different.

Managers make a point of playing down their authority to an extent where they seem almost scared by its exercise; direct orders are rare, and managers make a point of being able to talk on equal footing with everybody, including shopfloor workers.

This egalitarian attitude can also be seen from the low spread of wages and salaries. In talking about good results obtained, Scandinavian managers will invariably refer to the team as being responsible for the success, knowing that they would be ill advised to take the credit alone.

Our respondents would also stress the informal and non-hierarchical nature of meetings; anybody present can speak their mind, and the atmosphere is relaxed and calm, though disciplined. It is not accepted to shout or lose one's temper; feelings are not considered a good basis for work and people go to great length not to hurt the sensibilities of others. If they have grievances of a personal kind, they will keep them to themselves and take care not to stir up conflicts. Problems of personal chemistry are preferably dealt with on a general level. Instead of saying directly to someone that you do not like the way he handles things, you may talk to his manager in order to put procedures on the agenda. Even if people do not get along personally, they are expected to maintain a decent working atmosphere in the group. That, at least, is the ideal, though in some cases people have to be moved around in the organization to solve such problems. One of the reasons for going to such lengths to avoid conflict is the stress put on cooperation and teamwork. The attitude is 'kick the ball, not the person'.

Here again we can point to relative differences between the three countries in that we found the Swedes most conflict avoiding. Indeed it was impossible to make any of our Swedish respondents admit to the existence of any conflicts at any time. Norwegians were also cautious not to provoke confrontations and open conflicts, the Danes perhaps less so.

Along with this restraint in personal relationships we find a degree of decency in the way the workforce is treated. Human issues and considerations will be in the forefront, not just the bottom line, as will be concern about the environment and the local community in which the company is operating.

## CONCLUSION

Our cases illustrate that successful Scandinavian management builds on the strengths of the culture, context and history in Scandinavia. These strengths include fair decision-making processes in management founded on discussion before decisions, together with the dissemination of information, up-skilling and the empowerment of the employees, all promoting a sense of common destiny and a real possibility of influence. On the other hand, our cases also illustrate that not all companies have been able take advantage of these potential strengths. In those companies management lacks clear direction in essential strategic questions, responsibility tends to be diluted and the workforce is resistant to change. Not all Scandinavian management is good Scandinavian management.

## COUNTRY CLUSTER THEORY

Before discussing the existing country cluster theories, we would like to show how our study contributes to the status and understanding of the cluster concept. It does so first of all by using a different methodology from prior studies. While all other cluster studies are quantitative, *ours is qualitative*, based on multiple interviews in companies matched by industry across the three Scandinavian countries. Our view is that our three countries – Norway, Sweden and Denmark – can indeed be regarded as a cluster; what this study demonstrates is what it means in practical terms to be a cluster, namely that it has implications for management behaviours at a general level and particularly for:

- the nature and understanding of the hierarchy;
- for decision making and the way decisions are made;
- for interpersonal relations and interactive style;
- for attitude to conflict and confrontation; and
- for attitudes to the environment.

There is, however, nothing absolute about this; there are exceptions to the behaviours that we have described, there are counter examples, and there will be modifications and change over time. In short, these descriptions are largely but not invariably true, they are *pro tempore* generalizations, which allow for counter examples, and they should not, we hope, be taken as stereotypes nor be made into stereotypes, an obvious danger whenever we try to systematize cultural knowledge.

What the cluster does not inform is company strategy, which, as we have seen, is primarily determined by the industry dynamics and by more general economic and business trends external to the managers. Nor does it tell anything about particular company cultures, except in so far as they are shaped by national, in this case Scandinavian culture.

Turning next to existing writing on cluster theory, a long-standing line of research has indeed attempted to establish clusters of countries based on their relative similarity according to values and relevant organizational variables. The obvious definition of a cluster is that the countries in a cluster are more like each other than another country from outside the cluster (Javidan and House, 2002). A key source on country cluster research is the Ronen and Shenkar article (1985), which reviews eight empirical studies using data on employee work attitudes. In spite of some discrepancies, in their synthesis Ronen and Shenkar still group Norway, Sweden and Denmark together with Finland in a separate Nordic cluster.

Since the Ronen and Shenkar review, three more comprehensive quantitative studies have been undertaken. One conducted by Schwarz (1994) is the Schwartz Value Survey Program, comprising 38 countries and using a 56-item questionnaire on 41 different occupations. This study, however, includes only Denmark and only one occupation, that of teachers, so that is not central to the present discussion of business and management.

A second recent and ongoing study is the Global Leadership and Organizational Behavior Effectiveness Research Project (GLOBE). It was started in 1993 and it is a multi-phase, multi-method project in which investigators are examining the inter-relationships between societal culture organizational culture and organizational leadership. It includes 62 cultures/countries representing all major regions throughout the world. The cultures are examined in terms of nine dimensions: performance orientation, future orientation, assertiveness, power distance, humane orientation, institutional collectivism, in-group collectivism, uncertainty avoidance and gender egalitarianism. One of the present authors contributed as country co-investigator. Publications have started to appear from this study (see *Journal of World Business*, 37, 2002), and a book anthology edited by Robert House et al. is in preparation. This study includes two of our countries, Sweden and Denmark, but unfortunately not Norway.

To construct their clusters the initiators of the GLOBE study used the results of previous empirical quantitative studies along with other factors such as common language, geography and religion, and perhaps most importantly historical accounts. As a result of their analysis they proposed to group the nations into ten distinct clusters as shown in Figure 7.1.

In this Figure we find Sweden and Denmark along with Finland in a group called 'Nordic Europe'. Subsequently, discriminant analysis was used to test the empirical validity of the proposed clustering statistically, and the result was that 59 of 61 societies were found to be classified accurately into the hypothesized clusters. The two countries not accurately classified were both Central American.

The researchers found the following characteristics for the Nordic cluster (Gupta et al., 2002): moderately strong practices of uncertainty avoidance, future orientation and institutional collectivism, as well as gender egalitarianism. The Nordic cluster also has weaker practices of in-group collectivism, performance orientation, assertiveness and power distance. This

| **Anglo cultures** | **Eastern Europe** | **Arab cultures** |
|---|---|---|
| UK | Hungary | Qatar |
| Australia | Russia | Morocco |
| South Africa (white sample) | Kazakhstan | Turkey |
| Canada | Albania | Egypt |
| New Zealand | Poland | Kuwait |
| Ireland | Greece | |
| USA | Slovenia | **Southern Asia** |
| | Georgia | India |
| **Latin Europe** | | Indonesia |
| Israel | **Latin America** | Philippines |
| Italy | Costa Rica | Malaysia |
| Portugal | Venezuela | Thailand |
| Spain | Ecuador | Iran |
| France | Mexico | |
| Switzerland (French | El Salvador | **Confucian Asia** |
| speaking) | Colombia | Taiwan |
| | Guatemala | Singapore |
| **Nordic Europe** | Bolivia | Hong Kong |
| Finland | Brazil | South Korea |
| Sweden | Argentina | China |
| Denmark | | Japan |
| | **Sub-Sahara Africa** | |
| **Germanic Europe** | Namibia | |
| Austria | Zambia | |
| Switzerland | Zimbabwe | |
| Netherlands | South Africa (black sample) | |
| Germany (former East) | Nigeria | |
| Germany (former West) | | |

*Source*: Gupta et al. (2002).

*Figure 7.1 Societal cluster classification*

characterization is supported by Smiley (1999) (cited also in Gupta et al., 2002), who notes that Nordics tend to be modest, punctual, honest and high-minded, and that wealthy people in Nordic countries generally dress, eat and travel in the same style as the middle class, all of which reflects an underplaying of assertive, familial and masculine authority and an emphasis on certainty, social unity and cooperation.

Since we do not yet have the exact rating of the countries on each dimension from the GLOBE study, it may be helpful to comment on some of the characteristics in terms of the way they are defined. The 'uncertainty avoidance' dimension is the same as that used in the Hofstede studies. We might, however, argue that the reason for Denmark's low position on this dimension lies in the nature of the three questions asked to form the Uncertainty Avoidance Index (stress, mobility and rules) (see Schramm-

Nielsen, 2000), and can further be explained by the fact that the Danish society has been built in such a way as to avoid uncertainty for its inhabitants (Schramm-Nielsen, 2000). Contrary to the popular interpretation of Denmark's low position on this dimension, it does not mean that Danes can cope with high levels of insecurity. It is the other way round: Danes do not feel insecure because they live in a secure environment. Consequently, the respondents in the Hofstede study had little reason to feel insecure. At this stage we cannot comment on the findings of the GLOBE study on this dimension for lack of details, but we can confirm that the Swedish society is no more insecure than Danish society, and our findings show that the Swedes are rather more rule oriented than the Danes and have lower mobility due to the business structure (many large companies), the geography of the country, and the fact that most families are dual career families.

It follows from the above that the characteristic of 'institutional collectivism', sometimes called 'societal collectivism', is also strong. It reflects the degree to which organizational and societal institutional practices encourage and reward collective distribution of resources and collective action. Gender egalitarianism is defined as the extent to which an organization or a society has minimized gender role differences and gender discrimination. From Chapter 2 it will be seen that in all three Scandinavian countries women make a substantial contribution to GNP by high participation on the labour market, and also by high participation in the national parliaments. Furthermore, laws on parental leave try to equalize the work burden and the career breaks in case of childbirth.

Among the dimensions examined we have performance orientation. It refers to the extent to which an organization or society encourages and rewards group members for performance improvement and excellence. This dimension includes the future oriented component of the dimension called 'Confucian dynamism' by Hofstede and Bond (1988). If we look at the wage differentials referred to in Chapter 2, we can confirm that our Scandinavian countries have what we might call weak practices on this dimension. The same can be said about the very small differences in pay between formally qualified and non-qualified workers, that is skilled versus unskilled, which is just SEK5–25 (US$1–3) per hour.

As to the last two dimensions 'assertiveness', defined as the degree to which individuals in organizations or societies are assertive, confrontational and aggressive in social relations, and 'power distance' in the Hofstedian sense of accepting differences in power, we can amply confirm that our respondents did indeed have weak practices in both. Managers in our study go to great lengths to delegate responsibility and to share power – that is, decision-making – with all layers of the hierarchy, and on their side employees expect to be heard and to be involved in decisions concerning their work. The attitudes to 'the higher ups' are non-deferential and the communication style informal and simple. 'Assertiveness' is one of the most interesting dimensions, since our study clearly shows an un-assertive, non-aggressive and non-confrontational style. Instead our respondents stressed the importance of cooperation, horizontally and vertically in the organization, and of striving for consensus as far as possible. The non-aggressive and non-confrontational attitude find expression in the exact opposite, in conflict avoidance or conflict shyness, which as we have noted is especially strong in Sweden. Finally, the social norms of modesty, stemming from the Protestant ethic, obviously defy assertive behaviour.

In conclusion our research does support the central theoretical proposition of the GLOBE study, namely that 'Societal cultural values and practices affect what leaders do' and that 'the attributes and behaviors of leaders are, in part, a reflection of the organizational practices, which in turn are a reflection of societal cultures' (House et al., 2002: p.8).

The third and last culture theory that we would like to present is that of Inglehart (2000). His theory is based on data from three waves of the World Values Survey, which now covers 65 societies comprising 75 per cent of the world's population. Inglehart is concerned with the relationship between culture and democracy, and he supports two claims:

- Development is linked with a syndrome of predictable changes away from absolute social norms, toward increasingly rational, tolerant, trusting and postmodern values.
- But culture is path dependent: the fact that a society was historically Protestant or Orthodox or Islamic or Confucian gives rise to cultural zones with highly distinctive value systems that persist when we control for the effects of economic development (Inglehart, 2000: 80).

The rationale, drawn from previous research, is that 'the world views of the peoples of rich societies differ systematically from those of low-income societies, across a wide range of political, social, and religious norms and beliefs' (Inglehart, 1997: ch. 3). To make his point Inglehart examines cultures according to two sets of variables. One is traditional versus rational-legal values, and the other is survival versus self-expression values. He uses these values to plot each society's location on a global cultural map. According to Inglehart, factor analysis had revealed that the two above-mentioned sets of dimensions do tap scores of variables and explain over half of the cross-cultural variation.

Inglehart further states that they involve dozens of basic values and orientations. He explains the first set of variables as:

Societies at the traditional pole emphasize religion, absolute standards, and traditional family values; they favour large families, reject divorce, and take a pro-life stance on abortion, euthanasia, and suicide. They emphasize social conformity rather than individualistic achievement, favour consensus rather than open political conflict, support deference to authority, and have high levels of national pride and a nationalistic outlook. Societies with secular-rational values have the opposite preference on all these topics. (Inglehart, 2000: 83)

Still citing from Inglehart, the survival/self-expression dimension involves the themes that have come to characterize post-industrial society. One of its central components involves the polarization between materialist and post-materialist values. It is about a shift from emphasis on economic and physical security toward increasing emphasis on self-expression, subjective wellbeing and quality of life. This cultural shift is found throughout advanced industrial societies.

Societies that emphasize survival values show relatively low levels of subjective wellbeing, report relatively poor health, are low on interpersonal trust, are relatively intolerant toward out-groups, are low on support for gender equality, emphasize materialist values, have relatively high levels of faith in science and technology, are relatively low on environmental activism, and are relatively favourable to authoritarian government. Societies that emphasize self-expression values tend to have the opposite preferences on all these topics. And Inglehart ends the characterization of the dimensions by saying that societies that emphasize self-expression values are much more likely to be stable democracies than those that emphasize survival values.

Placing the 65 societies along the two sets of dimensions, the vertical axis corresponding to the traditional authority versus secular-rational authority, and the horizontal axis depicting the polarization between survival values and self-expression, Inglehart draws the map shown in Figure 7.2.

The groupings that Inglehart compose are along religious, ideological or geographic lines corresponding to Huntington's cultural zones (1993, 1996). One of Inglehart's conclusions is that

... religious traditions seem to have had an enduring impact on the contemporary value systems of the 65 societies, as Weber, Huntington, and others have argued. But religion is not the only factor shaping cultural zones. A society's culture reflects its entire historical heritage. (Inglehart, 2000: p.86)

Inglehart points out that 'the placement of each society on the figure is objective, determined by a factor analysis of survey data from each country. The boundaries drawn around these societies are subjective, guided by Huntington's division of the world into several cultural zones' (2000: p.87). He admits to the groupings being arbitrary and discusses the example of

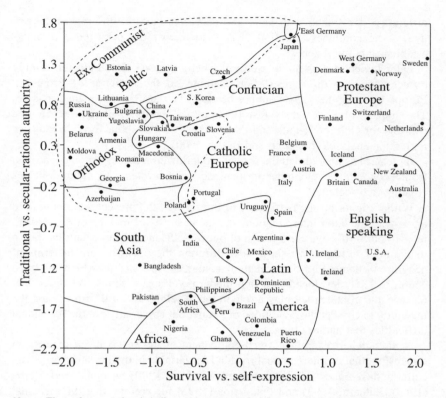

*Note*:   The scales on each axis indicate the country's factor scores on the given dimension.

*Source*:   Inglehart, 2000.

*Figure 7.2   Locations of 65 societies on two dimensions of cross-cultural variation*

Britain, which might as well have been in the group Protestant Europe, since Britain is Protestant and culturally close to those societies.

   The empirical positions of the countries also reflect their level of economic development, in as much as the top right hand corner represents high gross national product (GNP) per capita income, and the opposite bottom left hand corner the lowest GNP per capita income. Consequently, Inglehart can posit that economic development seems to have a powerful impact on cultural values. The value systems of richer countries differ systematically from those of poorer countries. He cites modernization theory as implying that as societies develop economically their cultures will tend to shift in a predictable direction, and his data fit the implications of this prediction. Economic differences are linked with large and pervasive cultural differences. Never-theless, he continues, we find clear evidence of the persistence of long-established cultural zones.

Later Inglehart asks the question of whether these cultural clusters simply reflect economic differences. For example do the societies of Protestant Europe have similar values simply because they are rich? His answer is no. The impact of a society's historical-cultural heritage persists when one controls for GNP per capita and the structure of the labour force in multiple regression analyses (Inglehart and Baker, 2000).

Inglehart has now turned the former modernization theory statement around from economic development influencing value systems to cultural values creating rich societies.

Without ignoring the pertinence of the former, the present authors tend to agree with the latter interpretation, and the best way of making our point is to refer to our bird's eye comparison of our three Scandinavian countries shown in Figure 7.1, where we show how different the countries are in terms of geography, demography and natural resources, in spite of which all three countries have developed into rich modern welfare societies. We agree that latitude and climate may play a role in the development of thriftiness and the ingenuity to combat the conditions of nature, but apparently not the individual difficulties that nature offers.

Next Inglehart examines a sub-component of the survival/self-expression dimension, that of interpersonal trust, a key variable in the literature on cross-cultural differences. He cites Coleman (1988, 1990), Almond and Verba (1963), Putnam (1993) and Fukuyama (1995) for arguing that interpersonal trust is essential for building the social structures on which democracy depends and the complex social organizations on which large-scale economic enterprises are based. It yields the map shown in Figure 7.3.

Figure 7.3 demonstrates that virtually all historically Protestant societies rank higher on interpersonal trust than virtually all historically Catholic societies. This holds true, Inglehart says, even when we control for levels of economic development: interpersonal trust is significantly correlated with the society's level of GNP per capita, but even rich Catholic societies rank lower than equally prosperous historically Protestant societies. Of the 19 societies in which more than 35 per cent of the public believe that most people can be trusted, 14 are historically Protestant, three are Confucian influenced, one is predominantly Hindu, and only one (Ireland) is historically Catholic.

In passing, Inglehart notes the striking correlation of these data with the Transparency International Corruption Perceptions Index. Here again we find our three countries, Norway, Denmark and Sweden, in the top right hand corner as the countries that are highest on interpersonal trust and among those with the highest GNP per capita.

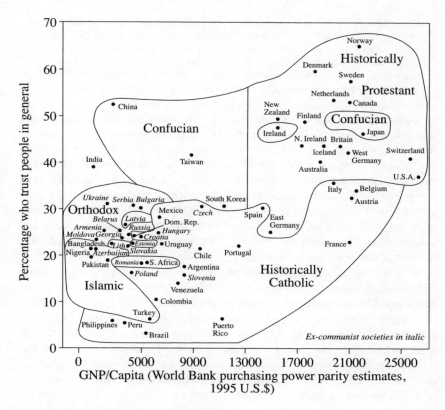

*Note*:   Trust by GNP/capita: r = 0.60 p < 0.000.

*Source*:   Inglehart, 2000.

*Figure 7.3   Interpersonal trust by cultural tradition and level of economic development and religious tradition*

Inglehart now makes a comparison between the Roman Catholic Church, which was the historical prototype of the hierarchical, centrally controlled institution, and the Protestant churches which were relatively decentralized and which over the centuries became gradually more open to local control and, we can add, right down to the individual parish church. And Inglehart continues:

> The contrast between local control and domination by a remote hierarchy seems to have important long-term consequences for interpersonal trust. Clearly, these cross-cultural differences do not reflect the contemporary influence of the respective churches. The Catholic Church has changed a great deal in recent decades.

> Moreover, in many of these countries, especially the Protestant ones, church
> attendance has dwindled to the point where only a small minority of the population
> attend church regularly. The majority have little or no contact with the church
> today, but the impact of living in a society that was historically shaped by once-
> powerful Catholic or Protestant institutions persists, shaping everyone – Protestant,
> Catholic, or other – who is socialized into a given nation's culture. (2000: p.91)

We can confirm that church attendance in the Scandinavian countries is not
just low, it is extremely low. Except for family celebrations such as weddings,
funerals and baptisms, it would be more correct to say that churches are practically empty, but when you ask people about their ethical standpoints it is
clear that Protestantism has a firm grip on people's mind-set in attitudes such
as egalitarianism, interpersonal respect and interpersonal trust. And the trust
goes further than the interpersonal level; over the last half century, the Scandinavians have built societies in which the authorities and public institutions
can be trusted to work for the citizens. The general attitude is that the state and
the institutions are there to serve the citizens, not the other way round.

At the level of our enterprises we have seen that, increasingly, cross
functional teams are created to work towards common goals and that they are
given extended authority and responsibility for getting there. This is a clear
expression of trust on the part of management. In turn the individuals are
expected to live up to the collective responsibility of the team, which demands
trust and cooperation among the team members. Another example is the
cooperative relationship between unions and management that has changed
over the past 20 years or so, from a confrontational attitude of 'them and us'
to a much more cooperative style of 'we are all in the same boat'. Today's
reality is that union representatives are being trained by their peers to
understand the mechanics of running of a business, and for its part
management is prepared to compensate workers and employees in an
equitable way, expressed in relatively high wages.

We began our discussion of the Inglehart country cluster theory by stating
that he is concerned with the relationship between culture and democracy. We
will approach this topic by quoting Inglehart to the effect that by the 1990s
observers from Latin America to Eastern Europe to East Asia were concluding
that cultural factors played an important role in the problems they were
encountering with democratization. Simply adopting a democratic constitution
was not enough.

Again Inglehart (2000) argues that economic development leads to two
types of changes that are conducive to democracy:

- It tends to transform a society's social structure, bringing urbanization,
  mass education, occupational specialization, growing organizational
  networks, greater income equality, and a variety of associated

developments that mobilize mass participation in politics. Rising occupational specialization and rising education lead to a workforce that is independent minded and has specialized skills that enhance its bargaining power against elites.

- Economic development is also conducive to cultural changes that help stabilize democracy. It tends to develop interpersonal trust and tolerance, and it leads to the spread of post-materialist values that place high priority on self-expression and participation in decision making.

Figure 7.4 plots the countries on a graph, where the vertical axis is the sum of the Freedom House ratings for civil liberties and political rights from 1981 through 1998. The horizontal axis reflects each country's mean factor score on the survival/self-expression dimension that we saw in Figure 7.2.

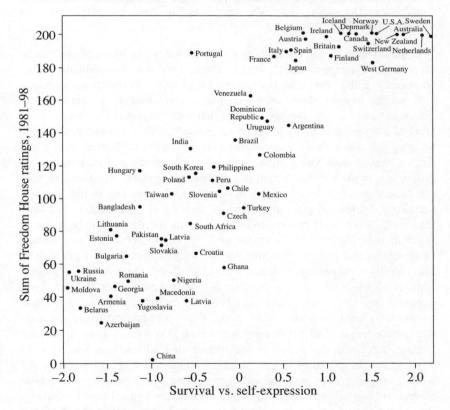

*Source*: Inglehart, 2000.

*Figure 7.4 Self-expression values and democratic institutions*

With this configuration of empirical data Inglehart shows that:

> ... a society's position on the survival/self-expression index is strongly correlated with its level of democracy. This relationship is powerful. It is clearly not a methodological artifact or merely a correlation because the two variables are measured at different levels and come from completely different sources. Virtually all of the societies that rank high on survival/self-expression values are stable democracies; virtually all the societies that rank low have authoritarian governments. (2000: 94)

In conclusion Inglehart states that:

> ... economic development seems to bring gradual cultural changes that make mass publics increasingly likely to want democratic institutions and to be more supportive of them once they are in place. This transformation is not easy or automatic. Determined elites who control say the army and police can resist pressures for democratization. (2000: p.95)

Inglehart later states that although rich societies are much likelier to be democratic than poor ones, wealth alone does not automatically bring democracy. If that were true, Kuwait and Libya would be model democracies.

It seems beyond doubt that economic development is conducive to democracy, and it has also been shown that with economic development the level of corruption is likely to go down (Paldam, 2002). However, there is a missing link. How do we explain that rich oil states like Norway and Saudi Arabia exhibit such vastly different models of society and such enormous differences in the way the wealth is distributed in society? The two countries can be compared in terms of the adversities of nature: one is hot, flat and seemingly barren, a great obstacle for feeding its population, but only seemingly, since with proper irrigation systems the desert can be made to flourish. It is almost entirely surrounded by water. The other one is cold, mountainous and just as uninviting for human living, making 81 per cent of the country completely uninhabited. Like Saudi Arabia, it is largely surrounded by water, and in contrast to Saudi Arabia, this fact has been exploited by the Norwegians. Until fairly recently, seen in a historic perspective, both countries were poor, their populations living on bare subsistence levels. And yet Norway has turned into a rich highly democratic welfare state, with democratic values permeating all levels of society right down to the shop floor of its enterprises, with modest wage differentials and with advanced gender equality including female participation on the labour market and one of the world's highest representation in a national parliament, as we have shown in Chapter 2. Inglehart's data do not include Saudi Arabia. Our qualified guess is that empirically it would be found in the bottom left hand corner of Figure 7.2. In Figure 7.3 it would be in the bottom right hand corner, and again in Figure 7.4 be at the bottom left hand corner. On all the measurements it would be exactly opposite Norway.

So how can we explain that? We can only explain it in terms of values and attitudes towards the individual, with everything that ensues from that. At this point we wish to stress that neither Norway nor the other Scandinavian countries have always been as democratic and egalitarian as they are today. There has been a gradual development from authoritarian ways to independence and participation of the individuals in public and organizational life, accompanied by a lessening influence of religious authorities. As at least part of an explanation we would like to point to one crucial point that has been an overarching element, namely education. It seems to us that once people become educated and knowledgeable, and especially if they are being trained in independent thinking and participation and given individual responsibility, they will no longer accept obedience and servitude, and those in power will have to understand that staying in power is dependent on their legitimation. If we were to point to key figures who have been especially instrumental in shaping the mind-set and attitudes of the population in our three countries, it would be Grundtvig in the case of Denmark and Norway and the Social Democratic party leaders in the case of Sweden (see national heroes cited in Chapter 2). The values of those key monumental figures have been fused into the education systems. Probably the best way of expressing the effect is to cite Barnard: 'The decision as to whether an order has authority or not lies with the person to whom it is addressed and not with the person who issues the order' (1938:163).

# REFERENCES

Almond, G. and S. Verba (1963), *The Covoc Ciætire*, Princeton, NJ: Princeton University Press.

Barnard, C.I. (1938), *Functions of the Executive*, Cambridge, MA: Harvard University Press.

Coleman, J.S. (1988), 'Social capital in the creation of human capital', *American Journal of Sociology*, 94, 95–121.

Coleman, J.S. (1990), *Foundations of Social Theory*, Cambridge, MA: Harvard University Press.

Fukuyama, F. (1995), *Trust: The Social Virtues and the Creation of Prosperity*, New York: Free Press.

Gupta, V., P.J. Hanges and P. Dorfman (2002), 'Cultural clusters: methodology and findings', *Journal of World Business*, 37, 11–15.

Hofstede, G. and M.H. Bond (1988), 'The Confucius connection: from cultural roots to economic growth', *Organizational Dynamics*, 16, 4–21.

House, R.J., M. Javidan, P.J. Hanges and P.W. Dorfman (2002), 'Understanding cultures and implicit leadership theories across the globe: an introduction to project GLOBE', *Journal of World Business*, 37, 3–10.

House, R.J., P.J. Hanges, M. Javidan and P.W. Dorfman (2004), *Leadership, Culture and Organizations, the GLOBE Study of 62 Societies*, London: Sage.

Huntington, S.P. (1993), 'The clash of civilizations?', *Foreign Affairs*, 72, (3).

Huntington, S.P. (1996), *The Clash of Civilizations and the Remaking of World Order*, New York: Simon and Schuster.

Inglehart, R. (1997), '*Modernization and Postmodernization: Cultural, Economic, and Political Change in Forty-Three Societies*', Princeton, NJ: Princeton University Press.

Inglehart, R. (2000), 'Culture and democracy' in L.E. Harrison and S.P. Huntington, (eds), *Culture Matters: How Values Shape Human Progress*, New York: Basic Books.

Inglehart, R. and W. Baker, (2000), 'Modernization, cultural change, and the persistence of traditional values', *American Sociological Review*, February.

Javidan, M. and R.J. House (2002), 'Leadership and cultures around the world: findings from GLOBE', an introduction to the special issue, *Journal of World Business*, 37, 1–2.

*Journal of World Business*, (2002), **37**(1), 1–89.

Paldam, M. (2002), 'The cross-country pattern of corruption: economics, culture and the seesaw dynamics', *European Journal of Political Economy*, **18**(2), 215–20.

Porter, M.E. (1990), *The Competitive Advantage of Nations*, Glencoe, IL: Free Press.

Putnam, R. (1993), *Making Democracy Work: Civic Traditions in Modern Italy*, Princeton, NJ: Princeton University Press.

Reve, T., T. Lensberg and K. Grønhaug (1992), *Et Konkurransedyktig Norge*, Oslo: Tano.

Ronen, S. and O. Shenkar (1985), 'Clustering countries on attitudinal dimensions: a review and synthesis', *The Academy of Management Review*, **10**(3), 435–54.

Schramm-Nielsen, J. (2000), 'How to interpret uncertainty avoidance scores: a comparative study of Danish and French firms', *Cross Cultural Management – An International Journal*, 7(4).

Schwartz, S.H. (1994), 'Beyond individualism/collectivism. New cultural dimensions of values' in U. Kim, H. Triandis, C. Kagitcibasi, S.-C. Choi and G. Yoon (eds), *Individualism and Collectivism: Theory Method and Applications*, Thousand Oaks, CA: Sage, pp. 85–119.

Smiley, X. (1999), 'Survey: the Nordic countries: happy family?' *Economist*, 350(8103): N3–N6.

Sölvell, Ö., I. Zander and M.E. Porter (1991), *Advantage Sweden*, Basingstoke and London: Macmillan.

Transparency International (1993–2003), 'Corruption perception index', accessed at www.transparency.org.

# 8. Present and prospect

The discussion of Scandinavian homogeneity in the previous chapter was concerned to reach a judgement valid for the present. Now we are considering the possibility of wider changes that may, as it were, pass through the present and impact on the future.

The previous chapter reached the conclusion of qualified homogeneity. This homogeneity might be expressed in terms of:

- a management style characterized by informality, equality and restraint;
- paralleled by generally flat hierarchies, compressed salary spreads and low fringe benefits;
- a consensual, participative and inclusive approach to decision making and change implementation;
- a reluctance by most managers to articulate their power, an inclination to reasonableness and quiet persuasion rather than to charismatic dominance; and
- a market and/or customer focus tending to promote coordinative mechanisms across hierarchies and between different departments.

It is difficult to find other countries that replicate this *combination* of values and practice. Such differences as there are between the three countries do not seem to us to be major or consequential in the context under review – that of business culture and management behaviour – but it will do no harm to reiterate these differences by type before moving the discussion forward.

First, there are differences of economic structure and what might be termed 'industrial legacy'. To take as an illustration the country with the most strongly differentiated profile, Sweden: one would recognize that Sweden industrialized earlier than the other two countries, that this industrialization was broader and deeper, that it generated more big companies, that these companies internationalized earlier and have attracted more cross-border investment and acquisition activity – this last fact being nicely caught in our Swedish case study companies, all but one of which were in non-Swedish ownership.

Second, some differences of degree have emerged, along the lines of Danish works councils having more limited functions than those of Sweden, Norwegian managers being more assertive than Swedish ones, and so on.

Third, differences in geography and demography between the three countries impact on some business activities. Again to take the strongest one, the very difficult terrain of Norway makes internal communications problematic which in turn impacts on physical distribution, which is rendered more of a challenge and serves to push Norway towards sea-based rather than land-based enterprise.

When it comes to the industries from which the matched companies are drawn some differences do surface, but they tend to be incidental or circumstantial or without obvious cause even if having demonstrable effect. So for instance the trucking industry is more concentrated in Sweden than in Denmark and Norway. And the relative fragmentation of this industry in Denmark does not seem to be consequential, but it does matter in Norway. Or, as was argued in the chapter on brewing, there are quite subtle, variable relationships between the brewing industry, the logistics industry and grocery retailing; yet these are only differences of degree, in countries having a similar pattern. In short, the differences which are thrown up are not theoretically interesting; one cannot do much with them that will raise our understanding of the cultural dynamics of business in Scandinavia.

Finally, the analysis offered early in the previous chapter tends to reinforce conventional wisdom, that the industry is a stronger determinant of both the strategy and operations of companies than is national culture.

We have wanted to re-run these differences both for the sake of completeness and to put them in their place. They do little more, that is to say, than qualify the picture of a Scandinavian homogeneity developed in the previous chapter, such that Norway, Sweden and Denmark are one of the best examples of a country cluster that the world has to offer.

Yet this identification of the Scandinavian cluster highlights another issue, namely that these Scandinavian countries are also embedded in the world economy and indeed are very much part of the Western business community, both of which have experienced change, some would say unprecedented change.

## EXPECTING CHANGE

The two key developments of the past 20 years have been an intensification of competition and globalization. Both have a variety of causes and feed off each other. Competition has been driven by several factors:

- the end of the 30-year boom following the Second World War, what the French call *les trentes glorieuses*, though it took another ten years for the fact that the easy post-War growth period had really gone for good;

- this long post-War boom had led to market saturation in many cases, or at least to mature markets;
- there has also been overcapacity in many industries, probably in most industries, for 20 years or more; and
- in turn this overcapacity has derived from productivity growth in the West, the industrialization of much of what used to be called the Third World, and even the 1989–91 fall of European Communism contributed by releasing onto world markets unwanted industrial capacity that had previously been locked up in the Communist system.

This is not, of course, the whole story. There has been some compensatory growth in technical boom industries, services and entertainment, but our concern is to highlight causes of enhanced competition. Add to all this the fact that by the early 1990s all the Western governments had managed to get control of inflation and that not all the consequences of this had been foreseen. The end of (significant) inflation, especially when conjoined with the end of easy economic growth, tends to foster public sector shrinkage. Governments and other public bodies, that is to say, become reluctant to spend and worry more about public debt when this cannot be offset against future growth or be neutralized by inflation.

Curbing inflation also adds a new dimension to running a business, in that it renders company performance more transparent. Mediocre results are not spuriously enhanced by inflation, and individual performance is also easier to monitor.

All this of course is a spur to globalization. If competition in the domestic market is tougher than it used to be for some mix of the above reasons, then expanding sales and perhaps operations to other countries is a way of adding to revenue and spreading the costs of promotion and development over bigger production and sales volumes. And of course 'selling to other countries' encourages same industry competitors in these 'other countries' to want to sell into your country. So no domestic market is secure, everyone is trying to do it to everyone else and more industries become global in the sense that the same big companies face each other as competitors in all major markets, especially those of the triad – North America, Europe and Japan. Indeed this globalization has become an imperative in some industries, where companies however mighty are exposed if they are not internationally established at least across the triad. This imperative has given rise to 'war games' of the kind we saw in the 1970s and 1980s when Japanese companies would invade US markets with lower prices, while maintaining industry-norm prices in their other markets, safe in the knowledge that the US companies they challenged operated mainly in the domestic market and so could not 'do it back to them'. All this makes the international business arena very tense.

Competition drives globalization in another way. It puts pressure on costs.
And costs can be reduced by switching production to countries with lower
labour costs. What is more, developments in IT and telecommunications are
making it possible to outsource administrative work cross-border, to relocate
to developing countries everything from data processing to customer call
centres. This in turn drives the development of some of the developing
countries. And even if *average* incomes in these countries are still modest, the
group with Western style incomes has grown markedly and with it the desire
for more (Western) goods and services, leading to more international trade.

So with all this going on around Scandinavia, what kind of impact do we
expect?

## ON BEING A CLUSTER

Before facing up to this question there is another piece of the jigsaw that needs
to be put in place. If we have succeeded in making a reasonable case for
Norway, Sweden and Denmark being viewed as a cluster, this means two
things. First, and most obviously, that the three countries have common
features, beliefs and behaviours. But second, that the cluster countries differ
effectively from other non-cluster countries. We need to spend a moment on
this collective difference.

The things that have been cited both here and in earlier chapters include:

- a strong commitment to egalitarianism;
- leading among other things to a higher level of gender equality than is
  the norm in most Western countries;
- and to a flat wage structure;
- plus a strong commitment to democracy;
- including industrial or workplace democracy;
- a commitment to negotiation and to consensual regulation, in
  organizational decision making, in wage bargaining and in industrial
  relations generally; and
- a tradition of high welfare provision and high welfare expenditure.

In the context of management, as we have seen, all this leads to styles and
behaviours which are egalitarian, consultative, participative, informal,
somewhat collectivist and non-confrontationist.

Most people have difficulty in naming non-Scandinavian countries that
share all these attributes, to a comparable degree. The Continental European
country most likely to be mentioned in this context is the Netherlands. Yet
there is some evidence of a departure from government sponsored welfarism

(McRae, 2001) in that country, and one of the present writers has gone some way to documenting over time the Dutch acceptance of a number of managerialist tenants at odds with the Scandinavian value-behaviour set outlined in the previous paragraph (Lawrence, 1986, 1991; Lawrence and Edwards, 2000). If we look outside Continental Europe, the United States promotes equality of opportunity rather than equality of condition. It is also fiercely individualistic (Hofstede, 1980) and has no problem with using power and rewarding individual achievement (Lawrence, 1996). There is also support from semantic differential studies and other evidence for the view that Britain resembles the United States more strongly in business culture than it does any Continental European country, notwithstanding differences of style and deportment (Lawrence, 1998). Israel does offer an ethos of informality comparable with that of Scandinavia, but it tends to be supported by a hectoring persuasiveness in a very loose organizational context (Lawrence, 1990).

So the question that is being framed is, if there are global trends, and there is a cluster of countries whose collective difference stands out, does this mean an impasse that will have to be resolved?

## EVIDENCE FROM THE STUDY

Part of our answer has to be to say that companies in our core sample do show evidence of the impact of some of the trends noted earlier in this chapter. An obvious example is industry consolidation. Indeed several of our companies owed their existence to M&A activity prior to the time of our research visit, including BGD, Procordia, Avesta Sheffield, Hansa Borg and Nidar. There were a number of cases of foreign ownership already noted, and also changes in the nationality of ownership during the time it took to complete the empirical work in all three countries, namely:

- Procordia passed from Swedish to Norwegian ownership;
- Dandy passed from Danish to British ownership;
- Kockums passed from Swedish to German ownership;
- Avesta Sheffield passed from British to Finnish ownership;
- Falcon Brewery passed from Danish to Norwegian ownership; and
- Ulstein sold its equipment division to the British.

Or again cross-border outsourcing of manufacture has become part of the 'new order' of business in the West, and once more there are examples of this in our core sample of Scandinavian companies. Two of the shipyards – Ulstein and Odense Lindø – were doing it, albeit not on a grand scale. In the case of

Odense Lindø it was given as a way of adding incrementally to capacity so as to produce up to the quota required or permitted by their owner, A.P. Møller. Danish chewing-gum producer Dandy at the time of our visit was a more substantial cross-border outsourcer with what was first a packaging facility in Russia and then a production site. Since our visit Dandy has largely passed into British ownership, and the substantial manufacturing site we had formerly visited in Vejle, Jutland, has now become a corporate office with a slim staff. Yet it is Swedwood, Swedish furniture producer and supplier to IKEA, which represents the ultimate in cross-border outsourcing in that all of its products are manufactured outside of Sweden. From the list of countries we were given it is clear that most of the outsourcing to Central and Eastern Europe was aimed precisely at cost reduction, something that has also been generally recognized as IKEA policy, though in one or two cases, for instance Canada, the outsourcing is probably driven by a desire to be close to both raw material suppliers and markets. Not that we should always regard Sweden as high labour cost country – stylish furniture-maker Fritz Hansen outsourced some wood-cutting and aluminium component production from suburban Copenhagen to Sweden 'where wages are 30 per cent lower'.

Though Scandinavian examples of this cross-border outsourcing can be found and have been offered, it would be fair to say that it has not been embraced with the manic conviction shown by British companies. Nor did we encounter in the core sample any instances of administrative process outsourcing cross-border.

None of our companies were the result of privatization initiatives by any of the governments concerned, the privatization of state-owned companies being a common theme across the West. Nonetheless some moves in this direction have occurred in our three countries. The Norwegian government, for example, offered 20 per cent of the shares of Statoil on the stock-exchanges of Oslo, New York and London in 2001. There has also been some measure of privatization or deregulation of the telecommunications industry in all three Scandinavian countries, and some railway privatization in Sweden.

As competition has grown in the West generally, the workforce has increasingly come to be regarded as 'a cost', something to be worked on. This reorientation in the West is encapsulated in the transition from old-fashioned personnel management to 'new-fashioned' human resource management (HRM) where the latter is thought to be distinguished by being:

- *proactive* rather than reactive, that is, management shoots for what it wants;
- *individualist* rather than collectivist, that is, employees are treated as individuals, regarding the value placed on them by the company and the reward they deserve for their performance; and

- *strategic* rather than routine, that is, the workforce is not taken as 'a given' but as a variable resource to be moulded to the business purpose of the company.

Interestingly very few of the personnel managers we interviewed in Scandinavia opted for the HRM badge, and the one or two with whom we queried this were dismissive of the HRM phenomenon, seeming to see it as a bit of a fad and as 'not invented here'. Nonetheless these Scandinavian interviewees did at several of the companies engage in criticisms of the workforce suggestive of the new competitive HRM view, including:

- references at several companies to over-manning, with the accompanying suggestion that it would not be easy to cure;
- references for underperformance of particular groups, say foremen or maintenance fitters;
- more diffuse references to constraints, to the limitations imposed by the past and deals done in the past; and
- references to a change resistant workforce that had not confronted the new realities.

It is fair to say that comments of this kind were not common across the sample of managers and companies, but neither were they isolated instances nor confined to any one of the three countries. Some of this will resurface in a final summary review of what for want of a better phrase we will call 'strengths and weaknesses'.

There was also some counter reflection of these sentiments in the interviews with trade unionists and/or works council members. Again these did not occur across the board, but there were several whose utterances were unexpectedly cautious or overtly critical. This qualified managerial dissatisfaction with some aspects of the workforce and working practice is reflected in the numerous rationalization and restructuring initiatives discussed in the previous chapter.

## STRENGTHS AND WEAKNESSES

Having looked at the muted yet perceptible impact of some global trends upon Scandinavia, it may be helpful to conclude with a summary restatement of the strengths and weaknesses of Scandinavian business and management. We are basing what follows on our own study of course, but also on a wider knowledge and experience and one that takes account of what has been written by others.

Having said this, the conventional formula of 'strengths and weaknesses' is not quite right, even though we cannot think of anything better. Put simply, some of what Scandinavians regard as their strengths may be regarded differently by people in other countries, and these same 'other people' may ascribe to Scandinavia weaknesses that are not so perceived by the Scandinavians themselves. We will return to this problematic at the end.

## Strengths

With this qualification let us start in a positive way.

## Background

If we treat the three countries as a collective, as a region, then they are nicely complementary. Consider that, put simply, the three countries have by tradition different core strengths:

- Norway: off-shore (shipping, fishing, oil plus hydroelectricity and aluminium).
- Sweden: manufacturing.
- Denmark: land, in the sense of agricultural production and food processing industry.

Any reader who feels this characterization is too flippant is invited to make a list of the six largest companies in each country.

It is also the case that the three languages are (largely) mutually comprehensible, which facilitates cross-border M&A within the region, as with Orkla and Procordia in our sample, and the easy deployment of managers and other staff cross-border.

## International

Much of our book has had a domestic focus, asking in effect: what are these companies like, how are they run, how do their managers behave? In addition if we raise the question of the international fitness of the Scandinavian region, it would be fair to make some points in their favour.

First, all three countries have open economies, are in favour of free trade, have favourable trade balances, are keen exporters, and in all cases foreign trade constitutes a significant proportion of GDP. Part of this openness is a readiness to learn from other countries and to take things from them – we have seen earlier, for instance, how Ekornes took expertise from the United States and how Ulstein accessed the London money market to finance its development.

Second, the region is characterized by near universal English-speaking ability. This is not an advantage enjoyed on the same scale by every country; in Europe the Scandinavian achievement is matched only by that of the Dutch.

Third, in discussions with Scandinavian managers, not restricted to our interviewees in the core study sample of companies, a respectful and discriminating attitude to other countries was discernible. This often gives rise to business advantage. This orientation to other countries is not peculiar to our region. Rather we would like to suggest that it is a feature of small countries generally. Big and powerful countries do not need to worry so much about such differences.

## General

We would like to argue that the two key values that suffuse the Scandinavian workplace are equality and consensus. These are values of Scandinavian society in general, though our concern here is with their impact on employing organizations. Starting with equality we would like to suggest that this:

- enhances organizational solidarity;
- reduces divisions within the workforce;
- underpins mechanisms of coordination across levels and departments within organizations;
- generally facilitates communication; and
- further facilitates dialogue across different skill-job-qualification levels.

These key values of equality and consensus overlap, and so it is difficult to separate out their effects in a clear-cut way. With this qualification we might suggest that the ethic and practice of consensus variously leads to:

- discussion before decision making;
- loyalty to the decision process; and
- participation by trade unions and by personnel at different levels.

As has been shown in the previous chapter, these factors have facilitated the acceptance of rationalization, restructuring and up-skilling.

Taken together these values of equality and consensus support integration and problem solving in production groups, often enabling them to 'get by' without foremen and sustain big spans of control. In Scandinavia close supervision is neither necessary nor welcome.

To these considerations it might be added that Scandinavia enjoys high levels of education, and that educational attainment is rather evenly distributed across society. That is to say, in matters of education and training, Scandinavia is not top heavy like for example France with its finely graded *grandes écoles* or 'bottom heavy' in the German sense of some 500 occupations for which a regulated three and a half year apprenticeship exists. At the same time high educational levels are not peculiar to Scandinavia; they are not uniquely enjoyed by countries in this region, but neither can this level of educational attainment be taken for granted in all Western countries. The United States, for instance usually comes out badly in international comparisons of educational achievement at secondary school level, especially with regard to maths and science – an area where Finland, Nordic if not Scandinavian, is something of a star!

Finally, the openness that was noted earlier vis-à-vis other countries also has a domestic dimension in the sense of a willingness to learn from other companies or industries. Just to focus for a moment on our Norwegian companies consider Nidar's adoption of BPR, Ulstein taking the matrix structure from the oil industry and Ekornes adopting CanBan from the auto-industry.

## WEAKNESSES

Scandinavian business is not marked by the presence of the 'killer instinct'. This killer instinct has as its prerequisites unrestrained individualism and the overt use of power, and these as we have seen are incompatible with core Scandinavian values.

In discussions of business the role of killer instinct is sometimes caught with contrasted sports metaphors – being tennis competitive as opposed to being golf competitive. Golf essentially is played against the external physicalities – the lie of the land, its contours and obstacles, the strength and direction of any breeze. It is played by man against nature. It is like polar exploration rather than war. But tennis competitive means beating a rival, doing everything you can to put the opponent at a disadvantage, exploiting their weaknesses, striking when they are unprepared – it is like war. So is much of modern business.

Consider a little story from Britain. The typical Christmas lunch in Britain is roast turkey eaten with a variety of vegetables of which the most traditional is Brussels sprouts. A few years ago the story went around that one of the grocery supermarket chains cornered the market in Brussels sprouts, denying its rivals of these vegetables. This forced the general public into the stores of this 'innovative retailer' if they wanted to do one-stop Christmas food shopping. Well, this is homely stuff which does not lead to dead bodies on the floor, but there is one winner and a bunch of losers.

Contrast this story with a bit of Norwegian folklore. You often hear in Norway tales of the successful fisherman. The hero will have bought a different kind of boat or fitted a more powerful engine, installed more sophisticated search gear or ventured to an 'off piste' fishing ground. He succeeds, becomes stinking rich and everyone thinks it is great. But note that there are no losers – apart from the fish!

Again because of the core value of consensus, decision making may be slow. It is not always slow, it does not have to be, but sometimes it is. And because of equality and decency and the reluctance to use power there is conflict avoidance, the ingestion of conflict other than working it out, the postponement or delegation of unpalatable decisions. All these have surfaced in the core study interviews, as instances or testimonies.

There is also a lack of geographic mobility, resulting from:

- size of country (Sweden and Norway);
- problematic internal communication (Norway); and
- skewed population distribution (all three countries) with high proportions living in the metropolitan area of the capital city.

These are all things which have been canvassed in earlier chapters. To this might be added the increasing incidence of dual-career families, where both partners need to move together or not at all. There is also evidence from our interviews of regional attachment and regional aversion of the 'workers will change company but not city' (Hansa Borg, Bergen) or 'people will drive four hours a day rather than relocate here' (company in south west Jutland) kind. It should be added that this does not always lead to low inter-company mobility. In Denmark, for instance, the factors reviewed above are offset by the relative absence of big companies in which one can have a lifelong career, as in say ABB in Sweden or Norsk Hydro in Norway, which leads to zig-zagging careers between more modest-sized companies.

If we try to put Scandinavia into an international context, not in the sense of a static comparison but in a psychodynamic sense, if we ask how do Scandinavians interact with foreigners (non-Scandinavians), what do people from other countries make of Scandinavia, then one would probably have to admit that Scandinavians are more likely than most to get conned in their business dealings with other countries. It is about value discontinuity. Scandinavia may believe in consensus and equality and dislike the articulation of power, but nobody else does, at least not with quite the same conviction. Indeed we had a few hints of this in the case study companies, with Dandy being wrong-footed in Poland by a rival American company, Hansa Borg being given the run-around by German and South African brewers over trademarks, and Swedes at Sheffield Avesta not being able to cope with the fact that the British usually have a meeting to fix the meeting – you do not have to approve of it, you just have to know that they do so that you can counter it.

Other sources often show flashes of this value discontinuity. In the 1990s there was a Dutch-led international telecommunications joint venture whose member companies included Sweden's Telia. This joint venture was known as Unisource and it ran from 1992 to 1997. According to its principal historian, van Marrewijk (1999), the Dutch were at first pleased and optimistic when Telia joined the alliance, believing that the Swedes were 'just like us' and feeling reassured by the two countries having close scores on Hofstede's (1980) cultural dimensions. But as the alliance wore on the Dutch became exasperated by the fact that the Swedes would never commit to anything in joint meetings, always wanted to go home and discuss it some more (slowly) and come back with a counter proposal (van Marrewijk, 1999).

There is another twist to this non-fit between Scandinavian values and those of some other countries. This is that business partners from some of these other countries who enjoy elite status in their own society and take the exercise of power for granted may not relish having these pluses neutralized by a Scandinavian insistence on equality and consensus. Being preached at makes it worse.

## TRADE OFFS

We began this discussion by urging that 'strengths and weaknesses' is not the right expression, but that we are using it out of convention. In practice we have got into cultural relativity where we are saying in effect: this works for them, but it would not work in some other society; the Americans do it this way, but the Scandinavians would not think of it; this might be considered a weakness elsewhere, but it is integral to Scandinavia, and so on. There is another way to construe these issues. This is to say that Scandinavian management involves some trade-offs, in terms of:

- consensus v management prerogative; that is, management's right to do what it wants and to decide alone;
- equality v individualism; that is, the pursuit of individual achievement and recognition, exceptional performance, elitism, differential reward;
- decency v killer instinct war games, unpopular decisions, doing what is nasty but maybe necessary; and
- social embeddedness v corporate freedom to choose on grounds of economic self-interest.

The first three will be clear and have been leitmotivs of the book. To elaborate for a moment on the fourth, Scandinavian companies tend to be more embedded in a network of social and institutional relations and obligations.

Companies in Scandinavia for the most part accept government regulation, recognize wage-bargaining partners, operate within a system of industrial democracy, embrace environmentalism and do more than the law requires, and accept implicit obligations to the communities in which they are located. If this sounds too grand, consider an example from among our Norwegian companies. Furniture maker Ekornes is located on the side of a fjord; the works and the community are on opposite sides of this fjord, and it is 14 kilometres to drive around the head of the fjord. Now there is a bridge, to the cost of which the company has of course contributed. But this bridge would not have been built if Ekornes had not been trusted by the community and its politicians. Ekornes does not now go down the Swedwood route and outsource production to Latvia.

We have reconfigured the issues in terms of trade-offs to underline the idea that these choices suit Scandinavia and are mutually reinforcing, but they do not necessarily suit other societies. In the United States, to take the obvious example, all these trade-offs would be rejected. And that rejection is not all bad: there are business and management gains from 'trading off' in a different way.

But if we try to reconcile the two themes of this chapter, the impact of global change and an attempt at a balance sheet for Scandinavian management, it might be fair to say that if change is the imperative then the Scandinavian decision process offers the best opportunity to adapt in a way that is not socially destructive.

If you are hoping to survive the apotheosis of turbo-capitalism, Scandinavia is probably your best bet.

# REFERENCES

Hofstede, G. (1980), *Cultures Consequences*, Beverley Hills, CA: Sage.
Lawrence, P. (1986), *Management in the Netherlands: A Study in Internationalism*, Report to the Technische Hoogeschool Twente, Enschede, The Netherlands.
Lawrence, P. (1990), *Management in the Land of Israel*, Cheltenham: Stanley Thornes.
Lawrence, P. (1991), *Management in the Netherlands*, Oxford: Clarendon Press.
Lawrence, P. (1996), *Management in the USA*, London: Sage.
Lawrence, P. (1998), *Issues in European Business*, London and Basingstoke: Macmillan.
Lawrence, P. and Edwards, V. (2000), *Management in Western Europe*, London and Basingstoke: Macmillan, Ch. 11.
McRae, H. (2001), 'Honey we've shrunk the state', *Fortune*, European Edition, 12, 25.
van Marrewijk, A. (1999), *Internationalisation, Cooperation and Ethnicity in the Telecom Sector*, Delft: Eburon.

# Index